In His Own Words

The Essential Speeches of Adolf Hitler

IN HIS OWN WORDS

The Essential Speeches of

— ADOLF HITLER —

Translated, compiled, and with commentary by

C.J. Miller

ANTELOPE HILL PUBLISHING

Antelope Hill Publishing
www.antelopehillpublishing.com

Paperback ISBN-13: 978-1-956887-12-9
Hardcover ISBN-13: 978-1-956887-13-6
EPUB ISBN-13: 978-1-956887-14-3

Dedicated to my fiancée, who is my dictionary, my muse, and my partner.

- C.J. Miller

Hitler speaking at a harvest festival in Bückeberg on October 3rd, 1937

CONTENTS

INTRODUCTION

C.J. Miller

Aside from his controversial historical legacy, and perhaps his iconic moustache, Adolf Hitler is best known for his impassioned, fiery speeches. It should go without saying that this book should not be taken as an endorsement of the content of these speeches or the deeds of the man who made them. It is rather an impartial, scholarly work, and as such is concerned with exploring the craft of his rhetoric, and framing the speeches within the historical context in which they were delivered. With detailed historical background sections outlining events leading up to and surrounding each speech, as well as dozens of explanatory notes embedded within the speeches, this work aims to bridge the gap between three genres which have heretofore remained mostly separate: Hitler biographies, general histories of the period, and Hitler speech collections. As it is aimed at the layman reader and casual student of history, it cannot hope to be comprehensive in any of these areas, but will give the reader a basic grasp of each, as well as introducing novel and insightful anecdotes, all contained within one accessible volume. The aim is not merely to present to the reader a selection of Hitler's spoken words on their own, but to elucidate the historical circumstances in which they were delivered, thus giving the reader insight into why they are significant, and perhaps even what made them effective.

Even the most hostile scholars of the subject have to acknowledge Hitler's oratorical ability, even if they feel the need to insist it was "the only thing he was good at doing"[1] and "his one real talent."[2] Indeed, his ability to move an audience through speech was his most important asset: there is a very real extent to which Hitler "spoke himself into power." And, at least regarding this particular skill, Hitler did not care for modesty: he was quite conscious of his own talent. In *Mein Kampf*, he relates his experience of delivering a speech at an early public meeting of the *Deutsche Arbeiterpartei* (German Workers' Party, DAP for short), the precursor to the NSDAP, in 1919. He writes: "Something that I always felt deep down in my heart, without really knowing, was here proven to be true: I could speak! After 30 minutes, the people in the little hall were electrified."[3]

Unfortunately, much of the effect is lost by transcribing spoken word into written word. Hitler himself propounded the superiority of speech as a means of reaching people, writing in *Mein Kampf*:

> *The force that has ever and always set in motion great historical avalanches of religious and political movements is the magic power of the spoken word. The broad masses of a population are more amenable to the appeal of rhetoric than to any other force. All great movements are popular movements.... In no case have great movements been set afoot by the syrupy effusions of literary aesthetes and drawing-room heroes.*[4]

In the second volume, he devotes an entire passage to detailing the superiority of speech to writing as a means of swaying an audience, because speech is delivered in real time, and can be adapted on the fly, so that a competent speaker can:

> *[F]ollow the lead of the broad masses in such a way that he will instinctively speak the words necessary to reach his audience's*

---

[1] Kershaw, *Hitler*, 77.
[2] Ibid., 105.
[3] Hitler, *Mein Kampf, Vol. I*, C. 12.12, 653.
[4] Ibid., C. 3.22, 225-227.

*heart.... He can read the facial expression of the audience to see,
first, if they understand what he says, second, if they grasp the
whole of his speech, and third, to what extent they are convinced of
the correctness of what was said.*[5]

Good thing, then, that this book is not designed to incite an
audience to take political action, but only as a historical inquiry.

Furthermore, Hitler's speeches, especially those that were part
of elaborate ceremonies at mass rallies, were visceral aesthetic
experiences quite unlike the dry and intellectual experience of
reading the same words printed on paper. Even in a crowded beer
hall, calculated theatrical flourishes were employed to create a
unique atmosphere. Historian and Hitler biographer Ian Kershaw
notes:

*[H]e used a beer table on one of the long sides of the hall as his
platform in order to be in the middle of the crowd – a novel
technique for a speaker which helped create what Hitler regarded
as a special mood in that hall.*[6]

Despite often speaking for an hour or two at a time, and
occasionally more, his speeches are generally described as
anything but boring. Kershaw describes how:

*[H]e observed the dull, lifeless meetings of bourgeois parties, the
deadening effect of speeches read out like academic lectures by
dignified, elderly gentlemen. Nazi meetings, he recorded with
pride, were, by contrast, not peaceful.* [7] *He learnt from the
organization of meetings by the Left, how they were orchestrated,
the value of intimidation of opponents, techniques of disruption,
and how to deal with disturbances. The NSDAP's meetings aimed*

---

[5] Hitler, *Mein Kampf, Vol. II*, C. 6.5, 199.
[6] Kershaw, *Hitler*, 90.
[7] Emphasis in original.

to attract confrontation, and as a result to make the Party noticed.[8]

Hitler went out of his way to study crowd psychology, reading the works of French theorist Gustave Le Bon for insight on how to communicate with the masses. Famous photos reveal him looking like quite the thespian as he practices dramatic, theatrically exaggerated movements, poses, and facial expressions that he might use in the performance of his speeches.

From the rowdy atmosphere of a beer hall gathering to the stupefying mass rallies in Nuremberg, a Hitler speech was an aesthetic experience deliberately calculated to produce certain emotions and effects in its audience. Indeed, a strain of scholarship has focused on National Socialism as a primarily aesthetic and artistic, rather than political, movement.[9] All of this is absent from the written word.

Nevertheless, it is still of historical value to study the written text of his speeches. Even absent the visceral aesthetic experience of his oration and the atmosphere surrounding it, the rhetoric is worth studying, and there is no better way to study it in a vacuum, so to speak, than by reading the bare text. Independent of any moral judgment of its content, it demonstrates a certain skill and consideration — consideration, especially, of its effect on an audience.

The accusation that Hitler spoke at a low level is so oft repeated it has become a cliché, and is only true to the extent that he shifted his register according to his audience. On average, the level of discourse may be simple — though I dare say hardly more so than most political speeches delivered today — but the reason for this should be self-evident: he wished to make himself as clearly understood as possible, to as many people as possible. Whether his revealed estimate of the intellectual capacity of the masses is patronizing and cynical, or simply realistic and strategically

---

[8] Ibid., 88.
[9] See, for example, Frederic Spotts, *Hitler and the Power of Aesthetics*.

sound, can be debated — but perhaps the best metric is whether it proved successful.

The frequent criticism that he is repetitive is also quite true, but the reason for it should likewise be self-evident: he addressed crowds in dozens of cities and towns across the country, in an age when mass communication was rather primitive, and, especially during his long campaign for power before he became Chancellor, the majority of these speeches were neither broadcast nor recorded. Almost any given rally was likely to include many people in the audience who were hearing him for the first time, and he aimed to make his main ideas and goals heard, understood, and remembered by as many people as possible. The sheer number of public speeches he delivered in his lifetime — estimates vary, but likely well over a thousand — makes it utterly impossible for them not to have been repetitive.

It also makes it utterly impossible for all of them, or even a significant portion, to be contained in one volume. Nor is that the goal of this project. A process of selection is always also one of omission, and certainly there are many other notable speeches which could have been included, but for the sake of brevity had to be left out. Speeches were selected first and foremost to give a broad picture of Hitler's vision of National Socialism as he presented it to the German public of the time. The secondary consideration was selecting speeches delivered around the time of significant historical events, those which addressed interesting, contentious, or seldom-studied topics, lesser-known speeches, and speeches from the early period of the NSDAP.

These are also only excerpts from his speeches. Nothing has been altered within the speeches, but significant omissions were sometimes necessary, as Hitler often spoke for two hours or more. The full transcripts of just a few of those would be enough to fill this entire volume. The decision as to what to include and what to leave out was determined primarily by what was most necessary for a full understanding of the subject on which he was speaking, and secondarily by what seemed most interesting and insightful.

For transcripts of these speeches in German, alternative translations in English, and excerpts from these and other speeches, see the Suggestions for Further Reading at the end of this volume.

The speeches have been arranged chronologically, with background sections preceding each speech, such that a sort of narrative emerges of the rise to power of the NSDAP and Hitler's time as Führer of Germany.

Other translations of most of these speeches exist in various collections, obscure archives, and websites scattered across the internet, mostly in partial form or in excerpts as they are here. The quality of these translations generally ranges from poor to questionable. In the major collections, the best translations are fairly accurate, and acceptable for the purpose of bare comprehension, but rarely as readable and natural as what I hope I have achieved with this project. In these all-new original translations of Hitler's speeches, the German has been abridged only as much as is absolutely necessary to make it as readable, easy to follow, and natural-sounding as possible for the modern English reader, with the aim of giving the reader a sense of the what the audiences of the time heard when they listened to a speech by Adolf Hitler.

THE 25-POINT PROGRAM OF THE NSDAP

February 24th, 1920

The program of the German Workers' Party has a time limit. Once the goals set out in the program have been achieved, the leaders will not set new goals merely in order to enable the continuation of the Party by artificially increasing discontent among the masses.

1) We demand the unification of all Germans into one Greater Germany on the basis of a people's right to self-determination.

2) We demand equal rights for the German people vis-à-vis other nations, and the abrogation of the peace treaties of Versailles and St. Germain.

3) We demand land and territory for the nourishment of our people and to settle our surplus population.

4) Only members of our people can be citizens. Only those who are of German blood can be members of our people, regardless of confession. Therefore, no Jew can be a citizen.

5) Anyone who is not a citizen will only be able to live in Germany as a guest, and will be subject to laws applying to foreigners.

6) The right to determine the governance and laws of the state must belong only to citizens. Therefore, we demand that every public office, regardless of its nature, whether at the national, provincial, or municipal level, may only be held by citizens. We will combat the corrupting parliamentary custom of appointing men to posts only according to party considerations, without regard to character or ability.

7) We demand that the state undertake to provide first and foremost for the employment and livelihood of the citizens of the state. If it is not possible to feed the entire population of the state, then members of foreign nations (non-citizens) are to be expelled from the Reich.

8) Any further immigration of non-Germans must be prevented. We demand that all non-Germans who have immigrated to Germany since August 2nd, 1914 be expelled from the Reich immediately.

9) All citizens must have equal rights and equal duties.

10) The first duty of every citizen must be to work, whether intellectually or physically. The activity of the individual must not be contrary to the interests of the general public, but must be carried out within the framework of the whole, and for the benefit of all.

Therefore we demand:

11) The abolition of unearned income, and the breaking of debt slavery.

12) Considering the enormous sacrifices of blood and property which every war inflicts on the people, personal enrichment through war must be regarded as a crime against the people. We therefore demand the complete confiscation of all war profits.

13) We demand the nationalization of all public trusts.

14) We demand profit-sharing in large enterprises.

15) We demand a generous expansion of old age pensions.

16) We demand the creation and maintenance of a healthy middle class, the immediate communalization of large stores to rent out to small businesses at low rates, and primary consideration for small businesses to supply goods to the state, the provinces, or the municipalities.

17) We demand land reform adapted to our national requirements, the establishment of a law to enable expropriation without

compensation of any land needed for the common good, the abolition of land interest, and the prohibition of all land speculation.

18) We demand ruthless prosecution of those who harm the common interest through their activities. Common traitors, usurers, profiteers, et cetera, are to be punished by death, regardless of confession or race.

19) We demand the replacement of Roman law, which serves a materialistic world order, by German common law.

20) In order to enable every capable and industrious German to attain higher education and thus to move into positions of leadership, the state must ensure a thorough development of our entire national education system. The curricula of all educational institutions must be adapted to the requirements of practical life. Schools must ensure that an understanding of the conception of the state is achieved as early as possible (civics education). We demand that exceptionally talented children of poor parents be educated at the expense of the state, regardless of their status or profession.

21) The state shall ensure the improvement of public health by protecting the mother and the child, prohibiting child labor, promoting physical training by means of establishing compulsory gymnastics and sport, and giving the greatest possible support to all associations engaged in the physical education of the youth.

22) We demand the abolition of the mercenary army and the formation of a people's army.

23) We demand a legal fight against deliberate political lies and their dissemination through the press. In order to facilitate the creation of a German Press, we demand that:

   a) all editors and employees of newspapers published in the German language must be members of the German people;

   b) non-German newspapers require the express permission of the state to be published. They may not be printed in German;

c) any financial interests effecting German newspapers, or their influence by non-Germans, must be prohibited by law; the punishment for these transgressions will be closing such newspaper operations, and the immediate expulsion from the Reich of the non-Germans involved in them;

Newspapers that work against the common good are to be banned. We demand a legal fight against the artistic and literary tendencies that exert a corrosive influence on our national life, and the closure of events that violate the above demands.

24) We demand freedom for all religious denominations in the state, as long as these religions do not endanger the existence or offend against the morals of the Germanic race. The Party as such represents the view of a positive Christianity, without binding itself to any particular confession. It fights against the Jewish materialistic spirit within and without, and is convinced that a lasting recovery of our people can only come about on the following basis: common good before individual good.

25) For the implementation of all this, we demand the creation of a strong central authority in the Reich, unconditional authority of the central parliament over the entire Reich and its general organization, and the formation of committees for the various estates and professions to implement the general laws enacted by the Reich in the individual states.

The leaders of the Party promise, if necessary at the risk of their own lives, to work relentlessly for the implementation of the above points.

WHY ARE WE ANTISEMITES?

Hofbräuhaus-Festsaal, Munich, August 13th, 1920

The Background

Most comprehensive collections of Adolf Hitler's speeches begin in 1922, when his speeches began to be systematically transcribed. Hitler began public speaking in a political capacity in 1919, and by 1920 was making enough of a stir in the tumultuous local political scene for several Munich newspapers[10] to take notice, but his speeches from this era were, for the most part, neither recorded nor transcribed. Throughout his entire speaking career, his speeches were generally loosely centered on a few key themes, and then almost entirely improvised, so there are no scripts or even detailed notes to draw from. If we want to gain an idea of the content of these early speeches, we must largely rely on police and intelligence records, as well as the Munich press of the time.[11]

The notable exception was the historically significant speech titled "Why Are We Antisemites?" The speech was delivered in the richly historical *Festsaal* (ball/festival room) of the *Hofbräuhaus*, Munich's largest brewery and public house, the same hall which barely a year earlier had hosted the headquarters of the short-lived Bavarian Soviet Republic, and in previous decades and centuries towering figures such as Lenin and Mozart. Now it was to be host to the NSDAP's largest public meeting to date, and the first in

---

[10] *Der Kampf, Münchener Post*, etc.
[11] Phelps, "Hitlers „Grundlegende" Rede," 390.

which Hitler spoke at length about the Jewish question, as previous speeches had focused mainly on issues such as the effects of the Treaty of Versailles, the goals of the Party, the role of workers, et cetera.[12]

This was not a light topic, even at a time when the general public was more receptive to antisemitic ideas. Even Hitler himself recalls that as a young man overhearing political conversations in which Jews might be discussed, "these references aroused a mild distaste," and at that time he "saw no other distinguishing feature but the strange religion." Consequently, his "aversion at hearing such remarks nearly grew into a feeling of abhorrence." The young Hitler "opposed the idea that [Jews] should be attacked simply because [they] had a different faith," and even when he was first exposed to crude anti-Jewish caricatures and screeds in Vienna's antisemitic tabloid papers, he "regarded them more as the products of jealousy and envy" of Jewish success, and had the impression that those forms of crude hatred were disreputable.[13]

He notes that even once he started learning more about historical and political issues surrounding European Jewry, he was still uncomfortable with antisemitism and full of doubts, and describes this learning process as "a great internal struggle between calm reason and spiritual sentiments."[14] When he read the antisemitic pamphlets, he was put off once again because "they all began by assuming the reader had at least some degree of knowledge about the Jewish question," and moreover because "they were partly superficial and their 'proofs' were incredibly unscientific."[15] He felt compelled to learn about the issue himself because "the subject appeared so enormous, the accusations so far-reaching,"[16] that he figured it must be an extremely important issue. If even some of the claims of the antisemitic pamphlets he read were true, after all, it would mean he would need to

---

[12] Ibid.
[13] Hitler, *Mein Kampf, Vol. I*, C. 2.20, 127-129.
[14] Ibid., C. 2.23, 135.
[15] Ibid.
[16] Ibid.

completely reevaluate his understanding of the world. According to his own version of events, it was only through many hours of long study and reading, and over the course of many months of personal observation, that he came to regard the Jews not merely as Germans who happened to have a different religion, but as a distinct people, and this was the first step on his path to developing what he calls a systematic understanding of the Jewish question.

This is also a major subject of the following speech. Whether this view is correct or incorrect could still be debated today — but more often, in fact, it is simply not seen as fit for discussion at all. Nonetheless, once Hitler began to perceive Jews as a distinct people and not as mere adherents of a different faith, he felt that he was able to notice them more easily, and observe their behavior, their interests as a group, and their role in German society. His newfound role as a propagandist for an upstart political party gave him a platform to endlessly propound these views to the German masses.

After Germany's defeat in the First World War, Hitler had remained in the service of the Army, being bounced around to various posts, first as a guard at a prisoner of war camp at Traunstein, then at Munich's main train station. During this period, chaos reigned in Germany, and in Bavaria especially: labor disputes and a growing restlessness on the political left coalesced into what became known as the German Revolution of 1918–19, with various factions of leftists competing and/or cooperating to seize power, and even forming a turbulent succession of revolutionary governments in the state of Bavaria.

Although Hitler still served in the military at this time, even being elected as his unit's representative for the soldiers' councils, and thus by extension technically served under these revolutionary governments, according to close comrades who knew him at the time, he had nothing but hatred for the chaos of the revolution and the Reds who carried it out,[17] to such an extent that once Munich was retaken by the *Reichswehr* and the rebellion

---

[17] Heinz, *Germany's Hitler*, 85, 92-94.

crushed, the officers put him in charge of rooting out former revolutionaries among the Army's ranks.

Shortly thereafter, Hitler was selected to become a military intelligence agent in an anti-communist educational program. Here he further developed both his political ideas and his extraordinary talent for public speaking, of which he himself was apparently quite conscious.[18] The Army intelligence at the time considered surveillance of the political scene for the purpose of preventing another revolution one of its primary objectives. To that end, and in one of the many historically fateful turns of events that seem to have constantly befallen him, Hitler was assigned to monitor the tiny *Deutsche Arbeiterpartei* (German Workers' Party, DAP for short).

Although only meant to monitor the activities of the Party, Hitler was impressed with their platform, and especially with the ideas expressed by Anton Drexler, then leader of the Party, and Gottfried Feder, its economic theorist. At a meeting he attended at which Feder was speaking, Hitler's response to heckling from a Bavarian separatist audience member apparently so impressed Drexler that he invited the young intelligence officer to join the Party. Although Army personnel were normally not allowed to join political parties, an exception was made for Hitler, and he became a card-carrying member of the DAP.

Hitler's oratory skill allowed him to rise through the ranks very quickly, becoming chief propagandist within months and officially beginning his career as a political speaker. It was Hitler who drew the crowds to the Party's meetings, and this gave him considerable influence over the direction of the Party. A competent artist, he designed the notorious swastika flag himself, and decided on the name change to the *Nationalsozialistische Deutsche Arbeiterpartei* (National Socialist German Workers' Party, NSDAP for short).

An early challenge to Hitler's growing power came from within the Party, when several founding members, including Party Chairman Anton Drexler, wanted to merge it with the rival

---

[18] Hitler, *Mein Kampf, Vol. I*, C. 8.6, 411.

Deutschsozialistische Partei (German Socialist Party, DSP for short, a nationalist party with a very similar platform to the NSDAP). Hitler balked at the idea of the Party being absorbed into someone else's movement, and, in a bold political maneuver, threatened to leave the Party. The other leaders all knew that without Hitler to bring in audiences and revenues from ticket sales and donations from his speeches, their party would not survive. He thus forced them into the position of pleading for him to stay. Hitler remained in the NSDAP only on the condition that it remain independent, and that he replace Drexler as chairman.

His gambit was fully vindicated: as the DSP declined and eventually folded, the NSDAP absorbed most of its membership, notably including Julius Streicher, the future publisher of the NSDAP tabloid newspaper *Der Stürmer*. Meanwhile Hitler, now in undisputed control of his organization, led the NSDAP to new heights. The following speech drew an audience of two thousand and, if the NSDAP's own transcription is to be believed, was frequently punctuated by applause, raucous cheering, laughter at Hitler's occasional jokes, and shouts of agreement. As the veracity of these audience interjections cannot be ascertained, seeing as the objective impartiality of the transcriber is questionable at best, most of these interjections are not included in this translation, except for a few near the beginning, just to give a flavor of the atmosphere in the hall.

The Speech

My dear fellow Germans! We are already used to being called monsters, and it is perceived as particularly monstrous that we are in the vanguard on the question that most unnerves certain gentlemen in Germany today, namely the question of opposition to the Jews. Our people understands so much, but this one thing we do not want to understand, and above all because the worker asks, "What does the Jewish Question have to do with the workers at all?" Indeed, the majority of our people today still have no idea what the actual situation is with regard to this question. The vast majority perhaps only deals with this question emotionally, and immediately judges: "Well, I have seen good and bad people among them, just as among ourselves." Very few have learned to judge from objective observation. This is where I will draw a connection with the word "work."

What does work actually mean? Work is an activity that one does not perform for one's own sake, but for the benefit of one's fellow men. If anything distinguishes man from animal, it is precisely his work, which is not only guided by instinct, et cetera, but is based on the pure recognition of a certain necessity. Hardly any revolution has had such a profound effect on this earth as this slow one, which has gradually turned the lazy man of primeval times into the man of work. We can assume here that this activity has followed three great stages:

First of all, the purely instinctive drive for self-preservation. We find it not only in man, but also in animals, and this instinctive drive for self-preservation later developed into another form of work, namely work for purely selfish reasons. This second stage of work was also gradually overcome and the third came: work out of a sense of moral duty, which the individual does not do only because he is compelled to do it. Today we can see it everywhere, the work which millions of people do without being driven to it constantly, which binds thousands of intellectuals to their study day after day, through the night, without perhaps being materially compelled to do this work, which makes hundreds of thousands of German workers wander into their home gardens after the end of the workday, and we can see that today millions of people cannot live at all without some kind of occupation. And when I said earlier that this may well be a slow but perhaps the greatest revolution that mankind has undergone so far, then one must assume that this revolution too must have had a certain cause, and this cause is again the greatest Goddess on this earth, the one who is able to drive man to the extreme: the Goddess of Hardship.

We can trace this hardship on this earth back to ancient times, especially in the northern part of the world, in those enormous ice deserts, in those places which offered only the most meagre existence. Here man was forced for the first time to fight for his existence in practice; what the smiling south offered him in abundance without work, he had to win through his labor in the north, and so perhaps the first groundbreaking invention was born here: in these cold stretches man was forced to seek a substitute for the only gift of heaven that makes life possible, the sun, and the man who first artificially produced the spark later appeared to mankind as a god: Prometheus, the fire-bringer. The north forced people to further activity: making clothing, building their own dwellings, caves, and later houses; in short, it practically gave birth to the principle of work. Without it, existence up there would have been impossible.

Even if it was still modest, it was already an activity that had to be planned in advance, which the individual knew that if he failed to carry out, he would hopelessly starve to death in the following hard winter. And at the same time a second development took place: the enormous hardship and the terrible privation acted as a means of racial purification. What was weak and sickly could not survive this terrible period, but sank prematurely into the grave, leaving a race of giants in strength and health. And a further characteristic was born in this race. Where men are externally muzzled, where their sphere of action is externally limited, their inner life begins to develop; externally limited, inwardly unlimited; the more man must depend on himself due to external forces, the deeper his inner life becomes, and the more he turns inward. [...]

These three achievements — the recognized principle of work as a duty, a necessity, not only for the individual and out of egoism, but for the existence of the whole clan, even if that was often only a very small group of people; secondly, the necessity of physical health and thus mental health; and thirdly, the deep inner spiritual life — these gave the Nordic races the ability to expand over the rest of the world and form states.

Even if this power could not be expressed in the far north, it became capable of taking effect at the moment when the ice shackles fell away and man moved down to the south into a favorable, happy, free nature. We know that all these people had one sign in common: the sign of the sun. They created cults based on Light and created a sign, the tool of fire generation, the whorl, the sun cross. One finds this cross as a swastika not only here in Europe, but just as much in India and Japan carved into temple posts. It is the swastika of the communities once founded by Aryan culture. [...]

So we must ask ourselves: What about the Jew and the formation of states? Does the Jew also possess the power to build states, and so on? We must first of all examine his attitude to work, how he actually perceives the principle of work, and you must excuse me now for quoting a little book called the Bible. I do not wish to claim that everything in it is necessarily correct, for we know that Jewry worked on it very liberally, but at least one thing is certain: that it was not written by any antisemite! [*Laughter from audience.*] This is significant because no antisemite could have written a more terrible indictment against the Jewish race than the Bible, especially the Old Testament. We must pick out one sentence: "By the sweat of thy brow shalt thou earn thy bread." And it says here that this was determined as punishment for the Fall.

Ladies and gentlemen! This is where a whole world separates

us, because we cannot see work as a punishment, otherwise we should all be convicts. But we do not want to see it as a punishment either. I must confess: I could not be without work, and hundreds of thousands and millions would perhaps endure three, five, ten days, but could not live ninety or a hundred days without activity. If this paradise really existed, this so-called land of milk and honey, our people would not be happy there. We seek the chance for activity no matter what, and if Germans have no other possibility, we will make do with bashing each other's heads in, at least temporarily. [*Laughter from audience.*] We would not be able to endure absolute rest.

Here we see a great difference, for a Jew wrote this down, and whether it is all true or not, it corresponds to Judaism's conception of work itself; for them, work is not a self-evident moral duty, but at the most only a means for the preservation of one's own self. That is not work in our eyes; for if I explain that word in this way, then any activity at all by which one supports oneself without regard for one's fellow men could be called work. And we know that this work once consisted in the plundering of travelling caravans, and that today it consists in the coordinated plundering of indebted peasants, industrialists, townsfolk, and so on. The form has changed, but the principle is the same. We do not call it work, but robbery.

If already this first fundamental concept separates us, a second one immediately separates us further. I explained to you earlier that this great period in the North purified the Nordic races. This means that everything inferior and weak gradually died out of these races and that only the healthiest bodies remained. Here, too, the Jew differs, for he did not become purified, but inbred; he has, to be sure, multiplied unsurpassably, but only in his own circles, and without any selection pressure, and thus we see the growth of a race which bears all the defects inherent to inbreeding.

Finally, the Jew still lacks the third trait: inner spiritual experience. I do not need to describe how the Jew appears in general. You all know him. That incessant restlessness which never gives him the opportunity to gather himself inwardly, to give himself over to a spiritual mood! At the most solemn moment his eyes dart about, and you see how even during the most beautiful opera, the man is still calculating dividends. The Jew has never possessed an artistry of his own. He has had his temples built by foreign builders, first by Assyrians, then, during the second reconstruction, by Roman artisans. He personally has left no cultural arts, no other visual works, no buildings, nothing at all. And musically, too, we know nothing except that he is capable of copying the music of others well. I do not wish to conceal the fact that today we have many famous conductors from their ranks, who have become famous thanks to a Jewish press that is coordinated down to the last whistle.

If a people lacks these three qualities, it cannot be state-building. This holds true, for the Jew, through the long centuries, has always been nomadic, albeit on the grandest scale. He never had what we would call a state. It is a great misconception, even among us today, that Jerusalem was the capital of a Jewish nation-state. First of all, in those days the gulf between the Jews of the tribe of Judah and Caleb, and the northern Israelite tribes was still practically unbridged, and it was only David who succeeded in bridging this gulf and gradually creating a union through the unified cult of the God Yahweh. We know precisely that this cult chose Jerusalem as its sole seat of power only at a very late stage, and that only from that moment on did the Jewish people receive a headquarters, exactly like they have today in, for example, Berlin, or New York, or Warsaw, etc. It was a city in which, thanks to their other abilities and characteristics, they gradually gained the upper hand, partly by force of arms and partly by force of trumpets. Even then the Jew lived primarily as a parasite on the body of other peoples, and it had to be that way; for a people who do not want to perform work themselves — the sometimes thankless work of forming and maintaining a state, working in the mines, in the factories, in construction, all this work so unpleasant for a Hebrew — such a people will never found a state itself, but will always prefer to live as a third party in another state, where this work is done by others and he is only a middleman in business, a merchant at best, or translated into today's German: a robber, a nomad, who undertakes the same raids he once undertook.

Thus it becomes immediately apparent why the whole project for the foundation of a Zionist state is nothing more than a comedy. The Chief Rabbi in Jerusalem has now assured us that "the most important thing would not be the founding of this state, because it is very doubtful whether this can yet be realized. But it is also not necessary, because Jewry needs this city at the most as a spiritual center. In fact, we have already become the masters of a whole series of states; we dominate them financially, economically and also politically." Thus, the goal of this Zionist state is nothing more than to pull the wool over the eyes of the unsuspecting. They try to explain that so-and-so many Jews have found themselves wanting to go there as farmers, as workers, even as soldiers. [*Laughter from audience.*] If they really had this instinct in them, the German Reich would need these ideal people today to cut peat, to work in the coal mines, they could participate in the development of our great projects, our hydro-power plants, our lakes, and so on, but it does not occur to them. The whole Zionist state will be nothing but an academy for their international schemes, and from there everything will be directed, and every Jew will receive, as it were, an immunity as a citizen of the Palestinian state. And besides, he will naturally keep our rights as a citizen. But if you should catch a Jew red-handed, he will longer be a German citizen, but a citizen of Palestine! [*Laughter from audience.*]

One might say that the Jew cannot help it, that it all stems from his race, he cannot overcome it, and therefore it does not matter whether the individual is good or evil; he must act exactly according to the law of his race, from which he cannot detach himself, as do our people. Even when confronted with the fiercest Spartacist, [19] the sheep-like good-naturedness of the present

---

[19] Referring to a member of the *Spartakusbund* (Spartacist League), a communist organisation named after Spartacus, the leader of a Roman slave rebellion. The

German shines through, for he only turns his rage against "the other side," and is good-natured enough that he does not notice who is pulling the strings. The Jew is everywhere a Jew, who resolutely represents the interests of his race, whether consciously or unconsciously.

We can already see that there are two great racial differences here: Aryanism means a moral conception of work and thus what we so often talk about today: socialism, community spirit, the common good before self-interest; Jewry means an egoistic conception of work, and thus Mammonism and materialism, the opposite of socialism. And from this trait, which he cannot overcome, which is in his blood — he himself recognizes this — from this trait alone comes the absolute necessity for the Jew to act in a state-destroying manner. He cannot do otherwise, whether he wants to or not. He is thus not capable of forming a state of his own, for that more or less always presupposes a great deal of community spirit. He is thus only able to live as a parasite in other states, as a race within other races, as a state within other states, and we see here quite clearly that the race in itself does not have a state-building capacity if it does not possess definite traits which are inherent in the race, which must be in its blood, and that conversely a race which does not possess these traits must have a and state-destroying effect, regardless of whether the individual is good or evil.

We can trace the fate of Jewry from the earliest times. It is not necessary that everything written in the Bible should be true word for word, but on the whole it gives at least an impression of the history of Jewry as the Jews wrote it for themselves, and there we see that the Jew writes this work quite innocuously. It does not seem outrageous to him when he describes how, by cunning and deceit, he penetrated and contaminated race after race, was always

---

Spartacists split off from the Social Democratic Party (SPD) in 1914 due to that party's support for Germany entering the First World War. The Spartacists spurned the more moderate and parliamentarian methods of the SPD, preferring direct action, including strikes, demonstrations, and a failed Spartacist Uprising. They later formed the Communist Party of German (KPD) and joined the Comintern.

expelled, and, without being offended, sought out another. How he pimped and haggled when it came to his ideals, ready to sacrifice even his family. We know that a gentleman recently stayed here, Sigmund Fraenkel, who most recently wrote that it would be quite unfair to accuse the Jews of having a materialistic spirit, for just look at the sunny, intimate family life of the Jew. This intimate family life did not for a moment prevent their own patriarch Abraham from immediately pimping his own wife to the pharaoh of Egypt, just so that he could do business. And this is their patriarch and progenitor. And just as the Lord Papa was, so the sons have become, and have never spurned these deals, and you can be sure that they do not spurn them even today. Anyone who was a soldier will remember that in Galicia or Poland he could see these Abrahams standing at every railway station. For thousands of years the Jew has been forcing his way into other races, and we know very well that whenever he has lived somewhere for a long time, the signs of collapse have made themselves felt, and that in the end the peoples have no choice but to rid themselves of the unwanted guest or to perish themselves. We know that heavy plagues came upon the nations; there were ten of them that came upon Egypt — we are experiencing the same plague today — and finally the Egyptians ran out of patience. When the chronicler describes that the Jew was the acquiescent one and finally left, it cannot have been so, for they had hardly left when they began to long for the fleshpots again. So it seems that in reality they did not fare so badly. But even supposing it to be true that the Egyptians used them in building their pyramids, this is quite the same as if we today proposed to give this race gainful employment in our mines, quarries, etc., and just as today you would not see this race go there voluntarily, you would probably not see them build pyramids voluntarily in Egypt, and there was no choice but to force them. What hundreds of thousands of others do as a matter of course, to the Jews represents another chapter of Jew-baiting and pogroms. […]

What does the term "industrial capital" actually mean? Ladies and gentlemen! We are reproached, especially in the factories: "You are not fighting industrial capital, but only stock exchange and finance capital." Very few understand that industrial capital cannot be fought at all. What does industrial capital even mean? It is a factor that changes gradually in size, only a relative concept. Once it meant needle and thread, the workshop, and perhaps the few pennies of savings that the master tailor in Nuremberg possessed in the thirteenth century. This was the sum that he needed in order to work, i.e. tools, workshop, and a certain amount of money to enable him to live for a certain time.

Gradually the small workshop became the great factory, and we see practically the same thing; for the small weaving frame of its time later became the mechanical loom, but the latter is just as much a tool as the loom of the most primitive design, and the workshop, once a small room, has become a great factory. But workshop and tool, machine and factory, in and of themselves do not generate value, but are only a means to an end, only generating value when work is done with them. The thing that produces value is work. And the few cents that perhaps the small master craftsman possessed in order to get through hard times, in order to buy materials, have increased tenfold and a hundredfold and stand before us again today—only now we call it capital for the maintenance of the business in bad times, i.e. working capital.

I would like to emphasize one thing: tools, workshops, machines, or factories, working capital, industrial capital—you cannot fight against this at all; you can perhaps see to it that it is not abused, but you cannot fight it. This is the great fraud perpetrated on our people, and it is perpetrated in order to divert them from the real struggle, in order to tear them away from the capital that ought to be fought, and must be fought: loan and finance capital.

This form of capital arises in a fundamentally different way. While the smallest master craftsman is dependent on the fates that may affect him day to day — on the general situation, in the Middle

Ages perhaps on the size of his town and its prosperity, on the security of this town — today too this capital, industrial capital, is bound to the state, to the people, dependent on the will of the people to work, but also on the possibility of procuring raw materials to be able to offer work, of finding customers who will actually buy the product. And we know perfectly well that a collapse of the state can, under certain circumstances, devalue the greatest assets, rendering them worthless. This is in contrast to the other form of capital, stock exchange and loan capital, on which interest is paid quite evenly without any consideration of whether or not the owner, on whose estate, for example, these 10,000 marks lie, goes to ruin himself. The debts remain on the estate. We can see that a state has debts, for example the German Reich has bonds on the Alsace-Lorraine railways, and these bonds must bear interest, even though we no longer own the railways. We know that the railways today fortunately have a deficit of 20 billion, but their bonds must bear interest, and although they were partly sold sixty years ago, and have already been repaid four times over, the debt remains, the interest continues to accrue. And while a great nation no longer gains anything for this enterprise, but still has to bleed, this loan capital continues to grow, quite evenly, regardless of any outside disturbance. Here we already see the first possibility, namely, that this form of multiplication of money, which is necessarily independent of all the events and incidents of ordinary life, because it is never hindered and always continues uniformly, will gradually lead to gigantic sums of capital which become so enormous that in the end they have only one fault: the difficulty of accommodating them.

In order to accommodate this capital, one must proceed to destroy entire states, to annihilate entire cultures, to abolish national industries, not in order to make them public, but in order to throw all this into the jaws of international capital, for this capital is indeed international: as the only thing on this earth which is truly international, it is international because its bearers, the Jews, are international due to their spread over the whole world.

And already here everyone should smack his head and say to himself, "If this capital is international because its bearers, the Jews, are spread internationally over the whole world, then it must be madness to think that this capital can be fought internationally by the same members of this race!" Fire is not extinguished by fire, but by water, and international capital, which belongs to international Jews, can only be broken by national force.

Thus this capital has grown and today dominates practically the whole earth with its immeasurable sums, incomprehensible in its great proportions, growing uncannily and, worst of all, completely corrupting all honest labor. For therein lies the dreadful thing: the ordinary man, who today has to bear the burden of paying interest on this capital, must see how, in spite of diligence, assiduity, thrift, in spite of real labor, he has scarcely enough left to feed himself and still less to clothe himself, while at the same time this international capital is devouring billions in interest alone, which he must help to raise, at the same time as a racial stratum spreads in the state, which does no other work than to collect interest and cut coupons for itself.

This leads to the degradation of all honest work, for every honest working person today must ask himself, "What is the purpose of my productivity at all? I'll never get anywhere, and there are people who can not only live practically without working, but who essentially even dominate us." And that is the goal.

One of the foundations of our strength is to be destroyed, namely the moral conception of labor, and this was also the brilliant idea of Karl Marx: to change the moral conception of labor, to organize the whole mass of people who were struggling under capital, and marshal them for the destruction of the national economy and the protection of international stock exchange and loan capital. We know that today 15 billion worth of industrial capital faces 300 billion worth of loan capital. This 15 billion in industrial capital is invested in productive value, while we have to pay back this 300 billion in loan capital, which we only receive by the spoonful in instalments of 6 and 7 billion, and which we use up in periods of one to two months to supplement our rations a little. And if we should ever recover, this 6 to 7 billion which is decreed to us today in completely worthless scraps of paper will have to be repaid later on in high-quality money, i.e. in money which is backed by practical work. This means not only the destruction of a state, but the donning of a shackle. [...]

Finally, the Jew's last resort is destroying everything that one would regard as necessary for a state to be considered cultured. It is perhaps here that his work is most difficult to recognize, but it is also here that it actually has the most terrible effect. We recognize his activity in art, how today's painting becomes a caricature of everything we might call true inner feeling. People always explain that you just don't understand, that this is the inner experience of the artist. Do you think that what a Moritz Schwind or Ludwig Richter created did not also reflect an inward experience?[20] At the end of the day, do you believe that Beethoven's chords do not also come from an inner experience and feeling, or that a Beethoven symphony is not also an inner experience? It is true inner experience as opposed to the other form, which is only a superficial swindle, deliberately put into the world in order to gradually destroy every healthy conception of the world, in order to gradually stir people into a state in which one no longer knows whether these times are crazy, or whether he himself is crazy.

Just as he works in painting, sculpture, and music, so he does in poetry, and above all in literature. Here he has a great advantage: he is the editor, and above all the publisher, of more than 95 percent of all the newspapers that are published. He makes full use of this power, and anyone who has become such an antisemitic monster as I am can smell where the Jew begins as soon as he picks up the newspaper. You can already tell from the title page that this is not one of us, but one of the people behind the scenes. One knows perfectly well that all his wordplay and cunning only cover up the inner hollowness of his spirit, only conceal the fact that the

---

[20] Schwind and Richter were both nineteenth-century painters of the Romanticist movement.

man knows no spiritual feeling or experience, and what he lacks in true spirit he replaces with a swarm of phrases, verbal tricks, and turns of phrase which seem maddening, but it is preemptively declared from the outset that whoever does not understand them is simply not sufficiently developed intellectually.

Speaking of literature, we must also jump to another chapter, in which we can appropriately admire Moritz Wolf and Salomon Baer. Our theatres, the places that Richard Wagner once wished darkened in order to produce the greatest degree of consecration and seriousness, in which he wanted to perform works that he was ashamed to call mere plays, and called instead "consecration plays," the place where there should be nothing but the highest elevation, the detachment of the individual from all sorrow and misery, but also from all the rottenness that we otherwise unfortunately encounter on God's earth, that is supposed to lift the individual into a purer air—what has become of it? A place where one is ashamed to enter today, lest someone should recognize you when you walk in. We see that a Friedrich Schiller may have received 346 *Thalers* for *Mary Stuart*, but that one receives 3.5 million today for a *Merry Widow*; that one earns millions today for the greatest kitsch, for which an author in ancient Greece would probably have been exiled from the state.[21]

And if the theatre has thus become a breeding ground for vice and shamelessness, then this applies a thousand times more to that new invention which perhaps originated from a flash of inspiration, and which the Jew immediately understood how to

---

[21] Two stage plays; *Mary Stuart* deals with the life of Mary, Queen of Scots and premiered in 1800; *The Merry Widow* is a light-hearted operetta by Austrian playwright Franz Lehár about a widow in a poor Balkan state who inherits a fortune from her late husband, and the convoluted machinations of government officials to make sure she marries a local and thus keeps her wealth in the country; it is bizarre and perhaps outright dishonest that Hitler cites this play as an example of the degeneracy of theatre, seeing as it was actually his favourite play, to the extent that it was performed constantly in National Socialist Germany, and he even had Lehár's entirely Jewish wife declared an "honorary Aryan" just because he enjoyed the play so much; perhaps at this time the play was a guilty pleasure of his, and later on with his power secured as Führer he felt comfortable dropping the pretence and openly proclaiming his love for this silly and racy operetta.

transform into the dirtiest business imaginable: the cinema. At first one could only attach the greatest hopes to these ingenious inventions. The easy transmission of profound knowledge to a whole people and the whole world. And what has become of it? The vehicle for the greatest filth and shamelessness. And so the Jew works on. For him there is no spiritual feeling, and just as his forefather Abraham pimped out his wife, so he finds nothing unusual about pimping girls today, and we can find him everywhere, in North America as well as in Germany, Austria-Hungary and throughout the Orient, throughout the centuries as the trafficker of human flesh, and it cannot be denied — even the greatest defender of the Jews cannot deny — that almost all these traffickers in girls are Hebrews. Here one can find truly horrific material. To Germanic sensibilities, there should be only one punishment here: death. For people who play fast and loose with this, treating as a business, as a commodity, that which for millions of other means the greatest happiness or the greatest misery, the penalty would be death. To the Jews, however, love is nothing but a business with which they earn money; they are ready at any time to tear apart the happiness of any marriage as long as they can get their thirty pieces of silver out of it.

We know that today they tell us that all that which is called family life is a completely outdated notion from the past, and anyone who saw the play *Schloß Wetterstein*[22] could experience here how shamelessly the most sacred thing left to a people is described as nothing more than a "brothel." So we should not be surprised if the Jew boldly attacks the last thing that many people still care about today, the last thing that can at least give many people inner peace: religion.

Here, too, we see the same Jew who has enough religious customs of his own for which others might easily mock him, but for which no one mocks him, because we never mock religion, as

---

[22] A play by the sexually deviant but non-Jewish German playwright Frank Wede-kind satirising bourgeois family life with the tale of a rebellious teenage girl who leaves her unstable home to become a prostitute.

it remains sacred to us. But he pulls it off, he reaches everywhere, destroys everywhere and can offer no substitute anywhere. Whoever is detached from religion today, in this age of the vilest deceit and fraud, has only two possibilities: either he despairs and hangs himself, or he becomes a thug. [...]

And when we see, for example, in these Jewish journals, how they dictate that every Jew is obliged to enter the struggle against every antisemite, whoever and wherever he may be, then it follows that every German, whoever and wherever he may be, must become an antisemite. For if the Jew has a racial determination, so do we, and we are obliged to carry it out. For it seems to us inseparable from the social idea, and we do not believe that a state can ever exist on earth with lasting internal health if it is not built on internal social justice. And so we have joined forces in this knowledge, and when we finally came together, there was only one big question: how should we actually christen ourselves? As a party? A bad name! Notorious, discredited in the mouths of everyone, and hundreds asked us, "Why did you call yourselves a party? When I hear that word I go mad," and others explained to us. "It's completely unnecessary for us to organize ourselves officially; it is enough to spread systematic knowledge of the danger of Jewry, and the individual, on the basis of this knowledge, can begin to remove the Jewish influence from himself." I very much suspect that this whole beautiful train of thought was devised by none other than a Jew himself. They then went on to tell us, "It is not necessary to organize politically; it is sufficient to take away the Jew's economic power. Only organize economically, that is where salvation and the future lie." Here, too, I assume that it was a Jew who first put forth this idea, for one thing has become clear to us: in order to free our economy from these vises, it is necessary to fight the pathogen in the politically organized struggle of the masses against their oppressors.

It was clear to us that systematic knowledge is worthless and its deepening can serve no purpose unless it becomes the basis for an organization of the masses to carry out what we feel is necessary on the basis of our knowledge, and that only the broad masses of our people can be considered for this organization; for in this we differ from all those who are still would-be saviors of Germany today, whether Bothmer or Ballerstedt[23] and so on, that we are of the opinion that this future strength of our people is not to be sought in the Odeon bar or the *Bonbonnière*,[24] but in the countless workshops into which that strength flows day after day and out at noon and evening, that the only hope of our people for the future lies in these millions of hard-working, healthy people.

We realized that if this movement does not reach the broad masses, if it does not organize them, then everything is in vain, then we will never succeed in liberating our people and we will never be able to think of rebuilding our Fatherland. Salvation will never come from above; it can and will only come from the broad masses, from the bottom up. And when we came to this realization and decided to form a party, a political party that wishes to enter uncompromisingly into the political struggle for the future, another voice rang out to us: "Do you believe that you few will be able to achieve this, do you really believe that you few men can do this?" For we realized that we were indeed facing an immeasurable struggle, but that nothing had yet been created on earth by men that other men could not destroy, and a further conviction arose within us that it could not be a question of whether we think we can do it. If it is right and necessary, then it is no longer a question

---

[23] Karl Graf von Bothmer was a monarchist and Bavarian separatist writer. Otto Ballerstedt was leader of the *Bayernbund*, a conservative Bavarian separatist league, and an early political rival of Adolf Hitler. The two men's organisations, while both nominally "right-wing," had strong ideological disagreements and an intense antagonism that even escalated to violence, with members of both groups storming the meetings of the rival group. On one occasion, Hitler himself led a group of National Socialists in a raid on a *Bayernbund* meeting. Hitler and his boys rushed the stage where Ballerstedt was speaking, beat him up, and threw him off the stage. The police arrived and arrested Hitler and the NSDAP contingent, and Ballerstedt insisted on pressing charges against Hitler personally. Hitler was convicted of breach of the peace and assault and sentenced to a fine and a short jail term. Ballerstedt was later assassinated as part of the purges of political rivals on the Night of the Long Knives. See Evans: *The Coming of the Third Reich*, 181 and Fest, *Hitler*, 160, 225.

[24] Places of leisure and decadence in Munich.

of whether we want to do it, but of our duty to do what we feel is necessary. We did not ask for money and supporters, but we decided to go forth, and when others are working for a whole lifetime to get perhaps a little house, or to create a carefree old age for themselves, then we truly consider it worth living to have begun this most difficult struggle. Should we win—and we are convinced that we will—we may go to the grave destitute, but we will have helped to bring about the great movement that will now sweep across Europe and the whole world.

First of all, we were clear about three principles which are inseparable from each other: socialism as the ultimate conception of duty, the moral duty of work not for one's own sake but also for the sake of one's fellow men, above all abiding by the principle of common good before individual good, struggle against all parasitism, and especially against easy and unearned income. And we were aware that in this struggle we could rely on no one but our own people. We were convinced that socialism in this sense can only be found among nations and races which are Aryan, and here we hope and are convinced, first and foremost for our own people's sake, that socialism is therefore inseparable from nationalism. For us, being nationalists does not mean belonging to one party or another, but rather examining every action to see whether it benefits the whole people, and love for the whole people without exception. From this conception we will understand that it is necessary to safeguard the most precious thing that a people possesses, the sum of all the active creative powers of its workers, whether of the fist or of the mind, healthy in body and soul. And this conception of the national immediately forces us to take a stand against the opposite, the Semitic conception of the people, and above all against the Semitic conception of work.

And if we are socialists, then we must necessarily be antisemites, since we wish to fight against materialism and Mammonism. And if today the Jew still runs into our factories and cries, "How can you as a socialist be antisemitic? Aren't you ashamed?"—The time will come when we will ask, "How can you as a socialist *not* be antisemitic?" The time is coming when it will be self-evident that socialism can only be carried out in the company of nationalism and antisemitism. The three concepts are inseparably linked. They are the foundations of our program, and that is why we call ourselves National Socialists.

Finally, we know how great the social reforms are which must be carried out, that Germany will not recover only on the basis of small efforts, but that we will have to make radical changes. We will not be able to avoid the national problem, or the problem of land reform, or providing for all those who work day after day for the national community in their old age, that their provision is not a pittance, but that they have a right to spend these old days in a way that is still worth living.

If we want to carry out these social reforms, they must go hand in hand with the struggle against the opponent of every social institution: Jewry. Here, too, we know perfectly well that systematic knowledge can only be the groundwork, but that behind this knowledge must come the organization which will one day put it into action, and in this action, the removal of the Jews from our people, we will remain adamant. Not because we begrudge them their existence — we congratulate the whole rest of the world on their visit — but because the existence of our own people is a thousand times more important to us than that of a foreign race. And we are convinced that this systematic antisemitism, which clearly recognizes the terrible danger of this race for every nation, can only be a guide, but that the broad masses will always perceive the matter emotionally, and will come to know the Jew first and foremost as the man in daily life who always and everywhere sticks out — our concern must be to awaken and stir up and incite the instinct against Jewry in our people until they come to the decision to join the movement that is ready to bear the consequences.

If we are told, "Yes, whether you are successful depends in the end on whether you have enough money," et cetera, then I believe I can say the following: even the power of money is limited; there is a certain limit beyond which, in the end, it is no longer money that rules, but truth. And we are all aware that once the millions of our workers have recognized who the leaders are who are always promising them today to lead them towards a blissful future kingdom, once they realize how gold is at play everywhere, they will throw the gold in their faces and declare, "Keep your gold, and don't think you can buy us!"

And we are least likely to despair even if we still stand alone today. If we see supporters everywhere we go, but nowhere the courage to organize, that should not make us mad; we have dared to fight and we must win nonetheless. I assured you before the voting that this election would not decide Germany's fate, that there would be no recovery after this election, and today I think most people will already agree with me. I guaranteed you this then because I knew very well that courage and the will to act were lacking everywhere, and I told you only one thing as our election program: let the others go to the polls today, to the Reichstag, to the parliaments, and stretch out in their club chairs; we want to get up on the beer hall table and sweep the masses along with us! We have kept this promise and will keep it in the future. Restlessly, unceasingly, as long as there is still a spark of strength in us and a breath in our lungs, we will go out and call upon all our people and speak the truth again and again until we can finally hope that this truth will triumph, that the day will finally come when our words will fall silent and action will begin!

[This is the end of the speech. There is a pause, followed by open discussion and a Question-and-Answer session. The discussion and questions were not recorded, but what follows is a series of Hitler's responses to the audience.]

Ladies and gentlemen! We are not at all as fearsome as our main enemy, and cannot immediately crush Jewry by ourselves, nor do we imagine it to be so easy. But we have decided that we will not come with ifs and buts, and that once the matter has been resolved, it will be done thoroughly.

To the gentleman who said it is all the same to him, if someone is a human being, he is a human being — that in itself I can accept, as long as this other human being does not get in my way. But if a great race consistently destroys the living conditions of my race, I don't say, "I don't care where they come from." In that case, I say I am one of those who, if they get a slap on the left cheek, give two or three back!

Then the gentleman said that our movement would mean a struggle into which the workers would be drawn. Yes, and they[25] promise our people God knows what kingdoms of heaven, as the fools have done for forty years, and now instead of the kingdom of heaven have nothing but a pile of rubble and misery. We do not go along with that. We do not promise a kingdom of heaven, only this one thing: that if you are willing to carry out this reform in Germany, perhaps the time will come again when the individual can live. If you carry out the glorious reforms which these other gentlemen here desire, you will in an even shorter time be faced with the necessity of embellishing this life by means of the very same decrees which their leader Trotsky, Lenin, and so on are now issuing: whoever is not prepared to fight for the blessings of this state will die.

Finally, he said they were opposed to any form of capitalism. Ladies and gentlemen! The Communists have hitherto fought only industrial capital and hanged only industrial capitalists. But name me one Jewish capitalist whom they have hanged. Three hundred thousand Russians have practically been murdered in Russia. The Soviet government itself now admits that. Among the three hundred thousand there is not a single Jew! But among the leadership, more than 90 percent are Jews. Is this persecution of Jews, or is it not, in the truest sense of the word, persecution of Christians?

---

[25] Possibly referring to the Social Democrats or the Communists. The context in Hitler's response to this audience member makes clear that he is contrasting his own fledgling party's mission with that of Marxist socialism.

Then you said you fought both loan capital and industrial capital. But you have fought neither the one nor the other so far. You cannot fight industrial capital; at most you can destroy it, then you can begin to build it up again with twelve-hour work days. And you have never fought the other! That's the one that funds you.

Then the second speaker explained that the cause of the revolution was only to be found in poverty. We would rather put it like this: poverty made Germany ripe for those who wanted revolution; read the writing of their lord and master Walther Rathenau, who even then ruled Germany, who explained precisely that the true and conscious practical purpose of the revolution was to oust the feudal system and replace it with a plutocracy. These gentlemen have been the financiers of this glorious movement. If their revolution had meant even the slightest danger to capital, then the *Frankfurter Zeitung* would not have announced triumphantly on November 9th, "The German people have carried out a revolution." Once we carry out *our* revolution, the *Frankfurter Zeitung* will be singing a different tune!

Then you went on to say, "Before the war, one never heard anything about the Jews." That was a sad thing, that so little was heard. But that does not mean that they were not there. But above all, this is not even true, for this movement has not existed only since the war, but has existed just as long as there have been Jews. If you go back in Jewish history and read that the Jews gradually wiped out the original tribes in Palestine with the sword, you can imagine that there was antisemitism as a logical reaction, and it has existed all the time up to the present day, and the pharaohs in Egypt were probably just as antisemitic as we are today. If before the war you had not only read their famous writers Moritz, Salomon, and so on – and I do not mean newspapers which from the outset bear the stamp of approval of the *Alliance Israélite*[26] – you

---

[26] An international Jewish organization based in Paris and founded in 1860 promoting Jewish interests, especially providing Jewish education and advocating for Jewish minority populations. On several occasions the Alliance also demonstrated

would have heard that in Austria there was already a huge antisemitic movement, and that in Russia, too, the people were constantly trying to rise up against the Jewish bloodsuckers, that in Galicia the Poles groaned and no longer worked, and sometimes rose up in despair against these drunken idealists who were systematically ruining the people. Unfortunately, we have only begun to understand this too late. But you say, "Before the war one heard nothing about it." But how sad are those who hear about it now and still don't have the courage to join with us.

Then you go on to say that Lenin did make some mistakes. We are grateful that you at least admit that your pope also made mistakes, but then you declare that *you* would not make these mistakes. First of all, if three hundred thousand people are hanged in Germany, if the whole economy in Germany is destroyed according to your pattern, then your statement that you would not make such mistakes means little. You have a poor idea of what the whole system of Bolshevism really means. It does not seek to improve the situation, but is there to destroy nations with these "mistakes." If you declare today that this has been done in Russia up to now, then that is a sad excuse, if first a people is decimated, a national economy is brought to the brink of total collapse, and finally this state, which practically only exists by the grace of Czarist officers, is forced to become imperialist and allowed to make conquests, then I declare that this is a peculiar policy. One thing I know is that if we do not have the iron will to stop the madness of war, that mutual mutilation, then we will perish.

Finally, you explain that precisely because loan capital is international, we cannot fight it nationally, because otherwise the international world will shut us out from everything. These are the consequences of relying on international solidarity. If you hadn't made us so powerless, we could give a damn whether this other

---

its considerable political clout, for example in 1867 they swayed the governments of France, Italy, Belgium, and the Netherlands to put pressure on Switzerland to grant full civil and political rights and privileges to the Jews by making it a condition of renewing their treaties with that country.

world is satisfied or not. But when you yourself admit that this international capital, which practically dominates Britain and France and North America, is in a position to close us off, do you then believe that the struggle against capital is being waged there? As long as this earth has stood, peoples have never become free through the will and deed of other peoples, but only through their own strength, or else they have remained slaves.

And then, at last, you too turn to the Bible, and that at least is a good sign in a communist! And you explain to me that I am a communist because of a peculiar agreement between the Bible and our Party program. What you assure me of here has already been assured to me by Dr. Gerlich, for example, and Mr. Hohmann called out to me, "If you stand up for what you have in your program, you are a communist!" Conversely, the *Post*[27] constantly tells me that I am an arch-reactionary, a completely deranged militaristic regressive.

[A heckler from the audience interrupts:] "The *Post* is itself reactionary!"

Would you please discuss that with the editor-in-chief and allow me to listen in? [Laughter from audience.] The *Kampf*[28] also emphasizes again and again that we are a bastion of counter-revolution. So I recommend that you first go to the *Post* and to the *Kampf* and explain to them that we are communists, because I couldn't care less what they call me, whether a reactionary, a pan-Germanist, a *Junker*[29], a heavy industrialist, or a communist—I am and will remain a German National Socialist, and I have my program before me, and as I said earlier, I will pursue it to the last spark of my strength and to the last breath of my lungs!

---

[27] The *Münchener Post*, a Social Democrat newspaper.
[28] A communist newspaper.
[29] The aristocratic land-owning class in Prussia.

FREEDOM OR SLAVERY?

Bürgerbräukeller, Munich, July 28th, 1922

The Background

The following speech was delivered at one of the many high points of political unrest in Weimar Germany. The whole Weimar period was marked by political polarization and extremely high political engagement. Difficult and serious questions of territorial sovereignty, regionalism, class relations, religion, labor disputes, the waning role of the traditional aristocracy, and coming to terms with the new parliamentary democracy, most of which had already been boiling up before and during the war, now began to boil over. Liberal historian Richard J. Evans points to the heated political atmosphere as a bad omen for the fledgling democracy, with "every spare inch of outside walls and advertising columns...covered with posters, every window hung with banners, every building festooned with the colors of one political party or another." [30] He even goes so far as to suggest that during the Weimar period "people arguably suffered from an excess of political engagement.... Elections met with none of the indifference that is allegedly the sign of a mature democracy."[31] Liberal democracy had not been around long enough for people to be checked out and depoliticized, hardships were keenly felt, the aftermath of defeat in the First World War effected everyone, and

---

[30] Evans, *The Coming of the Third Reich*, 118.
[31] Ibid.

as a result, tensions were high.

Mass mobilization and conscription during the war also had the effect that many of the political agitators and activists, whether on the left or the right, were veterans, and the appalling scale and horror of the conflict had desensitized many of them to violence, while the serious problems of Germany's present and future made them more willing to use violence to achieve their goals. Weimar Germany became an extraordinarily violent society: there were 354 political murders between 1919 and 1922 alone.[32] Political paramilitaries proliferated on the far-left and the far-right.

The revolution of November 1918 that swept away the *ancien régime* in Germany had been carried out primarily by Social Democrats and left-liberals, but the hard left was never quite satisfied with the results. While the Social Democratic Party of Germany (*Sozialdemokratische Partei Deutschlands*, SPD for short) was committed to parliamentarianism, the Independent Social Democrats (*Unabhängige Sozialdemokratische Partei Deutschlands*, USPD for short) and especially the Communist Party of Germany (*Kommunistische Partei Deutschlands*, KPD for short) grew frustrated with the half-measures, compromises, and slow progress inherent to democracy. The strong presence of the center-left in the Weimar government thus did not prevent the communists from attempting to carry out what they saw as the true revolution.

Meanwhile, many returning veterans with right-wing sympathies, or those who simply found it hard to adapt to civilian life after four years at war, refused to disband as ordered by the peace treaty, and formed *Freikorps* units: roving bands of soldiers offering their services as mercenaries and/or anti-communist forces. These heavily armed, highly experienced, well-equipped units operated as something like land pirates, often riding around the hinterlands on trucks and armored cars decked out in the infamous *Totenkopf*, the traditional black and white skull-and-crossbones insignia of the Hussar Cavalry. Violent clashes between

---

[32] Dreier, *Recht und Justiz*, 328.

communist revolutionaries and *Freikorps* units occurred frequently. In later years, many *Freikorps* members would make up the fighting base of the NSDAP.

Even in the realm of mainstream parliamentary politics, the Weimar period was characterized by short-lasting governments and frequent coalitions. A weak political center was constantly staving off attacks from the hard right and hard left, both of which were capable of inspiring passionate devotion, even fanaticism, among their followers, unlike the moderate parties of the center, and only this tenuous center was ideologically committed to the new democracy. Political violence was at a constant simmer, punctuated by occasional crescendos.

One such crescendo took place in Bavaria in 1919–1920 as an extension of the broader German Revolution that had already replaced the monarchy with liberal democracy. In early November of 1918, tensions were already mounting. An anti-war socialist movement led by the Independent Social Democrats (USPD) was putting pressure on the government of Bavaria, which was still technically a monarchy, a holdover from a bygone era. On November 7th they held a mass rally that marched on the *Residenz* Palace in Munich. King Ludwig III of Bavaria and his family fled the city, abdicating the throne. USPD leader Kurt Eisner declared the formation of the People's State of Bavaria, with himself and the USPD at the head.

Kurt Eisner was an eccentric, a black-bearded bohemian, a drama critic, and a Utopian, with no formal administrative experience. His disavowal of Russian Bolshevik violence and extremism, and his insistence on peaceful parliamentary methods, made him unpopular with the left wing of his party and with the communists of the KPD, while his Utopianism, perceived incompetence to govern, role in inciting a munitions worker strike during the war, and acknowledgement of German war guilt drew hatred from the right. The new government, largely inexperienced and saddled with preexisting social and economic problems, was unable to function smoothly or provide basic services. The USPD was roundly defeated in the election of January 1919, but Eisner delayed and obfuscated in an attempt to hold on to his influence, refusing to call a parliament session to hand over power until credible death threats from the esoteric folkish Thule Society forced his hand.

Anton Graf von Arco auf Valley, a young aristocrat and Army officer, apparently decided to act on these death threats, perhaps in an attempt to prove himself, as he had been rejected from the Thule Society due to partial Jewish ancestry on his mother's side. On February 21st, 1919, Anton Arco-Valley gunned down Eisner, who ironically was on his way to the parliament at that very moment to resign. The result of this was several months of complete pandemonium in Bavaria.

The young aristocrat was shot and wounded in retaliation, but saved from a lynch mob and placed under arrest. In a bizarre turn of fate, he was first held in the same cell in which Eisner had once been briefly imprisoned for treason, and later moved from another cell to make way for Adolf Hitler after the failed Beer Hall Putsch.[33][34]

News of Eisner's death quickly reached parliament, where a session was underway. Erhard Auer, both a rival and colleague of Eisner as the local leader of the Social Democratic Party and minister of the interior in Eisner's coalition government, began to deliver a eulogy. Meanwhile a devoted supporter of Eisner, the local butcher, bar waiter, and member of the Revolutionary Workers' Council Alois Lindner, acting on a false rumor that Auer had been involved in Eisner's assassination, stormed into parliament with a rifle and shot Auer twice. Auer's supporters fired back, and an unfortunate Centre Party delegate was killed in the crossfire. In the chaos and confusion of the ensuing gunfight and its aftermath, parliament scattered, and was effectively dissolved.

---

[33] Evans, *The Coming of the Third Reich*, 157.
[34] Hall, *Hitler's Munich*, 119.

Pacifist and former schoolteacher Johannes Hoffmann tried to restore order with a moderate, patched-together, SPD-led coalition government that lasted mere weeks. In early April 1919, a group of anarchist and communist intellectuals proclaimed a dictatorship of the proletariat in the new "Bavarian Soviet Republic." Hoffmann fled to Bamberg in northern Bavaria and declared this the new seat of government, but the real power remained in Munich with the communist republic.

The new government was headed by Ernst Toller, a playwright, and included in other leadership positions such figures as Gustav Landauer, an anarchist social theorist, and Erich Mühsam, another anarchist author and poet. The new regime was so heavily composed of literary leftist intellectuals from the hip bohemian Schwabing district of Munich that it earned the moniker "the regime of the coffeehouse anarchists." Bavaria's universities were opened for free attendance to anyone over eighteen, except those who wished to study history, which was declared "hostile to civilization." A plan to collectivize Bavarian farms was announced, but never enacted. Newspapers were ordered to publish poetry instead of politics on their front pages. Other amateurish appointments included a waiter as military commissar, a convicted burglar as Munich police chief, and the highly eccentric Dr. Franz Lipp as Foreign Affairs minister, who declared war on Württemberg and Switzerland for refusing to provide him with locomotives, and in a telegraph to Lenin famously complained that Hoffmann had taken the key to the ministry toilet with him when he fled to Bamberg.

Meanwhile the Communist Party, not wanting to let the opportunity afforded by the situation in Munich go to waste and the revolution be crushed, stepped in to take over. A contingent of more serious, more hardcore, and more experienced communist operatives was dispatched from Berlin to take charge of the situation. Eugen Leviné, a hardened professional revolutionary and highly capable organizer, deposed the playwright Ernst Toller to become head of the government of the Bavarian Soviet Republic.

Leviné had been born in Russia, educated in Germany, and returned to Russia to participate in the failed 1905 revolution, for which he was exiled to Siberia. He managed to escape to Germany, where he served briefly in the Army as an interpreter and at a POW camp, but his lifelong devotion to communism never wavered, and after the war he helped found the Communist Party of Germany (KPD). In Munich, with the blessing of Lenin himself,[35] Leviné began a series of radical social and economic reforms, starting with confiscating all firearms from the bourgeoisie and "reactionary elements" to arm the workers, and organizing a twenty to thirty thousand strong Red Army from the workers and communist activists. Factories were placed directly under the control of workers' councils, luxurious apartments were seized and used for government headquarters or to house the homeless, a church was occupied and converted into a revolutionary temple devoted to the "Goddess of Reason," echoing Robespierre, and Leviné planned to abolish paper money. Even more worrying, aristocratic and wealthy bourgeois civilians were taken hostage in case of reactionary retaliation, and a proclamation was issued that Bavaria was to act as the vanguard for the Bolshevization of Europe.

From the perspective of the parliamentarian government, the situation was totally out of control. Hoffmann was still technically recognized as the nominal governor of Bavaria by the federal government. It fell to him to take power back from the radicals. In his first attempt, his small force of loyalists was heavily outnumbered by the Red Army of the Bavarian Soviet Republic, which strangely was led by Ernst Toller—apparently being deposed and replaced by Leviné had left no hard feelings, at least not enough to alienate him from the revolutionary forces—and were defeated in a skirmish outside Dachau.

Meanwhile, there were troubles on the home front for the revolutionaries. Preexisting economic problems had been exacerbated by the instability, leading to shortages, notably of milk,

---

[35] Evans, *The Coming of the Third Reich*, 159.

which, along with other supplies, was probably being held back by Bavarian farmers hostile to the communists. Confronted with news of the milk shortage, Leviné infamously dismissed it as trivial because "most of it goes to the children of the bourgeoisie anyway." [36] Private wealth and food supplies were seized and expropriated for the new regime. Members of the Thule Society were infiltrating the soldiers' and workers' councils to spread dissent, and were rumored to be stockpiling weapons and supplies. Furthermore, the aggressively radical social reforms had done little to endear the revolutionary regime to the traditionally conservative, deeply Catholic population of the Bavarian countryside.

In a desperate bid to regain control, the former schoolteacher and avowed pacifist Hoffmann made a sort of deal with the devil under orders from SPD President Friedrich Ebert, augmenting his loyalist forces with a formidable *Freikorps* contingent under Lt. General Burghard von Oven to crush the communist uprising. At the end of April, the government and *Freikorps* forces took Dachau and surrounded Munich. In preparation for their push into the city, the government forces and *Freikorps* airdropped leaflets urging the civilians to stay off the streets, and the workers and soldiers in the Red Army to surrender. Facing overwhelming odds, many took heed, removing their red armbands and abandoning their weapons, so that the fighting power of the Red Army was significantly diminished when the enemy forces entered the city.

The communists raided a secret headquarters of the Thule Society in a suite at the *Hotel Vier Jahreszeiten*, where they discovered weapons, supplies, and propaganda materials. They arrested seven members of the Thule Society to hold as hostages. The Society's spy network managed to hide several high-ranking members, including Dietrich Eckart, future founder of the *Deutsche Arbeiterpartei* and publisher of the Party organ *Völkischer Beobachter*. In a moment of panic upon learning that the city was surrounded, the Red Army executed all of its Thule Society hostages, as well as

---

[36] Hall, *Hitler's Munich*, 63.

two Army officers captured in the previous skirmishes outside the city, and one art professor and painter who had been arrested for the crime of tearing down a communist propaganda poster.

Enraged at the news of the hostage massacre, the Bavarian *Freikorps* and the *Marinebrigade Ehrhardt*, another vicious *Freikorps* unit that had also helped crush the Spartacist Uprising in Berlin, could no longer be held back. The *Marinebrigade Ehrhardt* was distinguished by the swastikas painted on their helmets, perhaps the first German military or paramilitary unit to use the emblem. Notably, future SA leader Ernst Röhm and future Deputy Führer of Germany Rudolf Heß were present among the counter-revolutionary forces, while on the other side, Hitler's future chauffeur and first leader of the SS Julius Schreck actually fought in the Red Army. The combined *Freikorps* and government forces stormed the city on May 1st, which coincided with Mayday, a holiday associated with the labor movement, encountering only light resistance until they approached the city center, where heavy street-by-street fighting took place in the afternoon. The Thule Society Combat League, still hiding in the city, made its own move at that time, occupying the *Residenz* Palace and the War Ministry. The Red Army dug in at a courthouse and a brewery and put up stiff resistance, but the *Freikorps* brought in artillery to shell the communist strongholds, and then cleared them out with flamethrowers. The Red Army retreated to the *Hauptbahnhof* (the central train station) to make its last stand. The fighting lasted two more days, but the communists' situation was hopeless.

The government and *Freikorps* forces were victorious by the morning of May 3rd. Estimates of casualties vary widely according to different sources, but all agree that at least several dozen government and *Freikorps* troops, dozens more bystanders, and several hundred communists were killed in the fighting. Hundreds more were summarily executed in the following days, often on mere suspicion of revolutionary activity. In one particularly bad incident on May 6th, a gang of *Freikorps* men, drunk and spoiling for a fight, slaughtered twenty-one innocent civilians, acting on a false rumor that they were involved in revolutionary activity. They were wrong. The victims had been members of the St. Josef Society, a Catholic workers' club. After this notorious mishap, the populace was outraged, and the non-Bavarian *Freikorps* were forced to leave the city in shame.

Many of the instigators of the revolution were killed, including Gustav Landauer and Red Army commander Rudolf Egelhofer. Ernst Toller and Erich Mühsam were arrested and given lengthy prison sentences. Eugen Leviné, who had come close to becoming Germany's Lenin, went into hiding, but was tracked down in mid-May and given a public show trial, where he was sentenced to death. In his trial defense, he famously never denied his charges or downplayed his role, but merely stated his case and received his death sentence impassively, with the remark, "We communists are all dead mean on leave."

On paper, Hoffmann's SPD government was restored, but on balance this period was a disaster for the left. The Social Democrats and Communists distrusted each other, and were never able to effectively cooperate after this point. The SPD in Bavaria now had to share power in a coalition with the centrist *Deutsche Demokratische Partei* (German Democratic Party, DDP for short) and the conservative *Bayerische Volkspartei* (Bavarian People's Party, BVP for short). Furthermore, military rule was enacted, with conservative Army generals installed as the commandant of Munich and the general commander of the new *Reichswehr* military district of Bavaria. The instability, radical social reforms, and privations brought about by this period inflamed a deep hatred of the left among many Bavarians, and the right made hay of the bitter experience of Soviet Bavaria and the specter of "Red terror" for endless anti-communist propaganda. The anti-communist right consolidated its power in Bavaria, which had already been traditionally conservative, and from then on was generally perceived as the most right-wing part of the country. This would be significant later on in terms of the government's frequent leniency in dealing with Hitler and the NSDAP.

The DAP, later to become the NSDAP, was founded during this period, but at the time it was only one group among many on the nationalist and right-wing scene. There were the esoteric folkish secret societies like the aforementioned Thule Society, nominally apolitical veterans' associations like *Der Stahlhelm* (the Steel Helmet), as well as right-wing "defense leagues." But the NSDAP and its fighting organization, the SA, were to be distinct from all of these. Hitler specifically mocked the types of role-players "who brandish Teutonic tin swords and wear tanned bearskins, with ox horns mounted over their bearded faces," and then "scatter when the first communist cudgel appears," [37] warning that no small secret society operating with cloak and dagger tactics could retake Germany, but only a mass movement. [38] He noted that both the traditional right-wing parties and the defense leagues were lacking elements crucial to success: "The so-called national parties lacked influence because they had no force that could effectively demonstrate in the street," while on the other hand, "the defense leagues...were masters of the street and of the state, but they lacked political ideals and goals." [39] Unlike these other various nationalist and right-wing groups, the NSDAP was to perfect the elusive formula for success by combining elements of folkish intellectualism, clear social policy, the street fighting capability of a mass movement to challenge communism, as well as a party-political apparatus ready to assume parliamentary seats and government posts.

Another crescendo of instability and violence in the Weimar period was precipitated precisely by one of these other groups on the far-right: the shadowy *Organisation Consul*. On June 24th, 1922, just over a month before the following speech was delivered, members of *Organisation Consul* assassinated Walther Rathenau, the Foreign Minister of the Weimar Republic, in a drive-by shooting.

---

[37] Hitler, *Mein Kampf, Vol. I*, C. 12.16, 661.
[38] Hitler, *Mein Kampf, Vol. II*, C. 9.14, 331-335.
[39] Ibid., C. 9.9, 311.

Rathenau was a moderate liberal politician and a tycoon of German industry who had been in charge of the War Raw Materials Department during the First World War. As his wealth and power increased during the war, the far-right accused him of profiteering. Furthermore, he had recently concluded negotiations for the Treaty of Rapallo with the Soviet Union, in which Germany recognized the communist regime as the only legitimate government of the Soviet Union, opened up trade, and renounced German territorial claims from the war. On balance, the treaty was mutually beneficial for both states, much to the chagrin of Britain and France, and it even included secret provisions to allow Germany to build its military capacity back up in Russian territory in exchange for training Russian officers at German military academies. Nevertheless, it opened Rathenau to accusations from the far-right that he had links to communism.

On the morning of June 24th, 1922, as he was being chauffeured from his home to the Foreign Office, his car was overtaken and cornered by another vehicle driven by Ernst Werner Techow. Erwin Kern opened fire on Rathenau with a MP18 submachine gun, dumping the entire magazine into the vehicle. Hermann Fischer then threw a grenade into Rathenau's car for good measure, before Techow sped off. Rathenau was killed instantly, but miraculously his chauffeur managed to survive both the hail of bullets and the grenade blast. Techow was shortly arrested, tried, and convicted for the murder, while Fischer and Kern went on the run, but were killed weeks later in a shootout with police. All of the assassins were young students and members of the secretive *Organisation Consul*, which had initially formed from the most hardcore and devoted remaining members of the *Marinebrigade Ehrhardt Freikorps* after it was forced to disband, and had carried out numerous such assassinations throughout 1921 and 1922, including that of Finance Minister Matthias Erzberger in August 1921. Aside from pure revenge and bloodlust, the logic behind the assassinations was to provoke the left into retaliation, beginning a civil war in Germany in which the *Organisation Consul* would graciously step in, help the nationalist forces crush the left, sweep aside the weak moderate democratic parties, and install a military dictatorship in Germany.

Instead, in response to the assassination, the Weimar government under Friedrich Ebert and the SPD passed the Law for the Protection of the Republic, banning any groups that engaged in, advocated, or even endorsed political violence, and giving the state broad powers to prosecute extremist groups and individuals.

It was in the aftermath of this assassination and the passage of this law, and in this general atmosphere of instability, polarization, and habitual political violence, that Adolf Hitler delivered the following speech, attempting to make sense of the political situation in Germany, and to frame it within a broader historical context.

The Speech

My dear fellow Germans!

A sudden commotion has come over the German people. Now even those circles are beginning to stir which until now have been deaf to the constant warnings that we have been trying to address to the mass of our people almost without interruption for the past three years. Of course, many people still do not know why they are upset. They believe that perhaps it is only about so-called special privileges, or about the restriction of freedom of speech, or about the politicization of the civil service, and so on. Certainly, all these are extremely serious matters. Today, however, it is about much more.

It is about a huge process of destruction of our people and our Fatherland. This is happening now before our very eyes. All these things would be trifles in themselves, if they did not represent characteristics of a process which has been taking place for many years and whose end will be a horrible one! We can all sense that now two worlds are colliding with each other, and not only here, but everywhere we look: in the now-oppressed Russia, in Italy, in France and in England, et cetera — a relentless struggle between the ideals of the national-minded and the nebulous International.

It is a struggle that now goes back almost 120 years. It began at the moment when the Jew received the right of citizenship in the European states. The political emancipation of the Jews was the beginning of a madness, for with it one gave full civic rights and equality to a people which was racially much more clearly and abruptly demarcated than all others, which always formed and will always form a state within the state. Perhaps not all at once, but it went just as it does today, and as it always has gone: first a little finger, then a second and a third, and so bit by bit, until at last a people which still in the eighteenth century appeared to be completely alien, came to possess politically the same rights of citizenship as ourselves.

And that's exactly how it went economically as well.

The mass industrialization of the people meant the concentration of great masses of workers in the cities. Large crowds came into being, unfortunately not properly handled by those who had the moral obligation to take care of them. In parallel with this, however, there was a gradual monetization of the entire labor force. The "share system" came into being, and as a result the stock exchange gradually became the conductor of the entire national economy, but the owners of this institution were and are without exception Jews. I say without exception, because the few who participate in it as non-Jews are in the end nothing more than screens, token Christians who are needed to keep up the pretense to the broad masses that these institutions are natural to all peoples and their economies, while in reality they are institutions which correspond exclusively to the essence of the Jewish people, and thus also spring from it.

At that time, Europe stood at a crossroads. It began to divide into two halves, Western Europe on the one hand, and Central and Eastern Europe on the other. Western Europe first advanced in industrialization. Especially in England, crowds of agricultural laborers, sons of farmers, or ruined farmers themselves, poured into the cities and formed a new fourth estate. But there is one important fact here which many fail to take into account. England, like France, had relatively few Jews. The consequence of this, however, was that the great masses concentrated in the cities did not come into direct contact with this foreign nation, and the aversion which would necessarily arise did not find sufficient nourishment. Finally, the Jews of England, who at that time numbered scarcely fifty to sixty thousand, were able to "Europeanize" themselves with playful ease to such an extent that they remained hidden from the primitive eye of the common man, and he could not notice them. As "pillars of the economy," but especially as the bearers of great capital, they no longer appeared as foreigners, but as Englishmen themselves! This prevented antisemitism from gaining fundamental power in these countries. The same was true of France. Precisely because of this, however, it was possible to introduce in these countries the system known as democracy. Precisely in these countries it was possible to establish a form of government that could mean nothing but the outweighing of intelligence and true energy by the sheer dead weight of the masses. In other words, it was possible there for the small class of Jewish intelligentsia hidden in the British people to manipulate the broad masses with playful ease in such a way that the latter, unaware of whom they were obeying, served the purposes of this small class. There, with press propaganda and control of information, it was possible to found the prototypical large parties. Even back then, there were always two or three groups that appeared to be fighting against each other, but in reality were all hanging on a gold thread, and everything was adjusted to a peculiar human characteristic: that man gets tired of something he has had for a long time; he wants something new. And so two parties were needed. One of them rules and the other one forms the opposition. When one party is played out, the opposition party comes to power, and the played-out party now takes its turn as the opposition. After twenty years, the new party becomes played out, and the game repeats itself anew. In reality, this is certainly an ingenious mill in which the interests of a nation are ground down. As is well known, such a thing is called "self-government of a people."

In the process, we always find two main buzzwords, "freedom" and "democracy," as figureheads. Freedom is understood to mean, at least among the authoritative bodies that actually govern, the possibility of plundering the broad masses without limits or resistance. The masses themselves, of course, believe that freedom means the exercise of a very particular freedom of movement, both freedom of movement of the tongue, and freedom to move about the streets, et cetera — a bitter deception!

On the whole we can say that England as well as France put on the chains of slavery already back then. With a bronze firmness these states are in Jewish chains, as long as the Jew himself does not feel the necessity and "expediency" of a change in this condition. This change will also occur there in the foreseeable future.

Now, what is the difference between this Western Europe on the one hand, and Eastern and Central Europe on the other?

Here, industrialization did not happen as quickly. The masses streamed more slowly from the static countryside into the cities. Only slowly did the large cities develop here, and it took a long time for a fourth estate to form in Germany as well. In addition to this, there was the fact that both in the East and in Germany the presence of the Jew was constantly felt by the broad masses because of his greater numbers, so that the whole people had an inner instinctive aversion to him among all classes, but most of all the peasant, the worker, and the honest petty-bourgeois. On the other hand, a part of our own aristocracy and a certain circle of merchants, to whom money and gold are everything, were the most quickly corrupted.

If political contamination was already more difficult because of the large number of Jews and the consequent aversion of the mass of our people, the difficulty was increased by a form of government which did not place ultimate authority in the hands of a weak-willed and irresponsible so-called majority, but which was traditionally anchored in a personal apex: the monarchy.

At that time the Jew had to admit to himself that in these countries the resurrection of an enlightened despotism would by no means be impossible. There were three powerful factors at the disposal of the head of state: the Army, with a huge, wonderfully well-coordinated officer corps; the body of civil servants with its enormous apparatus of completely dutiful officials; and a great broad mass of people who were inwardly still free from any poison. And if we add to this the fact that at that time the national intelligentsia in Germany was still almost exclusively predominant, that even wholesale trade was still in German hands, that above all the young, flourishing, rich industry was of German origin and

German ownership, and that further the enormous peasantry, the last reservoir of a nation's strength, was still completely uncontaminated and healthy, we understand the following consideration of the Jewish people, who at that time were gaining political equality: when, through industrialization, a new fourth estate is formed in the cities, there is a danger that this fourth estate will fraternize with the monarchy and that, on this basis, a "people's kingdom" or "people's empire" will come about, willing and ready to deal the death blow to the international financial powers. [...]

Therein lay a grave danger for Jewry. If the broad mass of the then-forming labor force had come into national hands, and had then seized the nation as a true social catalyst, if the liberation of the individual estates had taken place organically step by step, and if the state form had later been based on this, then what many hoped for on November 9th, 1918 would have come about: a national, social state. For socialism as such is anything but an international creation. As a noble conception it has grown exclusively in Aryan hearts and reaches its intellectual apotheosis only in Aryan minds. It is completely foreign to the Jew. He will always and forever be the born private capitalist of the most exploitative kind! And it is no coincidence that the great pillars on which some later mistakenly tried to build the foundation of a so-called "people's enlightenment," were all without exception opponents of the Jews. Voltaire and Rousseau, as well as our German Fichte, and many others, they all without exception had been united in the realization that the Jew is not only a foreign body, different in his whole being, which is entirely harmful to the Aryan, but that Jewry as a people for itself stands against us and will stand against us as a mortal enemy, always and for all time.

Jewry has made a politically truly ingenious step. This capitalistic people, which first brought the unscrupulous exploitation of human beings into this world, knew how to take the leadership of this fourth estate into its own hands. The Jew became the founder of the social-democratic and communist movements. And with extraordinary skill he gradually played the leadership exclusively into his own hands by two methods. One he used on the right, the other on the left, but he had his apostles in both camps.

On the right, he endeavored to exacerbate all the existing problems by emphasizing as much as possible those qualities which were repugnant to the man of the people, the poor devil, so that the latter would be incited as much as possible. It was he who increased and drove the greed for money to the extreme. He was the one who preached unscrupulousness in the use of any and all means as a matter of course in business dealings, and by his competition forced the others to join in. He was the one who pushed hard-heartedness in the ruthless use of these means to such an extent that the saying, "Business, too, marches over corpses," became self-evident. But it was he in particular who increased gaudiness in the most disgusting form to such an extent that it could only become a grave insult to the broad masses. While he thus corrupted the people on the one hand by his evil example, he destroyed them also in terms of blood. More and more Jews wormed their way into the families of the upper classes, and it was from the Jews that these families took their wives. The consequence of this, however, was that in a short time the leading stratum of the nation became completely alienated from its own people.

All of that was the prerequisite for his work on the left side. And he exploited these prerequisites brilliantly. [...]

And he succeeded further by ingenious use of the press to influence the masses so much that the faults of the left were seen by the right as the faults of the German worker, and the faults of the right appeared to the German worker as the faults of the so-called bourgeoisie. Neither of them noticed that the faults of both sides were the intended result of malicious foreign incitement. And only in this way does it become comprehensible that history's bit of staircase wit could occur: that stock exchange Jews became leaders of a German workers' movement. [...]

And in all this, one can see how they work together so wonderfully, the stock market Jew and the workers' leader, the financial times and the workers' rag. They both pursue one direction and one goal, whether *Frankfurter Zeitung* and *Münchner Post, Berliner Tageblatt* and *Rote Freiheit* or *Rote Fahne*. [40] They operate wonderfully together. While the company attorney Moses Kohn stiffens the resolve of his company so that it faces the demands of its workers as rigidly as possible — that is, intransigently — his brother, the workers' organizer Isaak Kohn, is in the factory yard stirring up the masses: "Look at them, they just want to oppress you! Throw off the chains!" et cetera. And above, his brother helps to forge these chains in the first place. On the one hand the financial times is eager to awaken the incessant addiction to speculation. Speculation on the crops and foodstuffs of the people proliferates in an unprecedented way. On the other side is the workers' rag, riling up the masses by telling them, "Bread has gotten more expensive, and this and that have gotten more expensive, don't tolerate it anymore, arise proletarians, down with so-and-so!" [...]

This process is practically complete in Russia. The whole of today's Russia is nothing more than a ruined culture and a mature colony to be cultivated by foreign capital, which must nevertheless draw in Aryan minds as practical laborers, for the Jew is not fit for this either. Here, too, he is only rapacious and gluttonous. He knows no orderly economy and no orderly body of people. He steals everything over there in Russia. They take the diamonds away from the nobleman "to help the people." But then the diamonds disappear into foreign companies, never to be seen again. He seizes the wealth of the church, but not to feed the people, no; everything wanders away and disappears without a trace. He has become completely irrational in his greed; he cannot preserve

---

[40] *Frankfurter Zeitung* and *Berliner Tageblatt* were mainstream, business-oriented newspapers; the *Münchner Post* was a Social Democratic paper; *Freiheit* was a communist paper affiliated with the Independent Social Democratic Party (USPD); *Rote Fahne* was another communist paper.

anything; he has only the drive for destruction in him. Once he has destroyed everything, he will collapse along with that which he has destroyed.

It is a tragic fate that has struck the people of the northeast of our Fatherland. In the past, we were often supposed to get upset about some bandit who received his just punishment here or there. When an anarchist was put up against the wall in Spain, there was a great howl in our country about this "sacrifice of the most precious human blood." When a Max Hölz is brought before a court of justice in our country, the so-called "German" press never tires of reporting in long articles exactly how he, as the apostle of a higher conviction, is being unfairly condemned.[41] And if a stock exchange bandit is hanged somewhere in Hungary, then that is enough to boycott that whole state. Yes, there must be a boycott, because this state has a human life on its conscience, and we are so infinitely sensitive. [...]

Today, however, more than thirty million people have been slowly martyred to death in the East, some on the scaffold, some by machine guns and similar means, some in actual slaughterhouses, and millions and millions through hunger. And we all know that this wave of hunger is creeping on. It is all lies and deception, what is declared about the aid delivered there.

---

[41] Max Hölz (alternate spelling Hoelz) was a notorious communist agitator and militant with an interesting story of his own. A worker and veteran, he joined the Communist Party of Germany (KPD) after the war, and formed his own regional Red Guard, whose actions were so extreme and chaotic that even the KPD disavowed them and expelled them from the party. Hölz then joined the extremist, anti-parliamentarian Communist Workers Party (KAPD), which favoured violent direct action. More of a warlord than an ideologue, he took no interest in party politics. Instead, he and his motorised "expropriation squads" rode around the countryside on trucks and motorcycles decked out with red flags, occupying factories, bombing courthouses, robbing banks, freeing political prisoners, and eluding the authorities. He became something of a folk hero among the workers for stealing from the rich to give to the poor, gaining the moniker "The Communist Bandit." He was finally arrested in 1921 and sentenced to life in prison, but pardoned in 1928, after which he fled to the Soviet Union. He continued his outspokenness and rabble-rousing there, and voiced criticism of the communist establishments in Germany and in the Soviet Union. In 1933 he supposedly drowned in a mysterious "boating accident."

What does "aid" mean when on one side there is this greedy werewolf who eats up all this aid himself? [...]

They'll call you a reactionary, a monarchist, and a pan-Germanist if you criticize today's conditions. I ask you, what would be the state of Germany if there had been no criticism at all during these three years? I think that in reality there has been far, far too little criticism. Our people are unfortunately far too uncritical, otherwise they would not only have seen through many things long ago, but would have shut them down with their fists! Thus the crisis is reaching its climax. The day is not far off when the German Revolution will have to be pushed forward for the reasons mentioned above. The leaders know too well that it cannot go on forever as it is today. It will be possible to raise prices ten times by 100 percent, but it is questionable whether the Germans will accept a billion marks a day in salary, only to starve to death at the end of the day. It is questionable whether one will be able to maintain this great deception of the nation. The day will come when it will not be possible — and that is why we have to make provisions.

And so Germany is now entering that stage whose extremes Russia has already felt. Now, in a last grandiose push, the criticism and resistance — nay, the honesty — that is still present in us, is to be crushed. And this will happen all the faster, the more they see that one particular insight is beginning to take hold of the masses: the National Socialist doctrine!

Whether under ours or another name, more and more it gains ground everywhere. All these people cannot yet be in a party together, but wherever one goes in Germany, indeed almost in the whole world, there are already millions of thinkers who know that a state can only be built on a social basis, and secondly, that the mortal enemy of every truly social idea is the international Jew.

Every truly national thought is ultimately social; that is, whoever is ready to stand up for his people so completely that he really knows no higher ideal than the welfare of this people, whoever has grasped the meaning of our great song "Germany,

Germany above all," in such a way that nothing in this world is higher to him than this Germany, people and country, country and people, he is a socialist! And he who sympathizes with the poorest of this people's citizens, who sees in each individual a valuable member of the whole, and who recognizes that the whole can only flourish when it is not composed of rulers and oppressed, but when all, according to their ability, fulfill their duty to the Fatherland and the national community, and are valued accordingly, he who stands for the preservation of the strength and youthfulness of the millions of working people, and he who above all stands up to ensure that our most precious asset, our youth, is not prematurely used up in unhealthy, harmful work—he is not only a socialist, but a nationalist in the highest sense of the word! But it is the teaching of this insight which appears as the most threatening danger to Jewry as the leadership of today's revolutions. And it is precisely this danger that pushes him to strike as quickly as possible. Because he knows one thing for sure: in the end only this young movement can threaten him!

He knows the old parties. They are easy to please. A few endowments in the form of ministerial chairs and similar posts and they fall in line. He knows one thing above all: they are so simple-mindedly stupid. Every day they prove correct the saying that he whom the gods would destroy, they first strike blind.[42] They are struck blind, and so the gods must want to destroy them. Yes, just look at these parties and their leaders, Stresemann and whoever else.[43] They are truly harmless. They do not grasp the root of the problem. They all still believe that they can fight a battle, which is

---

[42] From Latin *Quos Deus vult perdere, prius dementat*, literally "Whom God wishes to destroy, he first drives mad"; in Hitler's German speech he said "strike blind" instead of "drive mad," either as an honest mistake, or to emphasise the short-sightedness of the mainstream parties.

[43] Gustav Stresemann was a politician of the conservative German People's Party (DVP). He served as Chancellor of the Weimar Republic for a brief period of 102 days in 1923, then served as foreign minister in various coalition governments until his death of a stroke in 1929. He is also known for popularising a modern variation on formal dress, substituting the formal morning coat for the less formal suit jacket. This semi-formal variation on morning dress is still referred to as "the Stresemann."

a battle like none other in this world, through leniency, humanity, and compliance. Through leniency they believe they can show the opponent on the left that they are willing to compromise in order to stop the deadly cancer somewhere in the middle.

No, and a thousand times no! There are only two possibilities: victory or defeat! [...]

We know that the so-called Law for the Protection of the Republic coming from Berlin today is nothing more than a means of silencing any criticism.[44] But we also know that they will now try by all means to make the last minds who see disaster approaching in Germany disappear in time. That is why the population of northern Germany is being whipped up against Bavaria by means of lies and distortion. They have the feeling up there that in one corner of the Reich the German people are not yet broken. And that is where we National Socialists have to intervene. We National Socialists are, by God, the most loyal supporters of our German Fatherland. In three years we have fought a battle, sometimes against death and the devil, but always and only for our German Fatherland. We have come so far that in the end we landed in prison ourselves for our efforts. But there is one thing we want to say: we distinguish between the German government and the German Fatherland. If some half-Asiatic scoundrel here in the *Landtag*[45] or in the Reichstag in Berlin accuses us today of not being loyal to the Reich, I would ask you not to grieve over it. The Bavarian people has proven its loyalty to the Reich with its countless regiments, which fought for the Reich and were often buried two or three times under the earth. We are convinced, and this is ultimately our only great faith, that the German Reich will once again rise out of this most bitter misery and all this hardship, different from how it exists now, not as a birth of misery and wretchedness, but that we will once again have a true German Reich of freedom and honor, a real Fatherland for the entire

---

[44] A law passed in response to the assassination of Foreign Minister Walther Rathenau banning all groups advocating or engaging in political violence.
[45] State legislative assembly of a German *Bundesland* (province).

German people, and not a haven for foreign crooks!

Today people speak incessantly about "federalism," et cetera. I beg you, don't rail against the Prussians while groveling before the Jews, but show yourselves stiff-necked against those now in Berlin. And if you do that, you will have millions and millions of Germans behind you throughout Germany, whether they be Prussians, Badeners, Württembergers, Saxons, or Austrian Germans.

What we did not "fear" at that time, but rather foresaw, because I never said that it *could* come, but always that it *would* come, because it *must* come and there is no way around it, has now come to pass. Because we foresaw this at the time, we resisted, and because we foresaw that today our task would not be complete, but that this too is only another step on the way into a morass of blood, we now ask you one last time: remain stiff-necked now and resist to the last!

We National Socialists, who for three years now have done nothing but preach, insulted and besmirched by all, mocked and ridiculed by some, blasphemed and slandered by others, we cannot go back! For us there is only the one straight path. We know that the fight that is about to begin will be a hard one. It will not be fought out in the Reich Court in Leipzig, nor will it be fought out in a Berlin cabinet; it will be fought out by those real factors that have always shaped world history up to now. I heard a few days ago in a ministerial speech that the rights of a state could not be eliminated by simple majority decisions, but only by treaties. Bismarck had something slightly different to say about this. He said that the fate of nations could not be determined by majority decisions, nor by treaties, but only by blood and iron!

There should be no doubt about it: we National Socialists will not let Jewry cut our throats without fighting back. In Berlin they might organize dinner parties with the Jewish executioners of Soviet Russia. Here they will never do that! They may today begin to set up the Cheka, the Extraordinary Commission, in Germany and let it operate freely; we will never submit to such a Jewish commission! We have the rock-solid conviction that if seven million people in this state are determined to stand up for their "No!" to the last, then the evil specter over the rest of the Reich will collapse into nothingness, for what Germany needs and longs for today is a symbol of power and strength!

So, at the end of my speech, I have to make a special request to those of you who are young. There is a very special reason for this. The other parties train their boys in mouthing off; we would rather train them physically. Because I'll tell you this: the boy who does not find his way to where the fate of his people will ultimately be decided, who only studies philosophy and sits behind his books or at home behind the stove — he is not a German boy!

I call upon you: join our storm divisions! No matter what slander and calumny you hear about them, you will know that they are formed for our protection, for your protection, and thus not only for the protection of the movement, but for the protection of a future Germany. And if you are blasphemed, and if you are besmirched, then hail to you boys! You already have the good fortune to be hated at the age of eighteen and nineteen by the worst scoundrels. What others have to fight for, this highest good of distinguishing the honest man from the bandit, falls into your lap as a bit of good luck in your youth. Be confident that the more they slander you, the higher you will rise in our esteem! We know that none of us could speak if it were not for you! We know and see that our movement would be crushed if you did not protect it. Today you are the defense of a movement that is called to revolutionarily transform Germany from the ground up, so that what so many expected on November 9th may come to be: a German Reich, a Germanic, and for our sake, a German republic!

Every battle must be fought to the end — better that it come sooner rather than later. And the one who goes into the fight with the most confidence from the start stands the most secure. And this highest confidence we can carry in our hearts, for whoever is the leader of the German people on our side today, by God, has nothing to gain, but everything to lose. He will have one great guarantee: whoever fights for us today cannot win great laurels at present, much less great wealth; rather, he is likely to end up in prison. Whoever is a leader for us today must be an idealist, if only because he leads those against whom everything seems to conspire.

And finally, take this one assurance with you: if this fight were not to come, Germany would never get peace. It would languish, and at best finally perish as a rotten corpse. But we are not destined for that. We do not believe in the downfall of our people; we believe that the disaster which today our Lord God sends upon Germany is the scourge which will whip us up to a new greatness, to a new power and glory, to a Germany which for the first time shall fulfill what millions of our best through centuries and millennia have inwardly hoped for: a Germany of the German people!

THE TRIAL SPEECHES

Munich People's Court
February 26th and March 27th, 1924

The Background

1923 was a particularly bad year for Weimar Germany. If 1919 was the peak of anti-Weimar and anti-democratic agitation from the left, then 1923 was the peak of anti-Weimar and anti-democratic agitation from the right. The reparations Germany was forced to pay, especially to France, as a condition of the Treaty of Versailles were a heavy burden on the German economy. The value of the mark was already depreciating quickly. When Germany fell behind on these payments, a vengeful France marched soldiers in to occupy the coal producing Ruhr region. The Social Democratic government's response to the Ruhr occupation was passive resistance in the form of a general strike. This caused the already inflated currency to collapse totally.

The horror stories from this fateful year are well-known: life savings rendered worthless in a matter of hours, increasingly ludicrous denominations of currency issued, from 5 million mark coins minted to 50 trillion mark banknotes barely worth the paper they were printed on, a wheelbarrow full of cash to buy a loaf of bread. The state was in a crisis.

The response in conservative Bavaria, where there was already a history of tension with Prussia, and now especially with the Social Democrat government in Berlin, was to declare a state of emergency and appoint reactionary aristocrat Gustav Ritter von Kahr as state commissar, essentially granting him dictatorial power. Now the power in Bavaria was shared among a triumvirate composed of Kahr, state police chief colonel Hans Ritter von Seißer, and Bavarian *Reichswehr* general Otto von Lossow.

This anti-communist reactionary government gave significant leeway for the far-right and nationalist scene to flourish, and Bavaria became known as a hotbed of right-wing political and paramilitary activity. By the end of the year, the NSDAP had grown to fifty-five thousand members.

Benito Mussolini's March on Rome of October 1922 inspired nationalists in Germany. The image of a nationalist strongman taking action and leading his men to seize power was evocative and powerful. It was around this time, too, that the Führer cult began to emerge, precipitated by some of Hitler's most ardent supporters rather than Hitler himself, though he did nothing to discourage it. He had primarily thought of himself as a propagandist whose task it was to instill in the German people a sense of national consciousness and prepare them for an as-yet unknown future leader who would save them, but his early speeches give no indication that he thought that leader would be himself. But as his influence grew, many supporters, and even just observers who heard him speak, came to be convinced that if anyone could do it, it was him. At one meeting, early Party supporter and editor of the *Völkischer Beobachter* Hermann Esser declared, "Germany's Mussolini is named Adolf Hitler." [46] In November 1922, the first rumors began to be whispered that Hitler might attempt a coup similar to Mussolini's.

The "Working Community of Patriotic Fighting Associations" was founded in February 1923 primarily by Ernst Röhm, a lifelong soldier who had enlisted in the Army long before the outbreak of the First World War, and stayed on in the *Freikorps* after it ended. He was present with the *Freikorps* forces that crushed the Bavarian Soviet Republic in May 1919, and joined the German Workers'

---

[46] Maser, *Frühgeschichte der NSDAP*, 356.

Party later that year, not long after Adolf Hitler, though he was always much more interested in military and paramilitary rather than political matters. His rank as a well-regarded and decorated Captain during the war gave him very valuable connections to high-ranking figures in the military and in nationalist politics, and his time as a supply officer gave him valuable experience in organizing and logistical matters, as well as access to surplus weapons and equipment. He became so important in supplying various paramilitaries that he earned the moniker "the machine gun king."

Röhm's valuable connections prepared the ground for Hitler's rise to prominence. He nominated Hitler for the role of "political leader" of the Working Community of Patriotic Fighting Associations, which included the *Bund Oberland*, the *Bund Reichskriegsflagge* (Imperial War Flag League), the *Kampfverband Niederbayern* (Combat League of Lower Bavaria), and the *Wikingbund* (Viking League). Hitler's role was to articulate the specific shared political goals of the Working Community. Röhm also introduced Hitler to the chief of the German Army Command, the highest-ranking military man in the country, General Hans von Seeckt, who also had reactionary anti-communist beliefs. Hitler and Röhm's bid to convince Seeckt to commit the military to drive the French out of the Ruhr proved unsuccessful. Their next hope was in appealing to the ruling triumvirate in Bavaria. Without Röhm's connections, none of these aristocratic officers would likely have had the time of day for Hitler, and in all probability they would have dismissed him as a beer hall rabble-rouser and roughneck. Indeed, this was the attitude that many continued to take towards him, but with his growing clout, thanks in no small part to Röhm's influence, Hitler was becoming a force that they at least had to contend with, if not respect.

Rowdier members of the NSDAP, and of the right-wing and nationalist scene more broadly, were itching for action, for their chance to take on the left and the Weimar government, and they would not be content with yet more speeches and bloviating propaganda. Hitler was under pressure to make things happen and to live up to the Führer cult that was growing around him. On Mayday of 1923 he proposed a counter-demonstration to the socialist left's traditional mass rallies, but the Bavarian authorities, justifiably fearing that the situation would descend into violence and get out of control, intervened, keeping the two sides far apart and heavily guarded. Once again the mounting energies and aggression of the nationalists were frustrated.

Hitler's next major propaganda success was at the massive German Day rally on September 1st and 2nd, 1923 in Nuremberg, with over one hundred thousand members of various right-wing and nationalist paramilitaries attending, including the SA. Multiple speakers addressed the troops, Hitler among them. This rally also afforded Hitler the chance to rub elbows and appear on stage with the legendary General Erich Ludendorff, a German folk hero due to his role in critical German victories of the First World War, who during the last years of the war had acted unofficially as something of a military dictator of Germany, and tacitly supported various nationalist causes and groups after the war. Ludendorff was by far the biggest name on the right, and was something of a symbolic leader of German nationalism.

The German Day rally resulted in the creation of the *Kampfbund* (combat league), an even larger successor to the Working Community of Patriotic Fighting Associations, incorporating several more groups. Once again, Hitler was appointed as the *Kampfbund*'s political leader.

It was in this capacity that Hitler, with the help of Ludendorff, appealed to the ruling triumvirate in Bavaria to take action against the federal government. There was already significant tension between these aristocratic reactionaries and the social democrats in Berlin, but in a series of meetings with Hitler, the gentlemen were noncommittal. They all agreed that something must be done, that things could not possibly go on like this, there was theoretical discussion of a coup—indeed, several times they even hinted they would support a coup—but the gentlemen of this triumvirate already had their own intentions to act against Berlin, and these did not involve the upstart corporal and rabble-rouser from Austria. The gentlemen were above all cautious: they would not act without assurance of support from the military, and this assurance was not yet forthcoming.

Hitler's supporters were restless. The state was in a crisis. Inflation was still not under control. The mood of much of the public, especially in Bavaria, was hostile to the government in Berlin. Hitler was more powerful than he had ever been. He did not want to let the opportunity slip away. He decided to force the issue.

On November 8th, 1923, a meeting was held at Munich's *Bürgerbräukeller* (Citizens' Brewery Cellar), where Gustav von Kahr was addressing an audience of about three thousand people. Hans von Seißer and Otto von Lossow were also present.

At around eight thirty in the evening, about six hundred SA men, armed from Röhm's weapons caches, surrounded the hall and set up a machine gun in the auditorium. Hitler and a squad of his closest comrades including Alfred Rosenberg, Rudolf Heß, Hermann Göring, and Max Erwin von Scheubner-Richter pushed their way into the overcrowded hall. Hitler jumped up on a chair, pulled out his pistol, fired a shot in the air to gain everyone's attention while Kahr was still speaking, and proclaimed that the national revolution would begin tonight.

While Hermann Göring addressed the crowd to calm them down, and another detachment of SA men took a car to pick up General Ludendorff and bring him to the hall, Hitler and his men brought the gentlemen of the triumvirate into the antechamber to push them to lead the coup and take up their roles in the new national government they would proclaim under Ludendorff. Much to Hitler's irritation, Kahr kept complaining about his speech being interrupted, and was worried about losing face in front of his supporters, as he did not want it to look like Hitler had bullied him into accepting a role in the coup. Frustrated, Hitler addressed the audience himself, whipping them up into a state of excitement about the national revolution about to take place.

One of Kahr's supporters, Dr. Karl Alexander von Mueller, later reported:

I cannot remember in my entire life such a change in the attitude of a crowd in a few minutes, almost a few seconds.... Hitler had turned them inside out, as one turns a glove inside out, with a few sentences. It had almost something of hocus-pocus, or magic about it.[47]

Hitler finished his speech by telling the audience, now firmly on his side, "Outside are Kahr, Lossow, and Seißer. They are struggling hard to reach a decision. May I tell them that you will stand behind them?" The audience roared their approval. In many ways, Hitler thus "spoke" the Beer Hall Putsch into happening, just as he would eventually speak his way into power.

Hitler returned to the triumvirate to assure them the audience would support them in a coup, but his bit of theatrics probably did nothing to assuage Kahr's concerns about saving face and appearing in control. He then ordered Göring and Heß to take some of their best men to take several members of the Bavarian government into custody.

General Ludendorff arrived on the scene around nine o'clock in the evening, having previously known nothing about the plans for a coup on this particular evening, though he had been in agreement that it would be necessary at some point, and now that the moment was upon him, he too urged the men of the triumvirate to lead it with him. Eventually, the gentlemen reluctantly agreed. Ludendorff, Hitler, and the triumvirate returned to the main hall, announced the formation of a new Reich government, all shook hands with each other, and then allowed the audience to leave the hall.

Meanwhile, from their staging point at the *Löwenbräukeller*, another brewery's beer hall on the other side of town, Röhm's

---

[47] von Müller, *Im Wandel einer Welt*, 162.

Kampfbund troops retrieved weapons from caches that had been prepared in advance and moved to seize several key targets around the city, including military headquarters, barracks, and government buildings.

Hitler made a crucial mistake when he left the hall with Ludendorff in charge to personally deal with trouble at the engineers' barracks, where the soldiers were refusing to cooperate with the *Kampfbund*. Ludendorff took the gentlemen of the triumvirate at their word that they would assist in the coup, and allowed them to leave the hall, where they immediately agreed with one another to go back on their word, which they felt Hitler had forced them to give against their wishes anyway. The gentlemen communicated news of the coup to the *Reichswehr* and police, and assured both that they were not going along with it.

Hours passed without word from the triumvirate. The *Kampfbund* troops that had managed to seize their objectives around Munich awaited further orders. Back at the beer hall, nobody knew quite what to do. The putschists did not yet know whether the police and *Reichswehr* would support or oppose them.

In the early hours of the morning, it was becoming apparent that the triumvirate had left the putschists twisting in the wind. The decision to marshal their forces and march anyway was probably influenced as much by confusion and desperation as it was by hope of success.

A column of over two thousand men set out from the *Bürgerbräukeller* towards the *Residenz* palace, joined by civilians as they marched. At first they encountered no resistance, even from police and soldiers, but eventually they were confronted with a police cordon that had been thrown up to block their march. That was when the shooting started.

To this day it is not known for certain who fired the first shots. In the following speech, Hitler forcefully insists that it was a rifle, not a pistol, that was fired first, which is significant because the police were armed with rifles, while only a few of the marchers, including Hitler, carried pistols. He vehemently denied the allegation that he or one of his supporters shot at police first.

Regardless, the shootout left eighteen men dead: fourteen National Socialists, and four policemen. Two more National Socialists had also been killed occupying the War Ministry earlier. Many more were injured, including Hitler, who dislocated his shoulder when he was dragged to the ground after the man marching beside him, Max Erwin von Scheubner-Richter, an early NSDAP member and one of the architects of the putsch, was shot dead. It was remarkable that Hitler escaped with such a comparatively minor injury, and Ludendorff escaped completely unscathed.

Heinrich Trambauer, a flagbearer of the fifth SA *Sturm* carrying one of the column's swastika flags, was shot down and badly wounded, and Andreas Bauriedl fell dead on top of the banner, bleeding out onto it and staining the flag with his blood. This flag later became known as the *Blutfahne*, and was revered as a quasi-holy relic of National Socialism, and would later be ceremonially touched to other NSDAP banners to consecrate them.

Hitler jumped in a car with some of his men and managed to temporarily escape to the countryside, but was arrested two days later. He was charged with high treason and held under heavy guard in pre-trial custody, likely as much to prevent an assassination attempt on him as it was to make sure he didn't escape. On February 26th he was brought before the People's Court for the first hearing of his trial. Presiding over the trial was Judge Georg Neithardt, the same judge who had previously tried Hitler for assaulting Bavarian separatist politician Otto Ballerstedt in 1921. Neithardt apparently had conservative and anti-communist political leanings, and treated Hitler, and especially Ludendorff, quite leniently at their trials.

The following speech is Hitler's response to the prosecution, which he turned into a propaganda opportunity to propound his ideas and lionize the NSDAP in full view of entire German public.

Hitler's Defense, February 26th, 1924

The Speech

It seems strange to me that a man who, as a soldier, became accustomed to blind obedience for nearly six years, should suddenly come into conflict with the state and its constitution. To explain this, I must to go back to my youth, because there indeed is the seed of the conflict between me and today's constitution and governing bodies. As a young man of sixteen and a half years of age, I was forced to earn my own bread. I came to Vienna when I was barely seventeen, and there I became thoroughly acquainted with three things. First, the social question. For the first time there I felt the great misery and hardship of the broad masses of society firsthand. Secondly, the racial problem in the city where East and West more or less meet. In Vienna one can study the racial problem better than anywhere in Germany, because there, according to my political conviction, the greatest enemy and adversary of all Aryan humanity emerges more strongly and sharply than in Munich, or in the rest of Germany in general. Thirdly, in Austria I became acquainted with that movement which was founded by a certain race, and which exploits the great needs of the broad masses in order to build up an organization whose consequences would inevitably lead to the collapse of the entire modern state — that is, the Marxist movement. I arrived in Vienna a cosmopolitan, and left an out-and-out antisemite, and a mortal enemy of the entire Marxist worldview. I then came to Munich and earned my bread here until the war came. [...]

I was convinced that the fate of Germany, and that of German Austria, would not be decided in the Austrian army, but in the German army; accordingly, I enlisted for service in the latter. [...]

When it was announced on November 7th, 1918 that the

revolution had broken out in Munich, I couldn't believe it at first. But by November 9th it became clear to me, and that night my decision was made: the great vacillation in my life, whether I would turn to politics or whether I would remain a builder, came to an end. I decided that night that if I got my vision back, I would turn to politics.[48] I came to Munich and a few weeks later I was with a reserve battalion. My further political development was relatively simple. I was active during the period of the Council Republics,[49] and as a result of my resistance during the Council period, came to the attention of my superiors, and was invited into the intelligence commission of Infantry Regiment II. Here I came into contact with the National Socialist German Workers' Party. At that time it was still called the German Workers' Party. The movement had six members; I was the seventh. [...]

The Marxist movement works with two powerful instruments. On the one hand, it employs an enormous propaganda apparatus, with mass influence. The bourgeoisie does not understand Marxism, does not know that the little boy who is taken out of school and inducted into this doctrine is thereby ultimately alienated from the state and society and, if this is consistently continued, soon becomes ripe to enter the trade unions as an apprentice, how he then becomes further and further alienated from his people, relies exclusively on manual labor, fundamentally rejects the intellect as bourgeois, and that this doctrine will lead to a monstrous force within the state, to an confrontation of the brute fist against genius and knowledge. Through this doctrine it becomes possible for a man of thirty to forty years of age to become a mortal enemy of his own brother, to call the comrades of his own German blood mortal class enemies, while he regards our real enemies — the English and French, or even the Hottentots[50] who

---

[48] At this time, Hitler was in a hospital being treated for injuries sustained in a poison gas attack, in which he was temporarily blinded.

[49] Referring to the brief establishment of communist regimes in Munich; *Soviet* is Russian for "council."

[50] A term originally applied to certain Khoisan tribes of southern Africa, which over time came to be a term for African peoples generally, sometimes seen as a pejorative

are completely racially foreign to him — as brothers. […]

The second instrument of this movement is an unprecedented terror. No movement has operated with such thorough knowledge of the nature of the masses as the Marxist movement. It knows that the masses have respect for strength and determination, and it has substituted brute power and brute will for the weakness and indecisiveness of the bourgeoisie, has ruthlessly subordinated the individual, and given the workers an ultimatum: either you be my brother, or I'll stove your skull in. […]

At first I was fighting a losing battle. Nevertheless, in the course of a few years, a movement has emerged from that small group of six men, which today comprises millions and which, above all, has made the broad masses national-minded again. We were clear that we could not get by with the old methods of whining and pleading. A government cannot protect an intellectual movement. Therefore, we decided on the following principle: for those who are willing to fight with intellectual weapons, we have the intellect; for the others, we have our fists! Our propaganda machine was joined by the *Sturmabteil* in order to prevent our movement from being terrorized and our supporters from being crushed. There were places where we could not hold a meeting for a long time. The SA had no military significance; its sole purpose was to be an organization capable of meeting terror from the left with even greater terror from our side. Until 1923, the SA never deviated from this purpose.

In 1923 came a great, bitter scandal. We had already realized in 1922 that the Ruhr would be lost. France's aim was not only to weaken Germany, but to break it up into small states in order to be able to hold the Rhine region. We knew, after the repeated declarations of weakness, that after the Saar region and after Upper Silesia we would also lose our third coal basin, the Ruhr, one loss after another. Our movement was thus at loggerheads with the bourgeois world for the first time. The folkish movement realized that the Ruhr could not be preserved by mere passive

---

associated with primitivism.

resistance, but only by reawakening the national will to resist. An active front in this sense had to be built up behind the Ruhr. This was impossible as long as the truce was maintained, which had already broken the neck of the German people in 1914.[51] We too wanted a united front, but not between people of whom one was prepared to climb the redoubt and sacrifice his life, while the other would stab him in the back.

Only fervent, ruthless, brutal fanaticism could have saved the situation at that time. The Reich government would have had to let the hundreds of thousands of young men who came home from the Ruhr to the Reich under the old colors of black, white and red,[52] flow together in a powerful national wave. In countless public rallies we advocated national revival. Instead, these young people were sent back. The government reduced the national resistance to a paid general strike. They forgot that an enemy like France cannot be prayed to death, still less lazed to death. Billions were thrown into this useless resistance, the German financial system was torn apart, and the conditions were created for the formation of those factions who, because they had forgotten how to work, because they had not been educated to be willing to make sacrifices, later attacked us as separatists. The national will, the great uprising of the nation, was allowed to wither and dry up, just as it did in 1914.

At that time I went to Otto Hermann von Lossow and explained to him that the resistance could only be led from the nationalist side. We must therefore vigorously support these elements. Our youth has only one thought — and let this be heard in Paris: that the day will come when we are free again. Lossow said at the time that there were two possibilities: either to support the resistance in an energetic form, or, if the whole thing fell apart, each state would

---

[51] Referring to the wartime parliamentary truce, in which the major parties of the Reichstag agreed to collaborate for the duration of the war. Hitler is essentially putting forward the idea that there cannot be a united front with the Marxist parties over the Ruhr issue, because they had stabbed Germany in the back once and would surely do so again.
[52] The colors of the old imperial flag of Germany, before the adoption of the Weimar colors of black, red, and gold.

have to look after itself. That, of course, would lead to the destruction of the Reich. I was inwardly very disturbed by this at the time; for my attitude is that I would rather be hanged if Germany should turn Bolshevik than perish under the rule of French sabres. It was then that the inner conversion of our movement took place, as is also emphasized in the indictment. The development of events in the Ruhr conflict proved us right. It showed that the backstabbers were more powerful than ever.

On May 1st we tried to see to it that at least in one town the Soviet flag could no longer be flown. The authorities opposed us for the first time. They protected the Soviet flag. After that I did not go to the military district command any more, since I saw that further talks were worthless. With pride I confess that it was our people who put up the only real resistance in the Ruhr. We wanted to initiate a propaganda campaign throughout Germany in a series of fourteen meetings with the slogan, "Down with the Ruhr traitors!" But a ban on these meetings took us by surprise. I had met Herr von Kahr in 1920. It was also after a putsch that he ascended to his ministerial chair. Kahr had given me the impression that he was an honorable civil servant. I spoke to Kahr for the first time when it was a question of disarming the *Einwohnerwehr*.[53] I implored Kahr not to disarm the *Einwohnerwehr*, because that would mean the loss of Upper Silesia. Herr von Kahr assured me that he would never agree to the *Einwohnerwehr* being disarmed, that we could rest assured with him. A few days later the *Etnwohnerwehr* was disbanded. I spoke with Kahr briefly a second time in a private conversation, but not since. It is not enough for a statesman to have a clean record; before the war that was what was demanded of the lowest civil servant. Kahr did not have other qualities that one must demand of a statesman in this situation: he did not have the iron fist to impose order. If Kahr had capable people behind him, he could achieve great things. But it

---

[53] Literally, "Citizens' Defence," a right-wing paramilitary group in Bavaria that existed in violation of the Treaty of Versailles, and was disbanded in June 1921 under pressure by the Allies.

was Pöhner standing behind him at that time. It was Pöhner, not Kahr, who did the work back then.

Von Kahr did not seem to me personally the man to fulfill the great expectations of the German people. He will, I said to myself, take a giant run-up, only to collapse when the fight is about to begin. [...]

I went to Lossow. I explained to him that I was not coming to him from political motives, because in my eyes he was politically a dead man. Lossow had indeed refused to obey the head of the *Reichswehr*, and it was naïveté to think that there was any other remedy than overthrowing him or fighting for what was right. [...]

Ludendorff was also convinced of this, saying, "What Lossow is doing is a battle from which he can only emerge victorious or fallen." I explained to Lossow at the time that I personally regarded the matter as a tremendous misfortune. The people had expected a gigantic wave, they had believed that the collapse would become the cause of a flood which would gradually take hold of the whole German people and drive out the Marxist International. From the struggle against Marxism, from the gigantic uprising, a dictatorship was to rise.

Now a man came and immediately declared himself dictator. Herr von Kahr could not fulfill the hopes placed in him; he was quite incapable of doing so. No one will dispute his outstanding human qualities. But I already said at the time that what is being demanded now is something else.

The struggle against Berlin, as led by Herr von Kahr, is a crime, unless one is determined to face the consequences, to incorporate the struggle into the German national uprising from the first minute on. I said that they had now turned the matter into a Bavarian rejection of Berlin's demands. The people, however, had expected something other than a beer price reduction, a milk price decree, a butter barrel confiscation, and similar impossible economic measures, where one had to ask oneself which genius had been consulted. Every failure was bound to increase the anger of the masses, and I pointed out that people would make fun of

Kahr's measures now, and be outraged later. I told Lossow, "If you lead the struggle to its end, then there can only be a political and military offensive. If you cross the Rubicon, you must also march on Rome. Or if you don't want the struggle, then there is only surrender." [...]

The struggle was to be directed northwards; it could not be led by a purely Bavarian organization. It only promised success if it was led by a force that could be seen as the coming German national army. Herr von Lossow recognized this as correct and asked me whom I had in mind. I explained, "You and Seisser must lead the fight yourselves, but Ludendorff comes to mind as the only man for the top."

I had seen Ludendorff in the field for the first time in 1918, and in 1921 I was able to speak to him personally for the first time. I realized that he was not only the most outstanding general in the field, but that he had now also re-learned and recognized the reasons that had brought the German nation to its downfall. The fact that Ludendorff was being pulled down by the others was one more reason for me to join him more closely. So I proposed Ludendorff, and Lossow and Seisser had no objection.

I further explained to Lossow that nothing could be achieved now with petty economic means. The struggle is with Marxism. To solve this problem, you don't need administrators, you need firebrands who are able to inflame national enthusiasm to the utmost. Kahr could not do that; the youth was not behind him. I could join, I declared, only on the condition that the political struggle be placed exclusively in my hands. But that was not impudent or immodest of me. I am rather of the opinion that when a man knows that he alone can do a thing, he must not be modest. [...]

When Lossow spoke of a *coup d'état*, when Kahr openly declared that he would give the signal to strike, this can only be interpreted as meaning that these people wanted to strike but always lost their nerve. Our last conversation on November 6th was basically nothing more than the absolute confirmation of my conviction: the gentlemen wanted to do it, but kept backing out. [...]

Lossow declared on November 6th that he was ready for a *coup d'état* under certain conditions. Now, it goes without saying that if a man does not find the courage to break loose, he cannot tell the others to break loose either. But we had to be convinced that the gentlemen were only waiting for a push. Our people and public opinion were pushing, and Herr Lossow and Herr Seisser only wanted a broadening of the foundation. So we were convinced that action would only be taken if the will came along with the want, so to speak. If, on the other hand, the matter was postponed, then things could pop off at a less favorable time, because our people could no longer be held back. In addition, Lossow had said that if the North did not strike out on its own, separation could not be avoided. I also remember the conversation with Lossow during the Ruhr movement, where he hinted that a foreign power might get involved. That's why it seemed to me that if the North were to give the impetus, things would be good. If it didn't, then perhaps the impetus would come from a faction that would let things fizzle out.

Therefore, the only option was to give the impetus myself. That is why I decided with two other gentlemen, whose names I will not mention, to give this impetus. We held a meeting the next day in which we agreed on the plan. I was immediately of the opinion that only a very few should be privy to the plan. I did not have to fear that afterwards I would be reproached for not having told the people beforehand what I intended to do, for all the gentlemen had expected nothing else. They hoped from hour to hour that salvation would come. All the older gentlemen who had families were not informed. When I spoke to Scheubner about whether Ludendorff should be informed, he explained that no, Ludendorff, as an officer, must not know anything about it. [...]

On the afternoon of November 7th I held the definitive and decisive meeting with the gentlemen, and the date of November 8th was finally fixed, because, as we had learned by chance at the last moment, Kahr was to hold a meeting on November 8th. That seemed to be the opportune moment to create this *fait accompli* most easily, and it was decided that the hall should be surrounded by our shock troops, that Lossow, Kahr and Seißer should be called out for a meeting, on the telephone or in some other way, that the hall should not be occupied and that they should be told very briefly: "Your Excellency sees that this is a *fait accompli*; now face the consequences from your previous speeches. There is no going back for you either way, but there is no going back for us either." We were of the opinion that what had been discussed for months would either be carried out by men, or rejected by cowards. [...]

The event itself, put very briefly, went as follows: I went to the Bürgerbräukeller at eight o'clock in the evening. There was a large crowd of people outside, and at first I thought that perhaps the police had somehow caught wind of the matter. I saw a large police detachment, another large police detachment was marching up from the bridge, and I knew that some of our shock troops were arriving in passenger cars. Whether the police had any idea of what was going on, I could not determine at first. In any case, I went in and left my companion, Herr Graf, who knew nothing about the matter, and simply told him, "When the shock troops arrive, go into the antechamber and wait for me. I'll be in there."

I went in and saw that the hall was overcrowded. I was let in because the police officers knew me. I immediately recognized that with this overcrowding it was completely impossible to ask the gentlemen to leave. It had been decided beforehand that I was to sit down at the table near the podium, but it was not even possible to get to the table. Then the gentlemen were to be asked to come out and I was to follow. That was quite impossible. No one could get in, not even by elbowing their way in. I immediately exited the hall again—the speech Herr von Kahr was giving was incomprehensible. There was now a feeling that, as things stood, a provocation might occur under certain circumstances. I went into the antechamber and told Scheubner to go immediately to Ludendorff and inform him. If Ludendorff did not want to come, I asked him to telephone me. I would then drive out myself. But I thought it impossible that Ludendorff would not do so if I asked him personally. Scheubner then went out, but came back and explained that the street outside the hall was full of people. Whether our shock troops would come was still a big question. I asked a police officer to have the street cleared, otherwise riots could break out in the hall. The police officer went out and cleared the street. I went into the hall at 8:34 p.m. with three men, my constant companions. We had a pistol with us, since it could not be ruled out that we would be shot at. The fact that we did not use the pistol to threaten Kahr was due to the fact that he did not appear to us in this environment as a terrible man who could only be kept in check by force of arms. Rather, he stood on his podium, trembling and pale.

I went in and got some quiet by shooting my pistol in the air. It was in the nature of things that I had to fire this shot, and only a gentleman who reads his speeches from drafts written by others could fail to understand such a thing. I then asked Kahr, Lossow and Seisser to come out. Then I was confronted by an officer. I found out later that it was Major Hunglinger. He had his hand in his pocket, and I had a feeling he was drawing a pistol. I held the gun up to his head and told him to take his hand out of his pocket. Nobody dared push my hand away. Hunglinger pulled his hand out and I lowered the pistol again. I then asked Herr Kahr, Herr Lossow and Herr Seisser to come out under the assurance that I would personally guarantee their safety. I was as much in control of my senses on that day as on any other day. I then led the gentlemen out into the antechamber; there was a line of blue-clad police, facing six to eight of us. I then cleared the antechamber and led the gentlemen in.

Kahr was so dejected and broken that I felt truly sorry for him; I felt even sorrier for Seisser and von Lossow, that I had to lead two officers out of the hall. I immediately apologized for this, and said, "Please forgive me for having to proceed in this way, but I have no other choice. The matter is now settled. There is no going back." The few sentences reported to the public are partly fabricated, and also partly taken out of context. His Excellency von Kahr supposedly stated, "To live or not to live, to die or not to die, is all the same to me." But in reality, Herr von Kahr did not stand there in a heroic pose during these minutes. I assured him once again that there was not the slightest danger to his life. That was when Kahr said that he was not afraid of that either, because to live or not to live was all the same to him. I answered Kahr by pointing to the pistol I had in my hand and smiling. "There are five shots in it: four for the traitors, and if it goes wrong, one for me."

I gave Graf the pistol to load to replace the fired cartridge. We did not threaten the gentlemen, but I reminded them of what they had discussed with us all along and asked them to face the consequences now. There would be no turning back or we would perish, although back then I assumed that they would go to prison with us if the whole thing fell apart, an opinion which I must correct today.

I asked the gentlemen to assume their new offices. Kahr raised the following objection: he said, "Yes, but one must also have an inner satisfaction in the matter, and after the way you led me out of the hall, people will not believe that I am doing this of my own accord. You didn't even let me finish my speech." I said, "Well, I had no idea that your speech would last so long."

I then went out and made sure that all the shock troops had arrived. Then I went back inside. But since Kahr declared that he feared that the proceedings in the hall might be misunderstood, I said to him: "Please, if you have reservations, I am prepared to go into the hall and speak. I will suggest in the hall that Herr von Kahr will take over, and there will then be thunderous applause. You will not be blamed for this; on the contrary, the people are waiting for it."

So I went into the hall and briefly explained that a decision would be made in the antechamber as to whether Herr von Kahr, Lossow and Seisser were prepared to accept the new government. I explained that the gentlemen were struggling with their decision, and that I considered it necessary for those assembled to decide whether they agreed with the proposed solution. There was an unheard-of applause in the hall, an incredible storm. I went out and said, "Your Excellency von Kahr, you may rest assured, you need not be ashamed in front of the people. When you come in, you won't be mocked; on the contrary, they will carry you on their shoulders!"

In the meantime Ludendorff arrived. He asked me whether the gentlemen had been informed of his coming. Then he explained that he was just as surprised as the others, but that the only possible decision had to be taken. [...]

What came next was self-evident. [...]

On our side it was certain that a struggle against the *Reichswehr* and the police was out of the question, for these were the two factors which were to bring about the change. Without these two factors the whole thing was futile. As long as we did not have the absolute conviction that Lossow, Seisser and Kahr did not want to take part in the matter out of their innermost convictions, we were obliged to carry out the matter honorably. It was therefore not out of recklessness that we held our ground at the morning meeting. The people stood up for us. As they are still standing up for us now, and will always stand up for us. The prisons to which our comrades are sent will become places of honor for the German youth.

Even in the early morning we did not receive any message that brought us positive clarity. Not even by noon was any communication brought to us. There were only two options: either to take the matter beyond Munich, or to stay in Munich and appeal to public opinion again. Ludendorff therefore said himself, "We are going into the city. In order to win public opinion, to see how public opinion reacts and how then Kahr, Lossow and Seisser react to public opinion. For they could not be so unreasonable as to take action with machine guns against the rebelling people.

So the decision was made to march into the city. We took the lead; after all, we don't do it like the communists, who seek cover in the rear when their men take to the barricades. My attention was drawn to the fact that I should inform Ludendorff that we might be shot at. I did so, but Ludendorff only replied, "We march!" [...]

We marched on. Ludendorff, Dr. Weber on his right, myself on his left, then Dr. Scheubner and the other gentlemen. As we advanced, green-clad police met us on the Ludwig Bridge, racking their bolts sharply and aiming their rifles at us. We marched on and they dispersed. They were not disarmed at that moment by advance disarming squads. If a man has his rifle ready to fire, he cannot be disarmed by another; he already has the advantage over him. Rather, they were deeply shaken, to be in such discord with everyone. They put down their rifles and stood aside. There were people with tears rushing into their eyes, who were completely broken. Our people marched through and it would have been difficult for them to shoot. If people were being disarmed in the rear, we did not see that in the front. On the contrary, there were individual shouts from civilians who joined in on the left and right and marched along, some of them pushing their way in. We shouted back, "Don't do anything, the police didn't do anything to us, we have no reason to harm them." The people then immediately stepped back.

There were young men of nineteen or twenty among them, recruits. You could imagine what a task it was for them to stand against us. They saw men facing them, many of whom had their chests covered with badges of honor from the World War. It was not necessary to go out of our way to harm them.

We arrived at Marienplatz. The enthusiasm was unparalleled, and on this march I recognized that the people were behind us, they recognized that this state of affairs could no longer continue. They could no longer be put off with ridiculous half resolutions and decisions. The people wanted those who once committed the monstrous crime five years ago to be called to account; they wanted a reckoning with the November criminals. That is what the people of Munich want, as far as they have a sense for the honor and dignity of human life and not for slavery. That was the wish of the broad masses, which resulted in an incredible storm of applause.

We marched on and finally came to the *Residenz*. Here, too, the same picture. A very weak police cordon had immediately dispersed, people stood aside, some even shouted "Heil!" Others didn't know what to make of it.

I must emphasize that everyone that marched forth with us was practically a civilian. Even Ludendorff went in civilian clothes. I had nothing but my raincoat, though I did have my armband; as usual, I wore my pistol strapped on the outside, not in my hand, but in my holster. It wouldn't have done me any good either. Ludendorff put his hands in his coat pockets. There was no one carrying a pistol, still less a rifle. In front were the two flag bearers, the only soldiers, on the left and on the right an attendant, no one else. We were all more or less unarmed.

That's how we arrived. A few meters from us I saw a short standstill and heard a shot. We had the feeling that the cordon, which had now become stronger, suddenly swarmed out at the *Feldherrnhalle*[54] — I thought they were *Reichswehr* because of the steel helmets — and stretched across the street in a triple line. So we linked arms in order to press forward, for the fact that we would march through was a matter of course. At that moment a shot rang out, not a pistol shot, but a rifle or carbine shot. One would trust a soldier who has heard shooting for four years to be able to distinguish the slight bark of a pistol from a rifle shot. It is indecent to make such an assertion. It was not a pistol shot, but a rifle or carbine shot. Immediately afterwards a volley cracked. I had the feeling at that moment that I had been shot in the left side. Dr. Scheubner, whose arm was linked with mine, fell to the ground, and I fell with him. I now felt as if I had dislocated my left arm from Dr. Scheubner's fall. Then a second salvo cracked and I had the feeling that I had taken a bullet to my left arm, because my first injury in the war had felt more like a blow than a cut.

I lay there for only a few seconds and immediately tried to pull myself together again. The shooting stopped again. When I got up,

---

[54] Literally, "Field Marshalls' Hall," a monument to the Bavarian Army.

there was only a little shooting, a single man shooting from Preysing alley. All I saw around me were dead and wounded, a single field of blood. In front of me were state police, some of them with weapons at the ready, and armored cars. Behind me, seventy or eighty meters further back, were our last men in the rear. I could not see Ludendorff anywhere. I had not fallen forward, but backwards, sideways. I only saw a tall gentleman in a black coat stained with blood, half-covered, and now, without a clear thought, I was convinced at first that it was Ludendorff.

At that moment I was faced with the question of whether to give myself up or go to the back, eighty meters to the last people behind me. I went to the back. There were still some shots from the *Residenz*, which is now no longer disputed, then from Preysing Lane, as well as from the front and perhaps also from our side some more stray shots. I went back and got into a car at the square near the revenue office. My whole left side felt paralyzed and I was convinced that I had been shot. I couldn't go into a house in Munich, because I would have been recognized and arrested immediately due to my notoriety. I therefore told the driver to leave Munich, and only return at night, for I did not know what kind of wound I had. In the woods, a doctor who had come with me examined me. He told me I was not wounded, but apparently had a dislocation. We drove to Uffing and I stayed there for three days. The doctor tried to set my arm; later it turned out that I had a broken joint and a broken collarbone.

During these days I was at first overcome by physical and emotional pain, especially because at first I feared that Ludendorff was dead. Only later did I learn through conversation in Uffing that Ludendorff was alive. On Sunday I arrived in Landsberg, after I had been surrounded by a crew of trucks and arrested after long preparations. In Landsberg I received newspapers over the next few days. There I was able to read that I was not a man of my word, that I had given Herr von Kahr my word of honor that I would never do anything without informing him, and even more, I had given him this word personally on the evening of November 6th,

1923. It was all printed in black and white in front of me. Supposedly I even declared in the next room, "Yes, I broke my word," threatening with the pistol and demanding a beer mug. In short, I now stood there as a completely disreputable scoundrel.

At that moment I actually regretted that I had not shared the fate of my dear comrades at the *Feldherrnhalle*. The most shameful of all was that the men who had worked with us all this time, now that we couldn't defend ourselves, as we were lying in prisons, some of us physically broken ourselves, were now coming up with lies upon lies. I never gave Kahr my word. And he now publicly states in the newspapers that I gave him my word of honor. It is not true: I never gave Lossow and Seisser my word not to do anything, but I said that I was loyally behind them, that I would not do anything against them. In the end I even said in a retraction, "Gentlemen! If you do not bring it to a decision now, I no longer consider myself bound in my decisions." But I did nothing against the gentlemen. What I did was not contrary to considerations of loyalty; I acted loyally towards them right up to the moment when our people went down in a hail of bullets. It is outrageous that at the moment when we could not defend ourselves, these most infamous lies were spread. The gentlemen knew that our deed did not rob us of the hearts of our supporters; that is why they wanted to rob us of our honor and the reputation of our members.

At that moment I really didn't want to know anything more of this lying and slanderous world. And when, in the course of the next few days, during the second week, this campaign of slander continued, and when one after the other people were brought to Landsberg, all of whom I knew were innocent, whose only guilt was that they belonged to our movement, who knew nothing of the matter, who were only arrested because they shared our opinions, and the authorities feared that these opinions would be expressed, then I made the decision to defend myself and to fight to the last breath. That is why I have entered the courtroom: not to deny anything or to deny responsibility; no, I am protesting against Lieutenant Colonel Kriebel declaring that he is responsible for what happened. He has no responsibility. I alone bear it. I alone wanted the matter in the end. The other gentlemen only acted with me. I am convinced that I did not want anything bad. I bear the responsibility and will also bear all the consequences. But I must say one thing: I am not a criminal because of this, and I do not feel like a criminal because of this; on the contrary.

If I am now more or less reproached as to how I, of all people, could come to do such a thing, since I do not even have Bavarian citizenship, I must say the following: I do not have the citizenship of the present state, but I once acquired citizenship in the state that was Germany for me, namely the German Army. I received the national diploma in my military passport, which directs me to the district office of Munich. And if the day should ever come when I am assigned this responsibility, then I will know where I belong.

Secondly, if I do not get naturalized as a German citizen, it is because I know that it is bitter when one has to renounce one's Fatherland in order to be German. But I believe and hope that the time will come when German citizenship rights will extend beyond fragmented and petty borders, from Königsberg to Strasbourg and from Hamburg to Vienna. But it seems to me easy for a weak-minded administrator to expel a superior man, just as it is easy for a superior rogue to escape justice.

I am convinced that it would be unprincipled for a man who stakes his blood to have a certificate issued by a Berliner who, in my eyes, does not deserve to be German, or is not German at all. From my youth, I have never felt Austrian. Individual Austrians really can't help what our ruling house has done in German history. On the contrary, as a pan-Germanist I fought against this ruling house in my youth. The day must also come when Austria becomes part of Germany, and it would be disgraceful if I, who advocated this the most, were to renounce my homeland in order to acquire a right of citizenship that is a mere empty phrase, since it cannot be affirmed any better than I have affirmed it. I have defended the right of citizenship as an obedient soldier as well as within the homeland without grumbling. If I stand here as a revolutionary, I stand here as a revolutionary against the revolution.

I myself cannot plead guilty. I confess to the deed, but I cannot plead guilty to high treason, because there is no high treason against the traitors of 1918. It is impossible that I have committed high treason, because it cannot lie in the deeds of November 8th and 9th, 1923, but in the whole attitude and in the whole action of the months before. It does not lie in a single deed, but in the discussions on this deed beforehand. If I really did commit treason, I am surprised that those who did the same as me at that time are not sitting by my side. I cannot plead guilty, since I know that the public prosecutor himself is legally obliged to bring charges against those who committed the same crime as we did and also discussed it with us; I mean Herr von Berchem, von Aufsess, Kahr, Lossow, Seisser, and all the others. That the public prosecutor has not brought charges against these gentlemen must be a mistake. I confess, as I have said, to the crime and deny any guilt as long as the same is not applied to the gentlemen who wanted the same thing as us and planned it in meetings, which can be shown privately. As long as these gentlemen are not beside me, I reject the guilt of high treason. I do not feel that I am a traitor, but the best German who wanted the best for his people. I now ask the Judge to address to me such questions as he deems necessary.

Hitler's Closing Arguments, March 27th, 1924

The Background

The following speech is Hitler's closing argument before sentencing. At the end of the trial, Adolf Hitler was sentenced to five years for treason, a remarkably light punishment considering the coup attempt he had led. Ludendorff was completely acquitted. A hostile judge could have sentenced Hitler to death, or at the very least deported him to his native Austria after his sentence. As it was, he was sentenced to *Festungshaft* (Fortress Confinement), a form of prison sentence that placed him under heavy guard, but did not include forced labor, and the court declined to deport him in consideration of his military service to Germany. His cell was comfortably furnished, he was allowed visitors almost daily, and was even able to wear his own clothes. Photographs of Hitler in his cell show him and his visitors wearing traditional Bavarian dress, and look more like a night out at the beer hall than the punishment of a man convicted of treason.

Hitler used his time while he was imprisoned in Landsberg to compose *Mein Kampf*, giving his own version of his early years, his time in the war, how he had come to hold his beliefs, and the early years of the NSDAP.

He also reflected on the lessons learned from the failed putsch. The most critical point of failure was the attempt to go ahead with the putsch without the support of the police and *Reichswehr*. Hitler became convinced that party politics and a mass movement was the path to power, not a paramilitary coup. He reoriented his efforts towards taking power in Germany by legal means only, building up a credible party, campaigning nationwide, and contesting elections.

On balance, the putsch itself was a miserable failure, inadequately planned and organized, almost on the spur of the moment, which had realistically had very little chance of success from the beginning considering that the support of the police and military had not been secured. Yet Hitler managed to make the best possible use of the situation, turning the entire affair, from the failed putsch, to his trial speeches, to his publication of *Mein Kampf*, into an epic propaganda spectacle that drew national and even international attention to the previously relatively obscure upstart corporal from Austria and that strange new nationalist movement from Munich, the NSDAP.

The Speech

Honorable Gentlemen!

In the indictment I read the following statement: "Admittedly, what happened in November 1918, the ousting of the federal Princes by the Council of People's Deputies, was a crime of high treason. At that time, the new government took over the whole Reich in a very short time, the supreme power of government was in fact in the hands of the People's Deputies, and thus the state of affairs was made legal. This is recognized law." If this theory were true and became law, the fetters of Germany could never be loosened, for it would mean that we too are defeated, cast down and gagged by power. But might is not identical with right.

Frederick the Great once uttered a statement that clearly defines the relationship between might and right. He said that the law is worthless if it is not defended by the point of a sword. In other words, the law was still worthless if there was no power to back it. I will point out a few practical examples from recent history. In April 1919, a small band of criminals overthrew the current revolutionary government and set up a new one of their own; the Soviet flags were brought out, and those men unquestionably took actual power. Nevertheless, this power did not exist legally. And even if the Soviet powers were to seize the whole of Germany and the whole of Europe, the day would come when they too would fall.

We can see the same thing in Hungary. There, too, Bela Kun set up a Red regime; he, too, took absolute power and asserted himself everywhere. A small group of freedom fighters helped to reimpose the true law; a small minority technically tyrannized Hungary at that time, but this minority actually represented the true Hungarian people.

How did Bismarck handle the constitutional conflict? He disregarded the constitution, parliament, and the overwhelming majority and ruled, relying only on the state's means of power: on the Army, on the body of civil servants, and on the Crown. This was described in the opposition press as a breach of the constitution and high treason. What legalized Bismarck's act? His act might indeed have been high treason, had it not been out of this deed that the blessing came which led the German people to its unity, to its highest achievement and freedom. On the day on which the German Emperor was crowned, high treason was legalized before the German people and the whole world.

We have two new *coups d'états* happening before us: the Turkish general Kemal Pasha opposes the central government of Constantinople; he goes so far as to reject even the sacred authority of the head of the Mohammedan religion. If we ask what ultimately legalized this act, the answer is the achievement of freedom for his people. Mussolini's deed was legalized by the tremendous work of purification; the March on Rome was legalized on the day when Rome was purged of the manifestations of the decay of political life.

What was the situation in Germany? What was the situation in our Fatherland in 1918? Germany was not then so miserable and corrupt as to make revolution a natural necessity. The later Social Democratic Minister of the Interior, Heine, declared that the former Reich was without a doubt the most orderly administered country in the whole world. And so it was. No state had such an honorable, principled body of civil servants as the old Germany, no nation had an army in which such a high degree of honor had become a tradition. As internally, so externally. Twenty-six foreign powers endeavored to bring this Reich down, and in four years of struggle they did not succeed—a proof of how formidable, strong and powerful this Reich was. There was no cause for revolution.

When we ask whether the revolution has succeeded, we must first examine what the revolution wanted. What did the revolution not promise our German people? A life of beauty and dignity and abundance, and less work than before. The struggle against the supranational power of international capital was preached, and what has been achieved? Here in the hall stood a general of the new Reich. He had to confess that the failure of this new power in the economic field was so appalling that the masses were being driven into the streets, but the soldiers who were supposed to shoot at the masses did not want to keep shooting at people who were driven to despair by the incompetence of their government. A more damning verdict cannot be reached. I do not want to talk about the hunger of millions, but only to point out the consequences of the destruction of our currency, which deprived thousands of people of the fruits of their labor.

Economically, this revolution has become a tremendous misfortune. Our largest agricultural regions have been lost, and in a highly treacherous manner, regions that are a prerequisite for the nourishment of the nation have been sold off. We heard about the right of self-determination of peoples, about the League of Nations, about the self-government of the people. And what came of all that? World peace, but world peace built on a field of our bodies. Disarmament, but only the disarmament of Germany so it could be plundered. The right of self-determination, yes, but only for every tribe of negroes, and Germany does not count as a tribe of negroes. A League of Nations, but a League of Nations only as a guarantor for the fulfillment of the peace treaty, not for a better world order to come. [...]

The best proof of what I have said can be seen in the speech of the prosecutor himself. The prosecutor explained that the root cause of these events lies in the shattered authority of the state. What remnants of legitimate authority still exist today ultimately go back to the germ of today's Reich. It was Friedrich Wilhelm who founded the authority of the state, it was the great King who declared of himself, "I am a servant of the state!" This applies in the same way right up to the old heroic Emperor.

We all still live by this state authority today. State authority was identical with the good of the people; it was not something opposed to the good of the people. Thomas Carlyle emphasizes that Frederick the Great's entire life was lived in the service of his people. [...]

The great debasement of the currency came, and what was felt most keenly among the people was that the man who had once been given 20,000 marks was now paid with 30,000 paper wipes.

Respect for the law has decayed bit by bit, because the law was no longer identical with morality. The legislators of today make laws without regard for ethics, morals, or decency. If the law is to be respected again in Germany one day, the first prerequisite is that the Reich emerge from its great misfortune. [...]

When did Germany's downfall begin? You know the slogan of the old German system in terms of foreign policy. It was preservation of world peace, economic conquest of the world. You cannot govern a nation with both principles. The preservation of world peace cannot be the goal and purpose of a state policy. Only the growth and preservation of a nation can be the goal. The world cannot be conquered by economic policy without this appearing as a threat to other nations.

What is the state? Today, the state is an economic organization, an association of people, apparently for the sole purpose of securing each other's daily bread. But the state is not an economic organization; it is a national organism. The aim and purpose of the state is to give a people the sustenance and the position of power it deserves. The German people are perhaps in the most bitter position of all nations in Europe. Militarily, politically, and geographically we are surrounded by nothing but rivals, and can only hold our own if we ruthlessly put power politics in the foreground. [...]

What we did was hardly appealing. I remember a time when the stereotypical calls used to come from the masses: "Down with the reactionaries! Warmongers, mass murderers!" Hardly any of us have not been beaten bloody. What we did, we did not do as demagogues, but in the feeling that it must happen, even if we should perish, not out of consideration of whether we would be victorious. We have acted in the consciousness that we are doing our duty, and we have done it. We have enlightened the masses.

And when I mentioned the name of the Quartermaster General sitting before you, the cry even came, "Down with Ludendorff!" If today a different cry rings back, and if people cheer us today, it is proof that the people are beginning to see clearly again, much to our joy. My friend Röhm also collaborated in this work of enlightening the masses in the *Bund Reichskriegsflagge*.[55] He too was prepared to be spat upon and beaten, but to emphasize: We are Germans and we are proud of it; we will not let our Fatherland down. [...]

Lossow said here that he had spoken to me in the spring and had not observed at that time that I was striving for any position for myself, but that I only wanted to be a propagandist. How small people think! I do not regard the attainment of a ministerial post as worth striving for. I do not consider it worthy of a great man to want to be remembered by history merely for becoming a minister. One would also run the risk of being buried next to other ministers, and names like Scheidemann and Wutzlhofer come to mind. I did not want to be buried in the same tomb with them.

What I had in mind from the first day was a thousand times more than becoming a minister. I wanted to become the breaker of Marxism. I want to solve this issue, and if I did solve it, the title of minister would be a joke to me. When I first stood before Wagner's grave, my heart overflowed with pride that here rested a man who forbade himself from being commemorated, "Here rests Privy Councillor Music Director His Excellency Baron Richard von Wagner." I was proud that this man and so many men in German history were content to hand down their names to posterity, not their titles. It was not out of modesty that I wanted to be a "drummer" at that time; that is the highest goal, all else is a trifle.

When the General State Commissariat was founded, I too underwent a change. Once I believed that perhaps I could lead the struggle against Marxism with the help of state power. January 1923 made me realize that this was hardly possible. The

---

[55] "Imperial War Flag Society," a short-lived right-wing paramilitary under Röhm's control that joined the *Kampfbund* and participated in the Putsch.

prerequisite for the defeat of Marxism is not that Germany should first be freed; Germany will never be free until Marxism is broken. At that time I withdrew and thought of nothing but strengthening the movement until it could sweep over the whole of Germany like a torrent. [...]

Herr von Kahr has stated here that he had hitherto not cared for politics until March 1920, when he was invited to get out of bed and enter politics. I take the view that the bird must sing because it is a bird. A man born for politics must do politics whether he is free or in prison, sitting in a silken chair or having to make do with a hard bench; the fate of his people will animate him, from early morning till late at night.

Kahr was even supposed to act as dictator once. I ask you to remember two statements made by this man. He said he didn't want to, but he was pushed. A second statement was that he had not pushed himself forward, but had been forced. He who is born to be a dictator is not pushed, but wants to be, is not pushed forward, but pushes himself forward. It is not presumptuous of a laborer to push himself to hard work; is it perhaps presumptuous of a man with a highly intellectual mind to brood for nights on end until he finally gives mankind an invention? He who feels himself called to govern a people has no right to say, "If you wish for it and fetch me, I will go along." He has the duty to govern. Do you think that this man, von Kahr, is the German Scharnhorst, Yorck, or Gneisenau, or the Freiherr vom Stein, for instance, who proclaimed with a hate-filled heart that he would crush Napoleon?

Ultimately what was missing from Kahr, in my eyes, is the characteristic of the great man. Herr von Kahr was popular. What he lacked was what Mussolini recently expressed in his proclamation, "I would not want to live in this world if I did not know that I was surrounded by a thicket of love and of hate." Kahr had popularity, but not the stones to endure hatred. He was not a heroic figure. Do you think it would be presumptuous of me, knowing this man so well, to declare at once, when he wanted to win me over, that a struggle under such leadership seemed to me to be hopeless? […]

People are surprised at our unity, despite different formal views. They say of me that I am ultimately a republican, of Pöhner that he is a monarchist, of Ludendorff that he is loyal to the House of Hohenzollern. It is proof of the power of an idea to unite such diverse people. Germany's fate lies not in the form of the republic or monarchy, but in the content of the republic or the monarchy. What I am fighting against is not the form of government as such, but the disgraceful content. We wanted to create the conditions in Germany which alone would make it possible for the iron grip of our enemies to be lifted from our neck. We wanted to create order in the national budget, expel the leeches, take up the fight against the international enslavement of the stock exchange, against the enslavement of our entire economy, the fight against the politicization of the trade unions, and above all, we wanted to reintroduce the highest duty of honor that we knew as Germans: the duty to bear arms in compulsory military service. And here I ask you: is what we wanted high treason? Finally, we wanted our people to rise up against the threat of enslavement, we wanted the time to finally come when we would not accept blow after blow in eternal sheep-like docility. […]

Now I have to address something that the prosecuting authority explains: we are subject to punishment because the enterprise failed. But the deed of November 8th did not fail. It might have failed if a mother had come to us and said, "Herr Hitler, you have my child on your conscience!" But I can assure you that no such mother came. On the contrary. Thousands of others came and stood in our ranks. And regarding the young men who fell, one day an obelisk to them will bear the inscription, "They too died for the liberation of the Fatherland."[56] That is the visible sign of the success of November 8th, that in its wake the youth will rise up

---

[56] In fact, a monument to those who fell during the Beer Hall Putsch was indeed erected by the National Socialists after they finally took control of Germany ten years later. Its inscription read, *Und ihr habt doch gesiegt* — "And yet you triumphed nevertheless."

like a storm tide and unite. That is the greatest gain of November 8th: that it did not lead to depression, but contributed to the highest enthusiasm of the people. I believe that the hour will come when the masses who are standing in the streets today with our cross flag will unite with those who shot at us on November 8th. I believe that blood will not divide us forever. When I learned that it was the police who fired, I had the happy thought, "At least it wasn't the *Reichswehr*." One day the hour will come when the *Reichswehr* too will stand by our side, officers and men.

The army that we have formed is growing faster day by day, hour by hour. Even in these days, I have the proud hope that one day the hour will come when these wild multitudes will become battalions, the battalions will become regiments, the regiments will become divisions, that the old cockade will be brought out of the dirt, that the old flags will once again flutter forth, that reconciliation will come at the eternal last judgment of God, to which we are willing to go. Then from our bones and from our graves will speak the voice of the only court which can sit in judgment over us. For it is not you, gentlemen, who will pronounce judgment upon us; judgment will be pronounced by the eternal court of history, which will dispense its own verdict upon the charge that has been brought against us. I know the sentence you will pass. But that court will not ask us, "Did you or did you not commit treason?" That court will judge us, the Quartermaster General of the old army, and his officers and soldiers, as Germans who wanted the best for their people and Fatherland, who were willing to fight and die. May you find us guilty a thousand times over. The goddess of the eternal court of history will smile and tear to shreds the prosecutor's motion and the verdict of this court, for she acquits us!

THE RE-FOUNDING OF THE MOVEMENT

Meeting of Party Members, Munich, February 27th, 1925

The Background

Hitler was released from prison on December 20th, 1924, and found the National Socialist movement in a sorry state without him. The end of the Ruhr occupation and the worst part of the hyperinflation crisis meant that the general population was less interested in radical politics, and this was reflected in shrinking support for fringe parties. The NSDAP and SA had been banned. In 1924, during Hitler's imprisonment, a successor organization to the NSDAP, the *Großdeutsche Volksgemeinschaft* (Greater German People's Community, GVG for short) was founded, first under the leadership of the aloof and somewhat unpopular folkish-pagan intellectual Alfred Rosenberg, then under the coarse-mannered roughnecks Hermann Esser and Julius Streicher. These figures were not widely seen as the best leadership material for the successor to the NSDAP, and the GVG had very little support outside of Bavaria.

But this was not the only organization claiming successorship to the National Socialist movement, or even the largest one. The *Deutschvölkische Freiheitspartei* (German Folkish Freedom Party, DVFP for short) had already been founded in December 1922, but in 1924 it rose to prominence to become the most important force on the nationalist scene in the absence of the NSDAP, and began to achieve electoral success at the federal level, especially in northern Germany, but in Bavaria as well. The DVFP attracted many former NSDAP members, including prominent organizers such as Gregor Strasser.

The *Nationalsozialistische Freiheitsbewegung* (National Socialist Freedom Movement, NSFB for short) was formed in April 1924, and unlike the GVG in Bavaria, which eschewed electoral politics, the NSFB began to contest elections.

Meanwhile, the SA was reformulated in a successor organization, the *Frontbann*, under the total control of Ernst Röhm, whom Hitler had left in charge in his absence and gave free reign to lead as he saw fit. On paper the *Frontbann* was affiliated with the NSFB, but in reality it was not entirely beholden to any particular successor organization. It was purely paramilitary in character.[57] Hitler was anxious to get out of prison and have the ban on the party lifted as soon as possible, and implored supporters to strictly abide by the law to avoid jeopardizing those possibilities. English author Wyndham Lewis, a contemporary of Hitler who lived in Germany during the later years of Hitler's rise to power, noted at the time:

> [W]hereas the communist is invariably armed, the Nazi has only his fists or sticks to defend himself with.... The Nazi organization lives under the perpetual threat of a Verbot, of suppression throughout Germany. In consequence the Nazi leaders recently have been compelled to issue orders to the effect that any National Socialist discovered in possession of firearms will be expelled from the party.[58]

In *Mein Kampf,* Hitler writes about how the violence at rallies between supporters and communist disruptors would be used by the police to get the meetings shut down, which was the goal of the counter-protesters in the first place.[59] The atmosphere of violence

---

[57] Noakes, "Conflict and Development," 9.
[58] Lewis, *Hitler,* 14.
[59] Hitler, *Mein Kampf, Vol. II,* C. 7.4, 229.

surrounding the rallies and their provocative nature were good for attracting excitement and attention, but also constantly threatened to become a pretext for banning the party and shutting down meetings, a tactic that liberal authorities have continued to use against nationalist dissidents ever since. But Röhm ignored Hitler's desire to use the SA as Party activists and political soldiers rather than preparing them to engage in armed conflict with the government. He continued to run things his way, and in Hitler's absence, the *Frontbann* acted essentially as Röhm's personal paramilitary. Even after the defeat of the coup attempt of November 1923, Röhm continued to scorn party politics. He was exclusively interested in acting as a warlord, with complete authority over his own troops. When the ban on the SA was eventually lifted in February 1925, the *Frontbann* turned back into the SA, and was reintegrated into the Party apparatus, but this disagreement was one of the seeds of future conflict with Röhm and the SA.[60]

There was confusion among committed National Socialists as to which of these organizations was the true heir to the NSDAP. Hitler agreed in principle to a merger of the movement with the DVFP, but only under certain conditions, one of which was that the movement remain based out of Munich. In the end he did not give a definitive answer.

In July of 1924, Hitler announced his decision to withdraw from politics for a while, both to focus on his book, and because he could not take responsibility for making decisions about the movement while he was in prison. This led to further confusion and disagreement, as Hitler loyalists were left to guess what his desires might be, while others with their own ambitions could invoke his name to get their way.

The DVFP and NSFB formed an electoral block in October 1924, a step towards unity, but the Bavarian GVG could not be brought on board, a prospect which was not made easier by the fact that the spokesman for the block, Gregor Strasser, wanted to exclude

---

[60] Kershaw, *Hitler*, 143.

GVG leaders Hermann Esser and Julius Streicher. Esser and Streicher, who both hated Strasser, in turn invoked Hitler's authority, countering that only he could decide whom to exclude.

Upon his release, rather than taking sides in any of these or other squabbles, Hitler devoted his attention to getting the ban on the NSDAP lifted. In February 1925, about two months after he was released from prison, the ban on the Party and the SA was lifted, as was the ban on the Party newspaper the *Völkischer Beobachter*. Cutting through the confusion and infighting that had plagued the movement in his absence, and still without ever having explicitly taken sides in any of the squabbles between various factions and personalities, Hitler declared his intention to re-found the old NSDAP. Loyalists, former members, and even would-be rivals flocked to him to declare their loyalty and rejoin the original party.

The following speech was delivered at a packed meeting of Party supporters at the *Bürgerbräukeller* in Munich. It concluded with many of the prominent figures of the movement joining Hitler on stage, even formerly bitter rivals shaking hands and, at least publicly, putting aside their differences to swear loyalty to the old party and its leader. With this rally, Adolf Hitler permanently cemented his role as the undisputed and absolute Führer of the National Socialist movement.

The Speech

My fellow Germans!

I do not address you today to give an account of times past. The last such meeting was on January 27th, 1923, at the Party General Assembly. We gave you the report on the period up to and including November 8th and 9th, 1923 in front of the entire public at the trial.

Today we are confronted with another question: What is to happen in the future?

The question of what should happen today can best be answered if we remember why our movement was founded.

So what were the causes for the formation of this new party? Think back to the year 1918. The German people, who were still at the height of their power in midsummer, had collapsed in a few months and now lay completely beaten, crushed and shattered on the ground. One question was on everyone's mind at the time: can we still come back from this deepest misery and unhappiness?

This question perhaps occupied the minds even of those who had helped to bring about the fall. In lucid moments, they too asked themselves if and when Germany would rise again.

At that time, however, one had to realize that the German people were facing a great question of destiny, on the answer and solution of which the existence of our nation would depend for all time to come.

The tragedy of our collapse did not lie in the military defeat, nor in the terrible peace deal itself, nor in the oppression that has set in since then; it lay not in the disarmament and not in the defenselessness, and not in all that has since befallen Germany in these long years; the tragedy lay in the fact that all this came about through our own fault, as well as the fact that millions of Germans not only did not understand this until the last moment, but on the contrary welcomed it, that hundreds of thousands cheered the defeat, that millions praised the disarmament, and others saw in all our oppression by the enemy a just judgment and the execution of a just punishment. Therein lies the tragic misfortune of the appalling calamity that has befallen us: that a large part of the German people no longer had any feeling for the misfortune of the Fatherland. And you see, this brings us to the fundamental question on whose answer the fate of the German nation will depend.

Will it still be possible in Germany to bring back the masses of those who no longer believe in their nationality, but see their brother in every enemy more than in their own nation, who are separated from them by party or ideology, will it be possible to lead this large mass back to a unified national community? Yes or No?

If this question is not resolved favorably, the German nation will be lost. For nations can indeed perish. It is madness to think that a great nation of sixty or seventy million is indestructible. It dies if it loses its instinct for self-preservation.

And eighteen million people in the German Reich are still of the opinion that the rights of our people on this earth are not based on our people's preservation *per se*, but are contingent upon the interests of others.

Ten million national-minded people stand against eighteen to twenty million anti-national people.

Ten million who are prepared to make the ultimate sacrifice for their nation and always seek justice in the name of their nationality, compared to eighteen to twenty million others who forget this.

This is the misfortune of the German people. But as long as this state of affairs persists and continues, any thought of a liberation of the German people is utopian.

And indeed, why? Firstly, why did we actually collapse?

We collapsed because the old empire had been sinning so badly for years, and because the Reich was denied the means it needed for its self-preservation. We perished because for a long time parliamentary shenanigans were committed with the most sensitive affairs of the whole nation, and because millions were no longer ready and willing to use their last resources to preserve the existence of their own nation and Fatherland, but were determined to sacrifice their nation and Fatherland for the existence of their party. We perished because the overwhelming majority of our pacifist, anti-national, and Marxist citizens no longer gave the state what it needed to survive.

Secondly, however, we perished in terms of foreign policy, because foreign countries recognized our internal political weaknesses all too well. Yes, they recognized the Achilles' tendon of the German Reich, and knew all too well how the balance of power in parliament was divided. They knew very well that any policy of active self-preservation would have to break down under the weight of the lukewarm, cowardly, and stupid in this country.

And today, as before 1918, it is always the same question: can this state of affairs still be changed or not?

In 1918, after the revolution, almost every attempt to lift Germany up again seemed hopeless at first.

In terms of foreign policy, the empire plummeted from its previous heights, in terms of domestic policy it was torn apart, and in terms of economic policy almost the entire national production gradually fell into the hands of foreign countries.

Every thinking person had to say to himself at that time that if things continued to develop in this way, Germany would perish hopelessly.

A change for the better no longer seemed possible. One had to ask oneself who could break this international power in the broad masses. For, my German comrades, the organized power of the International, which in Germany actually reaches from the moderate left-of-center all the way to the radical left wing of Marxism, was opposed politically only by a very weak formation: the German bourgeoisie.

Why, however, were the bourgeois parties, in their numerical weakness and pettiness, and in their lack of energy and real spirit of attack, unable to achieve a change of fortune in 1918 or later?

Let me give you the reasons very briefly.

Firstly, the recognition of the majority principle in parliament ensures that only a majority of people can bring about a change in things. But the bourgeois parties can never win majority support, for the bourgeoisie is formed primarily from the possession of intellectual and material goods — that is, from possessing property and intellect. Both, however, are present in this world only in a minority. A political movement based on these two foundations alone will always remain in the minority, and is thus condemned to insignificance in a system that gives rule only to the numerical majority.

Secondly, the path to power remains blocked for the bourgeois parties for all time to come, because the sins of the fathers are avenged upon them. The wrongs done by the previous generations in their attitude towards the broad masses over long decades are the cause of an everlasting grudge. For too many years, the plight of the masses was ignored and not cared for. For too many years, their lack of rights was not understood. Just ask yourself, which party was concerned with these people sixty or seventy years ago? Which party went out into the factories, workshops, and streets?

None of these bourgeois movements.

They all shunned the broad masses, and only when these masses began to organize themselves to fight for equal rights, and Jewry in all its cunning took the strings in its hands, did people on the right begin to realize that a new power in the state had thus begun to form: a new, fourth estate.

For too many decades these "lower" people were ignored, the bourgeoisie remained strangers to them and lost all instinct for them until on the one hand class conceit, and on the other class delusion, created an unbridgeable gulf by which the German people finally had to suffer its downfall. For, as a side effect of bourgeois class conceit, organized class consciousness now arose on the other side. The masses were systematically incited, and precisely by the people who, by God, were least concerned with bringing blessings to the broad masses, but rather saw in these masses only a tool to use to their own advantage. [...]

The bourgeois parties are born pacifist clubs. But this means that they lack not only the power and desire to attack, but also any possibility of going on the attack, for whoever wants to change a state of affairs must go on the attack himself and must not wait until he is attacked. This, however, was the most serious mistake of these politically bourgeois movements. They never went on the attack themselves, but were always happy simply to not be attacked.

They never had the courage to say, "There is our goal, there is the enemy, and now let's get on it and bring him down, and only when the last one is lying on the ground is our victory assured."

No, no, no. They were satisfied even if fate simply did not strike them too harshly in the next Reichstag election, if they were able to save a dozen more mandates, and as a last resort they kept telling themselves that surely the opponent would make such big mistakes in the next few years that the people would get fed up with him again, and then the movement's success would be secured once more by winning nine more parliamentary seats.

Of course, they could not attack at all. They were bound to their possessions, and these, whether intellectual or material, will always paralyze the will to attack.

And they did not even want to go on the attack. They were too "well-bred;" they were too "distinguished."

The foul smell rising from mass gatherings offends the sensibilities of these gentlemen. They had no love for the beer halls, and would still find it painful today if a great turn of events were to occur in the beer halls, although one might ask which is actually better — a parliament or a pub? [...]

But the most important reason why the bourgeoisie could no longer win over the broad masses is that it did not possess a fundamentally new worldview.

You must regard this, my dear German comrades, as the most important and most difficult characteristic. For when a movement fights forward today, with a certain goal in mind, then this movement also has an end point visible to all—one knows one has achieved success when one arrives at this goal. However, such a struggle does not end prematurely; on the contrary, it is driven forward relentlessly.

Conversely, defense is passive. Who can say when the goal is reached? In the best case, when the position seems secure, perhaps. And this is the difference between the bourgeois parties and those of the left: the bourgeois movements fight for the preservation of what they have; the left fights for the victory of its program, for the realization of its aims.

And this goal of theirs consists of breaking up the Fatherland, destroying the nation, destroying the national economy, and establishing international Jewish financial hegemony. [...]

Marxism, in the form of social democracy or communism, can be defeated as long as it is confronted with a doctrine of greater truthfulness but equal brutality. [...]

Now I ask you this: do you believe that a change will occur by chance, or are you convinced that when one sees doom inevitably approaching, it is one's duty, one's right, to rise up against it and to resist with all one's might, in order finally to go on the attack oneself?

That was exactly what we all had in mind when we founded the National Socialist German Workers' Party.

The goal then was clear and simple: fight the devilish power that has plunged Germany into this misery, fight Marxism and the spiritual bearer of this world plague and epidemic, the Jew. Fight not according to the bourgeois pattern, cautiously, so that it does not hurt too much. No, and no again!

When we joined together to form this new movement, we were clear that there were only two possibilities in this struggle: either the enemy will march over our dead bodies, or we will march over his!

The victory over this world plague will not be secured by winning a few parliamentary mandates, but only when the swastika flag flies above every workshop and every factory, and the last Soviet star has disappeared! [...]

But the art of all great popular leaders has always been to concentrate the attention of the masses on an enemy. This alone can bring them to that state of suggestible agitation without which great success is never achieved. Believe me about this: reason alone does little here. It is the right feeling that does more than all understanding. The intellect can deceive man; the sure feeling never leaves him. It is not for nothing that you see so many women in our movement and here in this hall, even in a movement that has fought in the most masculine way. You see them here because the feeling of women is predominant, and correctly tells them this is about the future of our children and thus about the future of our Germanness. And then there is no more wavering, no faltering the next day when the next hot new book fabricates some scientific way of deconstructing it; no, the feeling is steady; it does not waver and it does not give way.

Believe me, a Dr. Heim[61] may speak calmly of our "hysterical women," but women once brought Christianity to the nations, and they will ultimately lead our movement to lasting victory. And wherever she was missing, not only the woman herself would be missing, but with her also the youth, and thus the future. Be sure of this: the movement that has the fewest women also has the least strength, which is why you will find only a few ladies in the Democratic Party, for example.

Once it is clear that the movement has a goal to pursue, then it goes without saying that everything must be subordinated to this one idea. This should already be symbolically expressed in the name. And so the name National Socialist German Workers' Party was chosen.

"National Socialist" embodies the supreme goal of the movement, the combination of the liveliest national force with the purest social will. We realized that the hearts of the masses could not be won over merely by shouts of "Heil!"; they must come to the conviction that in the eyes of our people's movement, everyone

---

[61] Dr. Georg Heim, a conservative Bavarian separatist politician.

is equally regarded as a comrade of the people, that we do not want to see favors handed out, but rights established. And we do not at all see the future of our people in one-dimensionally developed intellects, but in a healthy people as such.

And we called it the German Workers' Party. Only those should enter it who are not ashamed to say, "I too am a worker, a productive person," for he who has not yet learned to pronounce this word with devotion is, by God, not the best German.

And that is why we also chose the swastika on a white background with a red field as our symbol. In this symbol, too, our aims should be expressed: the swastika as a symbol of work, the white as a sign of our national spirit, and the red as a sign of our truly social thought. In the swastika, however, another meaning is apparent—namely, the spirit which signifies work in this world, the spirit of Aryan idealism.

This is the symbol under which we are fighting against this global plague. But this is also the origin of our attitude towards the parliament.

We rejected parliament at that time. Why? The young movement did not want to create parliamentarians, but rather to train militants. We were convinced at that time that it was too early to go into such places and that what we need today are speakers, agitators, and apostles who go out into the masses to spread the new doctrine there, to try to lead these masses along, to organize them, and thus to win ever new members to strengthen and enlarge the movement. […]

This is how the movement began its work. It wanted to make up for what our bourgeois parties had failed to do. Above all, however, it wanted to reach out to the masses in order to spread a true national sentiment among them.

You know for yourself whether it succeeded. We started with nothing, and barely four and a half years later the name of the movement was on everyone's lips. The whole world has come to know it since then. And then came that sad day that you all know about too: that bitter day when, for the first time, people lost everything for the young movement, and thus most vividly testified to its spirit of sacrifice. The movement itself was then banned, its organization dissolved, and only with difficulty could the individual supporters try to continue working, and many, many went to prison.

Now a year has passed and the movement is free again. It is free again, in the sense that we are faced with the choice of forming it anew or abandoning it. Do not be surprised that for me there is only one choice.

Why am I calling the old movement, the old Party back to life?

You know that today there is a bitter quarrel raging within the movement. Do not ask me to take sides in this dispute. I still see in every Party member only the supporter of the common idea. Even today I do not see the individual before me, but the great idea, and if I should ever have any doubts about it, I need only close my eyes, and the picture rises before me of an hour when thousands were prepared to go to their deaths, if necessary, for this idea. Do not think that I have ever abandoned this thought. It is unshakably my guiding star, now and always. Every individual, however, who I believe has taken an iota of this thought into himself, is a brother in my eyes and belongs back among the old ranks. And I do not see my task as leader of the new movement in asking questions or in looking into the past. I see it only in one duty, namely to bring together again those who are drifting apart. But this I could not do if I were to take sides.

That is why I have taken up the old flag in the conviction that all those who felt anything at all for it will be able to rally under it once again. The old flag must again succeed in forming a single great, living movement out of the wild chaos that we find today. The old flag must again succeed in binding together the reluctant leaders, and instilling in the broad masses the conviction that this movement is not finished, but that even today it is still just beginning. [...]

And now, my dear Party Comrades, I come to a number of points of principle. When I raised the flag of our old movement again yesterday, I did so in the expectation that all those who remain National Socialists at heart will now rally around me. But I am not courting the great masses *per se*. I once declared war on this whole great current, and I swam against it for a long time. So it shall be the same for me today: whoever does not want to come into the common camp, stay away; but whoever intends to come, I say one thing to him: the quarrel has now come to an end.

Do not come to me with excuses. Do not say to me, "I can do everything you ask except this, and not that, and these others are guilty of such wrongs," et cetera. No. He who knows that he is free from all guilt, let him pick up the first stone, and then, friend, have courage and hurl it at me; for I too have failed, as every one of us has. No one has the right to strike his chest and cry out, "He is the guilty party, and I am pure as an angel!"

Whoever thinks like this bears the greatest guilt, for he is conceited and unjust at the same time.

There is a lot of talk today about "coming together." However, the first prerequisite for coming together is understanding. The first prerequisite for understanding is reconciliation. And those who cannot reconcile are, in my eyes, not worthy to work in such a movement.

Don't come to me now and say, "Yes, yes, but I represent this opinion in the interest of the movement itself."

Gentlemen, let me worry about the interest of the movement from now on!

You had nine months to preserve the interest of the movement. And I sometimes paced sleeplessly up and down in my narrow cell when I had to watch how the interest of the movement was being safeguarded! [...]

I turn to the women. I ask you above all, let only one feeling prevail now, the feeling for the obligation to faithfully administer the great good that we now have to carry on. Do not let it fragment and be dragged into the gutter, for every word we speak among ourselves in bad faith becomes a weapon against us in the hands of our enemies.

I believe we have a symbol that everyone can come to. The old flag has been almost dormant for fifteen months now. Today it has been raised again, and each individual can pledge allegiance to it once more. Anyone can come and join the ranks again. And those who believe they cannot do so can leave.

But whoever thinks he can attach "conditions" to his entry, does not know me well. I have been silent for nine months; now I lead the movement, and no one imposes conditions on me. If some gentlemen come to me, and one tries to demand that I impose this condition, and the other that I impose another, I have only one answer to give:

My friends, wait and see what conditions *I* impose!

I am not willing to have conditions imposed on me as long as I personally bear responsibility. And again, I am completely responsible for everything that goes on in this movement.

So I ask you once again to put aside everything that could divide you, and remember that today all of Germany is watching us. We are now gathered here in this hall, barely three or four thousand people. But the four thousand must become two or three million again in a short time.

This is the beginning of a new year for the movement. [...]

The hour is bitterly serious today. Our people are still dancing, while in reality death approaches. Our task is now to venture back into the morass and tell the people what they need to hear. I believe that in just one year many people's eyes will be opened. Some will have their illusions shattered, and people who still curse us today will one day stand in our ranks as new fighters. In the near future, however, your greatest task may be to win these people over.

So leave all the internal strife, leave the others—even if they attack me themselves, it doesn't matter. We don't want to argue about that either.

What we want is to reach out to the masses, to break them out of their present delusion and to reintegrate them into their nationality, so that one day the day may come when Germany will rise again under our flag.

And this greater goal, not the Party, is ultimately the goal for us. And if we thus put aside what divides us, we can do it all the more easily, since we all possess a common unifying ideal, a common good, the common, holy, German Fatherland.

WORKERS OF THE HAND AND WORKERS OF THE MIND

Schleiz, Thuringia, January 18th, 1927

The Background

In March 1925, Hitler was banned from public speaking in Bavaria, and many other regions shortly after that. Confined to speaking at private Party members' meetings, Hitler used this time to travel around Bavaria meeting local Party branches, and for a time again retreated from public life to finish the second volume of *Mein Kampf*. During this period, he deputized Gregor Strasser, who had previously won a seat in the Reichstag for the NSFB, to organize the Party in northern Germany on his behalf.

Strasser toured northern Germany tirelessly, establishing contacts, setting up Party branches, and campaigning ceaselessly on behalf of the movement. He was a highly effective organizer, and by all accounts a charismatic and energetic figure himself, and he took advantage of the leeway Hitler allowed him to shape the northern branches of the Party according to his own tastes. In these regions, more urban and industrialized compared to quaint and agricultural Bavaria, the urban working class was a stronger factor in politics. Strasser advanced ideas such as a Party labor union to challenge the unions affiliated with the left, and improving relations with Soviet Russia.

More important than any minor disagreements about economics or the finer points of National Socialist ideology, however, was the degree of independence with which the northern branches were beginning to operate. In hindsight, Hitler's relative neglect of the north compared to his stronghold in Bavaria, and his decision to take a vacation from Party affairs at this critical time, were probably tactical mistakes. A state of affairs arose where many branch leaders in the north knew Hitler only by reputation, but were personally beholden to Gregor Strasser, who had personally founded many branches and selected many of their leaders. Although he was born in Bavaria, Strasser became leader of a "Working Community" of north German NSDAP branches, and became the figurehead of the flavor of National Socialism that was developing there.

This "Working Community," guided by Gregor Strasser and Dr. Joseph Goebbels, even drafted a proposal for a new Party program. Conventional historiography on the subject usually states that this program was more left-leaning and socialistic, but on balance it does not seem to be any more radical than the original 25-Point Program of 1920; rather, it is in the same vein as the original program, but much more in-depth, with more concrete policy proposals and objectives.[62][63] The only point that was significantly more aggressively socialistic was the proposal to nationalize the land of large princely estates, which Hitler later rebuked explicitly at the conference in Bamberg where the new program was proposed.[64]

But there were two primary reasons for Hitler's rejection of the proposed new program, and neither of them was primarily ideological: first, the original 25-Point Program were vague enough to allow much more flexibility in interpretation, acting more as guiding principles than a series of concrete policy proposals. By this point in the Party's development, Hitler's own will and judgment were much more important in determining the

---

[62] Kershaw, *Hitler*, 245.
[63] Lane, *Nazi Ideology Before 1933*, 83.
[64] Kühnl, "Zur Programmatik der Nationalsozialistischen Linken," 324-335. This resource contains the full text of the program in German, as well as commentary. It is also available online in English at: https://arplan.org/2019/01/17/strasser-program

direction of the Party than any policy or document, and he wanted to retain his freedom of action and dictatorship over the Party without being tied down to any specific and concrete policy proposals and promises, especially ones that he had not had a hand in drafting himself.

More importantly, he saw the relative independence of the Working Community and Gregor Strasser's prominence within it as a potential challenge to his power, fairly or unfairly. At the Bamberg conference on February 14th, 1926, Hitler struck down Strasser and Goebbels' program proposal and reiterated that the original 25-Point Program was inviolable and immutable. He also disbanded the Working Community in a bid to avoid regional factionalism, insisting that the entire Party was a working community already. Strasser and especially Goebbels were upset, even disillusioned with Hitler for a time as Goebbels' diary indicates, but in the ensuing period Hitler made overtures to both of them, and won both of them to his way of thinking. Goebbels became especially infatuated with Hitler, and from this time on was incorporated into his intimate inner circle.

Strasser, too, continued to cooperate closely with Hitler. Unlike his brother Otto, who only reluctantly joined the Party in 1925 after previously being involved with the left, and later openly rejected orthodox National Socialism and Hitler's leadership, Gregor Strasser and the northern branches' brand of worker-oriented National Socialism were nowhere in direct contradiction to Hitler's National Socialism.

National Socialism was, after all, a revolutionary, not reactionary, movement. The socialism in its name was not, as historians in the Marxist tradition would have it, a mere cynical ploy to trick the gullible workers into supporting bourgeois nationalism against their own interests. Unlike both free-market theorists and Marxist socialists, though, Hitler believed economics were secondary, economic policy a tool to be wielded in the service of the people, and only ever as a means to an end. Indeed, a main topic of his speech on September 18th, 1922 is the subservience of economic concerns to political concerns.

But that is not to say that he was unconcerned with class issues. Indeed, it is a subject he spoke about constantly, including in the following speech. In *Mein Kampf*, Hitler admits that "those with whom [he] spent [his] younger days belonged to the petty-bourgeois class."[65] In the same passage, though, he demonstrates profound insight into the nature of class resentment, noting that the petty-bourgeoisie, though by no means rich themselves, and sometimes even worse off than skilled workers, often show an exaggerated distaste for the working class, and surmises that it arises mainly from:

> [T]he fear that dominates a social group that his risen only slightly above the level of the manual laborer — a fear that it may fall back into its old condition, or at least be again classed with the laborers.... Those who are only on the first rung of the social ladder find it unbearable to be forced into contact with the cultural level and standard of living from which they have risen.

Later on, he muses that precisely through their relative lack of education, the lower classes have been spared from some of the corrosive effects of Weimar liberal culture:

> This class doesn't include the worst elements in its ranks, but rather the most energetic. The sophistication of so-called culture hasn't yet exercised its disintegrating and degenerating influence.[66]

The NSDAP, as the name suggests, was intended from the beginning to draw supporters from the working class. Hitler noted that "The reservoir from which the young movement has to draw its strength will primarily be the working masses." [67] Party

---

[65] Hitler, *Mein Kampf, Vol. I*, C. 2.3, 77.
[66] Ibid., C. 11.16, 589.
[67] Ibid., C. 12.4, 627.

propaganda posters were deliberately printed in the blazing red associated with communism to attract attention. Hitler writes:

> *The ordinary bourgeoisie were shocked to see that we had also chosen the red of Bolshevism, and they regarded this as dubiously ambiguous. The suspicion was whispered among German nationalist souls that we also were merely another variety of Marxism, perhaps even Marxists, or better still, socialists in disguise. The actual difference between socialism and Marxism still remains a mystery to these people. The specter of Marxism was conclusively "proven" when it was discovered that we deliberately substituted the words "national country-men and -women" for "ladies and gentlemen" at our meetings, and addressed each other as Party Comrade. How often we roared with laughter at these silly faint-hearted bourgeoisie.[68]*

But the goal was not merely to provoke anger from the communists and conspiracy theories from timid conservatives, nor was the aim of attracting workers to the Party purely instrumental, to use them to gain power. Rather, taking care of the workers' interests and integrating them into the nation as a whole was fundamental to the National Socialist worldview. Numerous times throughout his speeches and in *Mein Kampf*, Hitler laments that so many workers are lacking in a national consciousness. Therein lies the crux of his hatred of Marxism, much more so than any disagreement about economic policy: Marxism exploits legitimate class grievances and labor issues to divide a people into bourgeois and proletariat, sets these classes against each other, and teaches them that they have more in common with members of their own class around the world than they do with their own countrymen of a different class, that for the German worker the real enemy is the German businessman, and when the workers believe and act on this message, the German businessman makes them his enemies as well. Hitler writes:

---

[68] Hitler, *Mein Kampf, Vol. II*, C. 7.2, 223.

The most difficult obstacle to the reunion of our contemporary worker with the national community doesn't consist so much in the fact that he fights for the interests of his fellow workers, but rather in the international ideas with which he is imbued, and which are hostile to nationhood and Fatherland. If inspired by the same leadership, the trade unions could turn millions of workers into the most valuable members of the national community, without thereby effecting their own struggles for their economic demands.[69]

This emphasis on the importance of national unity, preconditioned on mutual respect between classes, fair living conditions for all productive members of society, and recognizing the value of everyone who contributes to the national community, is the key theme of the following speech, and indeed one of the fundamental principles of the National Socialist worldview.

---

[69] Hitler, *Mein Kampf, Vol. I,* C. 12.4, 627.

The Speech

My fellow Germans!

I don't know if all the meetings here are this well attended, but I hardly think so.

Why, then, have you turned up in greater numbers today than usual? Simply because there is an election to be debated? No, not at all. You know very well that there have been elections for decades, and you also suspect that there will probably be elections in the decades to come. You have never been completely satisfied in previous years, and you will not be satisfied by the elections to come. What brings you here is not the hope that I will read you out a long recipe for a cure.

You do not expect the fulfillment of what the election speakers promise you. They themselves no longer believe they can perform miracle cures. What is actually decided by such an election? You know how things are today. Thuringia is no exception; here, too, it is not to be expected that a new worldview will suddenly come to the helm, but it is rather likely that coalitions will have to be formed again, whether of the right or of the left or in the center. The various partners in such a coalition ensure that the policy of the center remains, that if possible no one completely prevails, but that the previous general line of development more or less continues. You yourselves know what decisions are being made today in the German Reichstag, for example. The German Reichstag is not a sovereign institution. It has nothing to command and nothing to decide on except what has been prescribed for the fulfillment of the peace treaties.

The situation of the German people today seems to me like that of a sick person.

I know that many people say to us, "How can you keep saying that we are sick? Daily life goes on as before. This "sick person," you see, eats every day, works every day—how can you claim that he is sick?" But it is not a question merely of whether a people is still alive, whether the economy is working. It is by no means said that a person is healthy because he can still eat and work. The surest sign is the feeling of the human being himself; he feels whether he is healthy or sick. It is exactly the same in the life of nations. Nations are often sick for a long time—often for generations—without the individual members being able to fully explain the nature of the sickness.

A few days ago I was in Eisenach and stood on the Wartburg, where a great German once translated the Bible. At that time, the world was also sick. Many tried in vain to patch things up, until finally a very powerful figure came along, a great man who got to the root of the evil of his time. He triggered a movement that would not have completely eliminated human suffering, but which pointed out a new path that was decisive.

That is exactly how it is today. No one will claim that the German people is healthy. It is sick, and this feeling of being sick moves our whole nation today. Some, of course, feel good about it. There are those who flourish precisely when the nation is sick, whose flourishing is indirect proof of the general crisis. This crisis will always and forever be twofold. It is not only a crisis in material terms; it is above all a crisis in spiritual, moral, and ethical terms, even if most people do not want to believe this, because they feel only the material need. The latter could not occur if it were not for the spiritual crisis. This is especially true of the present time.

And this is also why you have come here. In this hall there are supporters and opponents of our movement. The supporters came to hear their leader, and the opponents came to hear the leader of this enemy movement. But those who believe fanatically in one idea—for example a religious idea—do not go when someone preaches another idea. If I am firmly rooted in my faith, then another one does not interest me at all. You have come here, even if you are perhaps not aware of it, because you are dissatisfied with what has gone before. Neither the man of the left nor the man of the right is satisfied.

I do not want to divide the German people into small parties, but into two broad halves: one half comprises those who call themselves and think of themselves as nationalists, the other half those who just as consciously call themselves internationalists. On the one side the national bourgeoisie and on the other the international proletariat. Within these two groups there is a continuous movement back and forth, in one direction or another. Why? The people are not completely satisfied with the results of their politics, but they sometimes feel that the tendency to which they belong at the moment is failing. They thus wander within the broader group, sometimes a little more to the left, sometimes a little more to the right, and search around, believing that perhaps in the other camp things can be better than before. […]

What political goal does the right have? I would like to ask you to put aside small daily goals — teachers' salaries, civil servants' pensions, et cetera. The political aim of the right wing of our people was, in general, as follows: to establish a great and powerful German Reich, a Reich of strength; to secure perfect freedom for this Reich through the cultivation of a sense of national honor, of national pride, and through the maximum development of national military power; to win for our people its place in the sun, and to retain this place; a national Reich, powerful externally and free internally. If we recall this goal today and compare it with reality, you must admit that it has not been achieved. We will talk about the reasons later. The fact is, Germany did not retain its power, its strength, or its greatness. The German form of government at home was not preserved. The organ of German defense, the source of strength of our people, was not preserved, nor has the final and most important thing been achieved — on the contrary! Of thirty million adult men and women, fifteen million reject the national idea outright. They say they are international, that they have nothing to do with the national idea.

It is not that we were close to the goal before, or that we were on the march to the goal. From decade to decade you on the right have moved further away from your goal, and today you are further away than ever. And you have grown old during this evolution. You can no longer hope to fight a battle against fate at sixty years old that you were once unable to fight at thirty or forty years old. This generation has failed and blundered, and now it is leaving world history — and not gloriously! It has inherited a great empire from its fathers and has squandered this inheritance miserably. I will address the reasons and the excuses later. First of all, I simply wish to establish that the political goal of the right was not achieved.

And what of the left? Its aim was to create a global coalition of proletarian states — that is, of states completely free from militarism and capitalism — the creation of a new world on the corpses of the vanquished anti-socialist states. And if here again you refrain from all explanations and interpretations and concern yourself only with the whole bare reality, then, my friends on the left, you must admit, your strict aim has also not been achieved. The world today is more divided than ever before. What is called the League of Nations is a ridiculous entity, ridiculous like perhaps our old German Reich before 1871. World history walks all over this so-called League of Nations as if it did not exist at all. The states are arming themselves day after day. Militarism has not been broken, nor has capitalism been broken, but has risen to become the general world order. And what we see in Germany — is this supposed to be the victory of socialism? Here, too, it is understandable that one is dissatisfied. His newspaper can tell him every day about the events of the day and so on, but he cannot get over the fact that he has to admit to himself at some point that the whole struggle has been in vain! Today, an army of the unemployed separates us from social well-being. It is not decreasing, but on the contrary increasing. […]

When I speak to nationalist politicians today and say to them, "Please admit that you have failed; fifteen million no longer want to have anything to do with the national idea, and that is the most appalling thing there can be," I get the answer, "Yes, but look at the people, they are riffraff. Go down among them now; the people are not worth talking to." There is only one reply to this: if it is true that fifteen million consciously reject the national idea out of wickedness, because they are rabble, riffraff, and scoundrels, then what is the point of any further political activity? With what material do the gentlemen of the right intend to save Germany? Their fragmented bourgeoisie perhaps? No, under such circumstances any further struggle is of no value, it is futile. Fate has spoken, our nation is destined to perish. But if that's the case then why not summon up the courage to go before the people and declare that, since they do not want to admit that they have failed, that they have no interest in politics, that there is no point in doing politics anymore? Yet these gentlemen stand up again to ask for your votes!

But it is not out of malice that fifteen million do not share the national feeling. You see, I cannot judge people by the situation of the moment. Of course, it is more convenient and easier to declare that fifteen million are swine, than to admit that one is mistaken or that one has misrepresented an idea.

One might say that people are worthless. Why worthless? I cannot assess the value of a person according to his wealth, his birth, or anything like that. All that means nothing; it is no measure of value! If I were to remove from society a good-for-nothing who had been born rich, I would do no harm to the nation, but if I were to take away a worker, of the hand or of the mind, who faithfully performs his duty, it would harm the nation. The value of a man depends on the value that his deeds create. A man does not become a poet or a thinker, a musician, a composer, a great inventor, et cetera, only by his own will; a higher nature gives him this disposition in the womb. A man may be praised because he is a genius, but his abilities mean nothing if he is not able to put them to the service of all. He can just as well be an ingenious criminal, a good-for-nothing or, as they say in Bavaria, a *Schwabinger*.[70] These

---

[70] A resident of the hip, progressive, Bohemian district of Munich; also a hotbed of leftist activity; Hitler's knowledge of the stereotypical residents of the district was likely firsthand, as he himself had once lived there before the war.

are the inhabitants of a district of Munich, a very special kind of people, where apart from a few exceptions, the females are characterized by particularly short hair, and the males by correspondingly long hair. These ingenious personalities — from whom only the most ingenious statesmen emerge now and then, such as a Kurt Eisner — if they were not there, the world would not suffer any loss. On the other hand, if I took away every street sweeper who conscientiously swept his square meter of the street, I would have to replace him with another. We should judge people according to the abilities given to them by nature, which they use for the common good. This standard completely excludes the accident of high or low birth, and makes man the forger of his own honor. [71] The most humble human being, if he honestly and truthfully fulfills his assigned work in the service of the national community, may be replaceable, but he is not dispensable. If this standard is applied, I cannot say that the fifteen million people of the left are worthless. You can't just take them away; you would have to replace them. Even if some of them are worthless, the first measure of value speaks for the fifteen million. Every intellectual invention needs many hands to be translated into real life. The national community needs them; only with them can it exist. These hands are no less valuable here than elsewhere. The German economy could not have begun its triumphal march were it not for the German worker. The industrialist would be astonished if he had to employ others instead of the German worker. He would not want to work with anyone else. He knows very well the value of the German worker. [...]

Just as the reasons from the right are not valid, those from the left are not valid either. The first major excuse is, "We were stupid to seize power on our own." Well that's your own fault! And the second is that if you ask a leader of the left, "What do you hope to

---

[71] This conception of fulfilling one's role in society to the best of one's abilities according to the propensities and talents with which one was born is consistent with Plato's theory of social morality, wherein moral good is equated with excellence (*arete*, which is also the root word of aristocracy — "rule by the best") at performing one's particular function (e.g. *The Republic*, 345a-346e).

achieve with your internationalist and Marxist thought, when fifteen million reject it altogether?" then here, too, you get the answer that these fifteen million are just worthless and useless; they should have their heads cut off. I have to say the same thing here as I said earlier about the other side. What is the value of a human being? It is determined by the value he provides to the community. Can the German worker of the mind really be called worthless? Certainly not! There are thousands and thousands of hands at work in a factory from which a locomotive finally rolls out. But don't forget that before all of them there were the engineers who designed the machines and the chemists who made the alloys. You can't say today, "Away with the engineer, he doesn't belong to our party, off with his head!" If it were only three or four, you could do it, but with fifteen million people you can't do it. If millions of workers did not offer their strength for the realization of intellectual ideas, or if the minds did not constantly give plans to the hands, the people would not be able to rise from a primitive state. The interaction of mind and hand has produced the society in which we all participate today. [...]

What is the definition of militarism? I am told militarism is the drill, militarism is the pomp and circumstance, militarism is the military in itself, it is armament, et cetera. But if the military organization itself constitutes militarism, then England is just as militaristic as Switzerland, or indeed today's Soviet Russia. And if drill constitutes militarism, then Soviet Russia is also militaristic, for I do not believe that the boot on the parade march sounds softer on Russian soil than on German—I do not believe it! But even armament has nothing to do with it; every state arms itself for its own purposes. You can say that in Russia they arm themselves for the purposes of the proletariat. In my youth I remember some large bakeries in Vienna, the Anchor Bread Works and the Hammer Bread Works. They were rival enterprises and each belonged to a Jew. One of them baked bread in the name of the proletariat. The bread from the Hammer was a little moist, it weighed a little heavier in the hand, and it was worse. They said, "But this bread is the bread of the proletariat!" If one could not stand it, the answer was, "Please, I would rather eat a loaf of freedom than a loaf of slavery." At the end of the day, however, people prefer better dry bread to the worse freedom bread. This is also the case in Russia today. You can say that Soviet militarism is the armor of the proletariat. I don't know that one dies more comfortably in such an army, but I don't believe so. I felt the thrill of looming death in my own body for four years. I think that would have been just as unpleasant for you in the name of the proletariat. And if you had repeatedly cowered in fear of death during heavy shelling, I believe that even if you had worn a red coat instead of a grey one, you too would have finally said, "Damn it, won't it end soon!"

One cannot define things so easily. This is also true of capitalism. What does capitalism really mean? There are three terms which, taken together, make up what Marxism calls capital: machines, factories or workshops, and working capital. My dear friends, these three components of production cannot be destroyed, even if the communist and syndicalist movement wish to do so. That is to say, they could be destroyed, but with the result that we would achieve in Germany what was achieved in Russia — namely, that we would have to beg international capital, as they did in Russia, to rebuild it and put capital at our disposal again. And then we would have to grant concessions, as Soviet Russia did to Herr Stinnes.[72] This was the same Herr Stinnes who would rather have cut off his fingers than have spoken ten words to a Hitler for fear of being compromised, who was presented here as the capitalist terror, who did business with the Soviet Union, who built up big hotels and big factories there. They say, "Yes, but there it was in the service of the proletariat." I don't believe that. I think Stinnes was always convinced that he was doing something for himself —

---

[72] Hugo Stinnes, a powerful German industrialist who had extensive business dealings with Soviet Russia, and was a main participant in an international consortium that aimed to use German, English, and American capital to rebuild Russia's economy in exchange for Russian natural resources and influence in the Russian economy; also a founding member and financier of the conservative German People's Party (DVP).

yes, as much as possible for himself, as little as possible for the proletariat. Besides, if these people are so devoted to the proletariat of other nations, then why not to their own? No, they do not think of it. [...]

The idea was put in the head of the German socialist that he could only be an internationalist, and he was taught that there are only other human beings. That is a blow against all experience, and a blow against their own existence. One might easily say that man is man, just as dog is dog, whether dachshund or greyhound; man is man, New Zealander or Teuton, Englishman or Zulu. Indeed, they are just as distinct from each other as one breed of dog from another. You know, it is really incredible that it was possible to preach the folly of internationalism to millions of people, and that people followed this idea, and that the Jew, who has been among us for thousands of years and yet remained a Jew, has managed to tell millions of us that race is completely meaningless, while for him race is of the highest importance. What would it mean, then, if race were meaningless? It would mean that if I took the Germans away from here today and put them in Central Africa, and brought the Negroes here, everything would look the same as if the Germans were here. The Negroes would create an equally cultivated state. Do not imagine that the jazz band would have created the culture that we have today. All that we see around us has been created by the collaboration of mental labor and physical labor over many millennia. And where do these inventors come from? Is there one significant invention that was made by a Negro? None at all. Even the most primitive work he has done he has borrowed from the White man. Today they train him until he can play a Wagner opera on the piano. That is more a proof of the trainer's ability than the Negro's ability. And it is like that with everything. A Negro can certainly clean a light bulb, but he can't invent it. We have areas where different races have been active for thousands of years. Where the Aryan goes, culture prevails; when he leaves, it gradually disappears, and if he returns after two thousand years, it may have been replaced by a desert, but he will bring it into being again. Culture is bound to people, and to certain peoples at that. If you take them away, in the long run there will be nothing left. [...]

Do not expect a people that is so sick inside to be redeemed by an election like the next one in Thuringia. Go ahead and cast your ballot again for the rotten and sick party structures, and know that in three years you will be gathered in the hall just as you are now, and you will be listening to someone again, but nothing will have changed in the meantime, only the misery will perhaps be even greater. You will not have helped your people towards a social state by promising them milk and honey, and you will not have established a national paradise of freedom within a world that oppresses you. The prerequisite for both ideals is freedom.

You will not achieve freedom for your people if you use only your fist or only your mind to achieve freedom, but mind and fist must work together. But you will achieve nothing at all until the division of the German people is eliminated. This division is only to the advantage of the international stock exchange and bank-jobber.

The two camps can no longer unite because too many people have an interest in their division. There are people who can only live from their division.

Believe me, you will never manage a reconciliation of the people in Germany using today's parties. This reconciliation is the task of National Socialism. Our national thought is identical with social thought. We are National Socialists, meaning that by "the people" we do not mean a particular class, nor an economic group, but the collective of all the people who speak our language and share our blood. We see no possibility of national pride when there is a well-fed crowd of entrepreneurs, and behind them the emaciated and exhausted working people of our nation, but only when workers of the mind and hand can exist harmoniously, well-fed and in good condition, side by side with each other. We want to lay the foundations for a new worldview in which only those who sacrifice themselves in ardent love for their whole people are considered great. We are convinced that no one in the world will hand us anything. No one else is furthering our cause; we alone must forge our own future. In our people lies the source of all our strength. If our people fall today, we fall with them. It cannot be good for us if our people are ruined. Our people and our state must prosper so that each individual member of it can live.

We are not pacifists; we know that the father of all things is struggle.

We see our people as a race, and we see its importance in the character of our nation, which must be based on a sense of responsibility to our people. We hold to the immutable principle that every decision requires responsibility. This is why the whole world opposes us, this is why we are considered dangerous to the state, and this is why I am forbidden to speak, why we are censored — because we want our whole German people to recover in body and soul from this cursed division!

THE INDUSTRY CLUB SPEECH

Düsseldorf, January 26th, 1932[73]

The Background

The federal elections of May 20th, 1928 saw the NSDAP receive 2.6 percent of the popular vote, resulting in twelve seats in the Reichstag. For many within the Party, the result was disappointing — it was less than they had won in the 1924 election under the *Völkischer Block* — but this was the first time the Party had representatives in the Reichstag exclusively representing the Party and its ideology rather than an electoral block. Prominent representatives included Gregor Strasser, fighter pilot ace and future head of the *Luftwaffe* Hermann Göring, economic theorist and early National Socialist Gottfried Feder, and master propagandist Joseph Goebbels.

A collapse in the price of agricultural products in the winter of 1928-29 led to an agricultural crisis in rural agrarian regions. Mounting debts to banks and financiers led to intense antisemitism among peasants and farmers, opposition to finance capitalism, and resentment towards the government for what they perceived as the exclusively urbanite interests of the SPD. The NSDAP

---

[73] Most sources indicate this speech as taking place on January 27th, as this was reported in the NSDAP newspaper the *Völkischer Beobachter*, but this appears to be incorrect, as contemporary sources make it clear that the speech took place on the evening of the 26th. See for example *Düsseldorfer Nachrichten* from January 27th, 1932, "Hitler sprach in Düsseldorf"; *Frankfurter Zeitung* from January 27th, 1932 (MA), "Hitlers Düsseldorfer Vortrag."

shrewdly embarked on a campaign to win over agricultural workers, peasants, and farmers. In numerous speeches, Hitler emphasized the importance of preserving and strengthening the peasantry, and Richard Walther Darré's *A New Nobility of Blood and Soil* formed the ideological underpinnings for land reform and agricultural policy that would be more favorable to peasants and farmers and maintain what National Socialists saw as a healthier urban-rural balance. The Party made inroads to farmers' interest groups, and began to receive strong support: by 1930, for example, they secured 27 percent of the vote in rural and agrarian Schleswig-Holstein, and 51 percent by 1932.

The Party was gaining ground nationwide. In a municipal election in June of 1929, the town of Coburg in Northern Bavaria even elected a full National Socialist town council.

In October 1929, a coalition of right-wing groups protesting the Young Plan, a new agreement for Germany's reparations payments, formed a Reich Committee for the German People's Petition led by the business magnate Alfred Hugenberg, formerly director of Krupp Steel, now the leader of the reactionary *Deutschnationale Volkspartei* (German National Peoples' Party, DNVP for short), as well as owner of a powerful media empire. Other members of the protest committee included the leader of the *Stahlhelm* veterans' association, the leader of the Pan-German League, and the powerful industrialist Fritz Thyssen. Admiring the youthful vitality and propaganda reach of the NSDAP, Hugenberg invited Hitler to join the committee, hoping to use his party to reach a broader audience and incite the masses against the Young Plan.

Now Hitler was rubbing elbows with some of the country's most important industrial figures and bourgeois nationalist leaders. The NSDAP temporarily began to receive favorable coverage in Hugenberg's newspapers, where previously they had been either ignored or dismissed as just another type of socialists.

The Party seized upon the onset of the economic crisis precipitated by the New York Stock Exchange leading to the beginning of the Great Depression in 1929 as an opportunity to offer concerned and dispossessed Germans a vision of a better future. Mass unemployment provided fertile ground for recruiting unemployed workers.

The Party enjoyed huge gains among students as well, with the National Socialist Students' League becoming the largest student organization in Germany by 1930. Far from being a party of old conservative reactionaries or vested interests, the NSDAP drew heavily from the youth movement. The youth and energy were on their side: in 1931, 40 percent of their membership was under the age of thirty.[74] Plainly the Party was on the rise, and quickly becoming a major force to be reckoned with in electoral politics.

In the September 1930 Reichstag elections, support for the moderate democratic parties of the center collapsed, especially the SPD, although they remained the largest party. The KPD and NSDAP both made huge gains, with the communists going from 54 to 77 seats, and the NSDAP going from 12 to 107 seats, securing almost 40 percent of the seats between them. The NSDAP became the second largest party in the Reichstag.

The communists and the National Socialists were the fastest growing political movements in Germany, and their supporters increasingly engaged in clashes and street fights with each other. The NSDAP deliberately conducted rallies and marches in communist strongholds to provoke them into attacking, allowing the SA to jump in and engage in "aggressive defense." This political street violence, echoing the troubled early days of the Weimar Republic, contributed to an atmosphere of politicization and polarization.

These developments allowed Hitler to appeal to skeptical, and sometimes even hostile, business elites, presenting National Socialism as the only viable alternative to communism, as he would in the following speech. Although they were skeptical of Hitler and wary of the collectivist tenets of the program, if trends continued and it came down to a Germany ruled either by

---

[74] Gerth, "The Nazi Party," 530.

communists or the NSDAP, they largely viewed the NSDAP as the "less bad" of the two options.

It must be understood that in this place and time, the bourgeoisie was the class historically associated with patriotism and social conservatism, while the working classes, under the influence of Marxism, were associated with internationalism and scorn for traditional social values—in some ways almost the reverse of the situation in much of the West today. This was what made it possible for Hitler to appeal to the patriotism and concern for social morality which many business leaders already possessed, as he would in the following speech, in an attempt to convince them to support his party, and view its socialism not as a threat to their class interests, but as an effort towards national unity and concern for the interests of the nation as a whole.

Despite the Party's tremendous growth, it was still perpetually plagued by financial difficulties. Other than a few donations from businessmen and industrialists in the 1920s, which amounted to a drop in the bucket compared with the Party's expenses, the NSDAP was funded almost entirely by members' fees, entry fees for speeches, and sales of its publications.

Viewed solely as an appeal to the business community for funding, then, the Industry Club speech would have to be regarded as somewhat of a failure. Donations trickled in, but these usually paled in comparison to the sums the same donors were giving to rival parties—they were merely hedging their bets so that they could claim to have supported whoever came into power, hoping thus to win favor with whatever government happened to be in charge.[75] Even in the 1932 presidential election, the majority of business leaders backed Hindenburg against Hitler, despite his appeals to them in this speech.

Businessmen and industrialists did donate to individual Party members in an attempt to influence the Party by supporting its "sensible" members, but there was no agreement on who these "sensible" members were: Thyssen donated directly to Hermann

---

[75] Turner, "Big Business and the Rise," 62-64.

Göring, whom he viewed as moderate and reasonable, while coal magnates supported Gregor Strasser.[76]

Historian Henry Ashby Turner, however, notes that "contrary to the belief of the Marxists, economic power did not translate readily into political power in the Weimar Republic."[77] Instead, the relatively little support Hitler received from these circles amounted to an abortive attempt by these circles to "make use of the energies and talents of the 'mass drummer' and then, having served their purposes, he could be tamed and fitted into their scheme of things."[78] On balance, Turner concludes that "the great majority of Germany's big businessmen had neither wanted a Nazi triumph nor contributed materially to it."[79]

In the latter part of the following speech, Hitler stresses that without the NSDAP, there would be nothing to stop the communist menace from ravaging Germany. He boasts of the numbers, strength, and dedication of the Party's storm troopers and activists, emphasizing that they would do anything for him, and then goes on to propound intolerance for anyone not aligned with the interests of the nation. Perhaps, then, as well as the assurance that his movement is not actively hostile to the business community as long as they "play ball," there is also an implicit warning here to these captains of industry, not only that the NSDAP is their only alternative to the communists, but also that if they're not going to actively support his movement, they had better at least stay out of his way.

---

[76] Ibid., 65.
[77] Ibid., 58.
[78] Bracher, *The German Dictatorship*, 116.
[79] Turner, "Big Business and the Rise," 69.

The Speech

If today the National Socialist movement is considered anti-business in broad circles of Germany, then I believe the reason is that we took a different position on the events which brought about the present situation than the other prominent organizations of public life. Even now, our view differs in many ways from that of our opponents.

We are convinced that the root cause of the present distress is not to be found in general world events, for this would also more or less preclude the possibility for an individual nation to correct its course from the outset. If it were true that German misery were only caused by a so-called global crisis[80] — a global crisis on which we as a people can naturally exert only a negligible influence — then the future of Germany would have to be described as bleak. How can a state of affairs change for which there is no direct culprit? In my opinion, the view that the global crisis is solely to blame will lead to dangerous pessimism. It is natural that the more the causes of a situation are removed from the individual's control, the more the individual will despair of ever being able to change his situation. The result will eventually be a certain lethargy, an indifference, perhaps even despair in the end. [...]

If someone tells me that foreign politics are primarily decisive for the life of a people, then I must pose a question: what does "politics" mean anyway? There are a number of definitions. Frederick the Great says, "Politics is the art of serving one's state by all means." Bismarck declares, "Politics is the art of the possible," based on the idea that everything in the realm of possibility should be done to serve the state and, according to the later transformation to the concept of nationality, the nation. Yet another believes that this service to the people can be carried out by peaceful as well as military means. Clausewitz says, "War is the continuation of

---

[80] Referring to the Great Depression.

politics by other means." Conversely, Clemenceau says that peace today is nothing but the continuation of war and the pursuit of warlike objectives by other means. In short, politics is and can be nothing other than the realization of the vital interests of a people and the practical implementation of its struggle for life by all means. It is thus quite clear that this struggle for life first takes its starting point from the people themselves, and that the people is at the same time the object, the value in itself, which is to be preserved. All the functions of this body of the people should ultimately serve only one purpose: to ensure the preservation of this very people for the future. I can therefore say neither that foreign policy nor economic policy is of primary importance. Of course, a people will need an economy in order to live. But this economy is also only one of the functions that a people needs in order to be able to exist. What is essential, however, is the starting point itself, namely the people itself. [...]

The whole structure of culture, in its foundations and in all its stones, is nothing but the result of the creative ability, the performance, the intelligence, the diligence of individual human beings. The greatest results come from the great achievements of individual God-given geniuses, average results from the deeds of human beings of average abilities, and overall results, of course, are the result of the application of human labor power towards utilizing the creations of geniuses and talented individuals. It is natural, however, that if the capable minds of a nation, who are always in the minority, are equated in value with all the others, a levelling of genius, a levelling of ability and of the value of personality will gradually occur, a levelling which is then falsely called the rule of the people. This is not the rule of the people, but in reality the rule of stupidity, mediocrity, half-measures, cowardice, weakness, inadequacy. It is closer to the rule of the people to let a people be governed and guided in all areas of life by its most capable individuals born for this purpose, than to let all areas of life be administered by a majority which, by its very nature, is unsuited to these areas. [...]

You gentlemen are of the opinion that the German economy must be built on the idea of private property. Now, in practice, you can only uphold such an idea of private property if it appears to be somehow grounded in logic. This idea must draw its ethical justification from the sense that it is a necessity of nature. It cannot be motivated merely by saying, "It has been this way up to now, so it must continue to be this way," for in periods of great upheaval, movements of peoples, and changes in ways of thinking, institutions and systems cannot remain untouched merely because they have existed in the same form up to now. It is the characteristic of all truly great revolutionary epochs of humanity that they march over such forms, sanctified only by age or even only apparently sanctified by age, with unparalleled ease. It is therefore necessary to justify the traditional forms which are to be maintained in such a way that they can be regarded as absolutely necessary, as logical and correct. And here I must say: private property can only be morally and ethically justified if I assume that people's achievements are different. Only then can I state that because the achievements of human beings are different, the results of their achievements are also different. If the results of people's achievements are different, it is expedient also to leave the administration of these results to people to an appropriate degree. It would be illogical to entrust the administration of the result of a certain achievement by one personality to the next best achiever, or to a group which, by the very fact that it did not create the achievement, has proved that it cannot be capable of administering the result. This means that it must be admitted that people are not economically equally valuable or equally important in all areas from the outset. If we admit this, however, then it is madness to say that there are necessarily differences in value in the economic sphere, but not in the political sphere! It is absurd to base economic life on the idea of achievement, on the value of personality, and thus on the authority of personality, but to deny this authority of personality in the political sphere, and to push the law of the greater number, democracy, in its place. Thus, slowly, a dichotomy must arise between the economic and the political conceptions, which one will try to bridge by aligning the former with the latter — has tried to do so, for this dichotomy has not only remained a mere empty theory. The idea of equality of values has meanwhile been elevated to a system not only politically but also economically. And not just in an abstract theory: no, this economic system is alive in gigantic organizations — indeed, it has already taken over a huge area in the form of a state.

But I cannot regard two basic ideas as possible for sustaining for the life of a people in the long run. If the view is correct that human achievement is different, it must also be correct that the value of human beings is different with regard to the attainment of certain achievements. It is nonsensical, however, to accept this only in relation to a certain field, in the field of the economy and its management, but not in the field of the management of the overall struggle for life, the field of politics. It is rather logical that if in the economic sphere I view the absolute recognition of achievements as the prerequisite for every higher culture, then politically I must likewise place the emphasis on achievement, and thus on the authority of the personality, first. But if, on the other hand, it is asserted that special abilities are not necessary in the political sphere, but that in this sphere there is an absolute uniformity of achievement, then one day this same theory will be carried over from politics to the economy. In the economic sphere, communism is analogous to political democracy. Today we are in a period in which these two basic principles are wrestling with each other on every frontier, and are already penetrating the economy.

An example: the practical activity of life is based on the importance of personality. This is now slowly being threatened by the rule of the majority. In the state, however, there is an organization — the army — which cannot be democratized in any way without giving up its essential character. This alone is proof of the weakness of a worldview — that it cannot be applied to all areas of life as a whole. In other words, the army can only exist by maintaining the absolutely anti-democratic principle of unconditional authority downwards, and absolute responsibility upwards, whereas democracy effectively means total dependence downwards, and authority upwards. The result, however, is that in a state in which the whole of political life, from the municipality to the Reichstag, is built on the idea of democracy, the army must gradually become a foreign entity, and become perceived as such. From the perspective of democracy, it is a foreign conception, a foreign worldview, which animates this entity. An internal struggle between the representation of democracy and the representation of authority will be the inevitable consequence, a struggle such as we are experiencing in Germany now. [...]

The most serious phenomenon is the fact that parallel to the gradual confusion of White European thought, a worldview has taken hold in a part of Europe and a large part of Asia which threatens to break this continent out of the structure of international economic relations altogether—a phenomenon which German statesmen still ignore today with astonishing flippancy. When, for example, I hear a speech which emphasizes that it is necessary for the German people to stand together, then I have to ask: does anyone really believe that standing together today is only a question of political goodwill? Can we not see that a rift has already opened up among us, a rift which is not merely a figment of a few imaginations, but whose ideology today forms the basis of one of the greatest world powers? Bolshevism is not just a mob raging in the streets of Germany, but a worldview that is about to subjugate the whole Asiatic continent, and which today reaches almost from our eastern border to Vladivostok!

It is presented to us as if these were purely intellectual problems of individual idealists or individual evil-doers. No, a worldview has conquered a state, and from there it will slowly shake the whole world and bring it down. Bolshevism, if its path is not interrupted, will subject the world to a complete transformation just as Christianity once did. In three hundred years it will no longer be talked about as a new idea of production. In three hundred years we will perhaps already know that it is almost a new religion, albeit one built on a different basis! In three hundred years, if this movement continues to develop, we will see Lenin not only as the revolutionary of 1917, but as the founder of a new world doctrine, with a veneration perhaps like Buddha. This gigantic phenomenon cannot simply be wished away. It is a reality, and will inevitably destroy and eliminate one of the prerequisites of the existence of the White Race. We can see the stages of this process: first the lowering of the level of culture, and with it the receptiveness towards culture, the lowering of the total level of humanity, and with it the breaking off of all relations with other nations, then the construction of an independent system of production with the help of the crutches of the capitalist economy. At the last stage, then, independent production with the complete exclusion of other countries, which of course will one day also have the toughest economic competitor on their borders.

I know very well that gentlemen of the Reich Ministry of Defense and gentlemen of German industry will reply to me, "We do not believe that the Soviets will ever be able to build up a truly competitive industry." Gentlemen, they would never be able to build it up from only Russian Bolshevik elements. But this industry will be built from the resources of the White peoples themselves. It is nonsensical to say it is not possible to build up industry in Russia through the forces of other peoples — it was also once possible to build up industry in Bohemia using Germans. Furthermore, Old Russia was already in possession of a certain level of industry.

If you go on to say their methods of production will never be able to keep up with us in any way, then don't forget that their lower standard of living will make up for whatever head start our methods of production might give us.

In any case, we will experience the following: Bolshevism will, if European and American thinking do not change, slowly spread across Asia. Thirty and fifty years are nothing when it comes to worldviews. Three hundred years after Christ, Christianity only slowly began to penetrate the whole of southern Europe, and seven hundred years later it finally took hold of northern Europe. Worldviews of such a fundamental nature can still prove their absolute ability to conquer five hundred years later, if they are not broken at the beginning by the natural instinct of self-preservation of other peoples. But if this process continues for even thirty, forty, or fifty years, and our state of mind remains the same, then, gentlemen, we will not be able to say, "What does this have to do with our economy?" [...]

In the life of nations, external strength is contingent upon the strength of the internal organization, but the strength of the internal organization depends on the stability of shared views on certain fundamental questions. What use is it if a government issues a decree to save the economy, but the nation as a living entity has two completely different views on the economy itself? One part says, "The foundation of the economy is private property;" the other part claims, "Private property is theft." Fifty percent profess one fundamental view, 50 percent the other. You may counter that these views are pure theory—no, this theory is necessarily the basis for praxis. Was this view only a theory, for instance, when it spawned the revolution in November 1918 that smashed Germany? Was it a completely irrelevant theory, and above all one that was irrelevant to the economy? No, gentlemen! I believe that such views, if they are not countered, will lead to a division among the people, for they do not remain theory. The government talks about "the patriotic way of thinking." What does "patriotic thinking" mean? Ask the German nation! One part professes it, the other declares that the Fatherland is a stupid bourgeois tradition, and nothing more. The government says, "The state must be saved." The state? Fifty percent see the state as a necessity, but 50 percent only wish to smash the state; they consciously feel themselves to be the vanguard not only of an alien national sentiment and conception, but indeed of an alien state. I cannot say that this is merely theoretical. It is not theoretical if in a nation only 50 percent at most are prepared to fight for the symbolic colors, if necessary, while 50 percent have raised another flag — a flag which is not of their nation, not of their state, but which represents a foreign state.

"The government will try to improve the morals of the German people." What morals, gentlemen? Morality, too, must have a basis. What seems moral to you seems immoral to others, and what seems immoral to you is a new morality to others. The state, for example, says, "The thief must be punished." Countless members of the nation, however, reply, "The owner must be punished, because the property itself is theft." If anything, the thief is glorified. One half of the nation says, "The traitor must be punished," but the other half says, "Treason is a duty." One half says, "The nation must be defended with courage," and the other half thinks courage is a folly. One half says, "The basis of our morality is religious life," and the other half sneers, "The concept of God does not exist in reality; religion is merely the opium of the masses."

Just don't think that once a nation is caught up in these worldly struggles, one can simply get around them by emergency decrees, that one doesn't need to take a stand on them because they are matters that do not affect the economy, or administrative life, or cultural life! Gentlemen, these struggles affect the power and strength of the nation as a whole! How can a nation still be a player on the world stage if fifty percent are Bolshevik-oriented and fifty percent nationalist or anti-Bolshevik? It is conceivable that Germany could become a Bolshevik state — it will be a disaster, but it is conceivable. It is also conceivable to build Germany up as a nationalist state. But it is unthinkable to create a strong and healthy Germany if fifty percent of its people are Bolshevik and fifty percent national-minded! We cannot get around the solution of this question! [...]

A historical example of the importance of unity within a people: in place of the lacking religious unity — for the two confessions[81] are firmly entrenched; neither can now overcome the other — a new platform is found: a new conception of the state, at first of a

---

[81] Meaning Catholicism and Protestantism.

legitimist character, and later slowly giving way to the age of the nation-state. On this new platform, Germany finds itself together again, and bit by bit, with the reunification of the Reich, which had disintegrated in the old turmoil, its power to affect the outside world increases again automatically and continuously. This increase in strength leads to those August days of 1914 that we ourselves were proudly fortunate enough to witness. A nation that seems to have no internal divisions and thus turns all its strength outwards! And in barely four and a half years we see the process regressing again. The inner divisions become visible, they slowly begin to increase, gradually its energy and power turn inwards. The internal struggle becomes paramount again. At last comes the collapse of November 1918. In reality, this means nothing other than that the German nation once again turns all its strength to the internal conflicts — outwardly it sinks back into complete lethargy and powerlessness.

But it would be quite wrong to think that this process only took place in November of 1918. No, the ideological division began to set in at the very time when Bismarck was unifying Germany. Germans began to see themselves as bourgeois and proletarians rather than as Prussians, Bavarians, Württembergers, Saxons, Badeners, et cetera. In place of a many-faceted rift, which could be overcome using state policy, a class division set in, which effectively leads to the same result, for the remarkable thing about the earlier state disunity was that under some circumstances a Bavarian was more likely to side with a non-German than with a Prussian. In other words, relations with the outside world were considered more possible than relations with one's own fellow Germans. Exactly the same result is now achieved by way of class division. Again, a mass of millions of people solemnly declare that they are more willing to enter into relations with people and organizations of a foreign people who think and act in the same way, than with their own people who are of the same blood but who think in a different way ideologically. Only in this way is it understandable that today you can see the red flag with hammer and sickle – the flag of a foreign state power – flying over Germany, that there are millions of people to whom one cannot say, "You too are German – you too must defend Germany!" If these people were prepared to do this, as they were in 1914, they would have to renounce their worldview, for it is quite absurd to believe that Marxism would have converted to the national cause in 1914 after all. No, in 1914, the German worker intuitively turned away from Marxism and found his way to the nation despite his own leadership. Marxism itself as a concept and idea knows no German nation, knows no national state, but knows only the Internationale! [...]

One thing has become clear to me: the previous world of party politics shattered and broke Germany. It is nonsensical to believe that the factors whose existence is historically inseparable from Germany's decline could now suddenly contribute to its resurgence. Every organization becomes the bearer not only of a certain spirit, but even of a certain tradition. If, for example, associations or parties have traditionally retreated from Marxism for sixty years, I do not believe that after the most terrible defeat they will suddenly break with the tradition which has become second nature to them and go from retreat to attack; I believe the retreat will continue. Yes, one day these associations will take the path that organizations with permanent defeats always take: they will make a pact with the enemy and try to achieve peacefully what they could not achieve by fighting. [...]

Developments have proven that this train of thought was correct in the end. Even if there are many in Germany today who believe that we National Socialists are incapable of positive work – they are mistaken! If it were not for us, there would already be no bourgeoisie in Germany today, the question of Bolshevism or no Bolshevism would have been decided long ago! Take the weight of our gigantic organization, by far the largest in the new Germany, off of the scales of national events, and you would see that without us Bolshevism would already be tipping the scales today – a fact of which the best proof is the attitude of Bolshevism towards us. It is a great honor for me if today Mr. Trotsky calls upon German communists to work together with social democrats at all costs, since the only real danger to Bolshevism is National Socialism. All the greater honor for me, because in twelve years we have built up a movement out of nothing against the whole of present public opinion, against the press, against capital, against the business establishment, against the administration, against the state — in short, with everything against us, we have built up a movement which today can no longer be eliminated, which is there, which one must take a position on, whether one likes it or not. And I believe that the position must be clear to anyone who still believes in a German future. You see before you an organization which does not only preach the theory of the insights which I described as essential at the beginning of my speech, but which embodies them practically, an organization filled with the most eminent national feeling, built on the idea of absolute authority of leadership in all fields, the only party which has completely overcome not only the international but also the democratic idea, which in its entire organization knows only responsibility, command, and obedience, and which thus for the first time integrates into the political life of Germany an organization of millions which is structured according to the principle of achievement. This is an organization which fills its followers with an irrepressible fighting spirit, for the first time an organization which, when its political opponents declare its very presence a provocation, does not suddenly retreat, but which brutally asserts its will and hurls back at them, "We fight today! We will fight tomorrow! And if you consider our meeting today a provocation, we will hold another one next week, until you have learned that it is not a provocation when the Germany of the Germans professes its will!" And if they say we are not allowed on the streets, we will go on the streets anyway! And if they say, "Then we will beat you down" — no matter how many sacrifices they impose on us, this young Germany will march on and on, it will one day completely reconquer the German street and the German man. And if we are reproached for our intolerance, we proudly confess to it—yes, we have made the inexorable decision to root out Marxism in Germany. We did not make this decision based on pure rowdiness, for I could think of a nicer life than being hounded through Germany, being persecuted by countless decrees, having one foot in prison all the time, and having no state rights to call my own. I could think of a more pleasant fate than conducting a struggle which, at least at the beginning, everyone regarded as a pipe dream. Finally, I believe I could also have taken up some post in the Social Democratic Party, and one thing is certain: if I had put my abilities at their service, I would probably even be fit to govern today. For me, however, it was a greater decision to choose a path on which I was guided by nothing but my own faith and my unshakable confidence in the natural powers of our people, which certainly still exist, and which, with the right leadership, will necessarily one day re-emerge.

Now a twelve-year struggle lies behind us. We have not only led it in purely theoretical terms, or put it into practice in our Party alone, but we are also ready to lead it on a large scale at any time. When I think back to the time when I founded this association with six other unknown people, when I spoke before eleven, twelve, thirteen, fourteen, twenty, thirty, and fifty people, when after one year I had won sixty-four people for the movement, to the time when our small circle expanded more and more, then I must admit that what has been created today, when a stream of millions of German comrades has flowed into our movement, represents something unique in German history. For seventy years the bourgeois parties have had time to operate. Where is the organization that could compare with ours? Where is the organization that, like ours, could if necessary bring four hundred thousand men out into the streets who have blind obedience in them, who will carry out any order, unless it is unlawful? Where is the organization that could have achieved in seventy years what we have achieved in barely twelve years, with means so improvised that one would almost have to be ashamed to confess to the enemy how impoverished this organization once was during its birth and early development.

Today we stand at the turning point of Germany's destiny. If the present development continues, Germany will one day inevitably end up in Bolshevik chaos, but if this development is interrupted, our people must be sent to a school of iron discipline and slowly cured of the prejudice of both camps. A difficult education, but one we cannot avoid!

If one believes that one can conserve the concepts of "bourgeois" and "proletarian" into the future, then one is either conserving German impotence and thus our downfall, or ushering in the victory of Bolshevism. If one is not willing to renounce those concepts, then I am convinced that a resurgence of the German nation is no longer possible. The chalk lines drawn by worldviews for peoples have historically been the death line more than once. Either we succeed in turning this conglomeration of parties, associations, unions, worldviews, class conceit, and class insanity into an iron-hard body of the people, or Germany will finally perish from this lack of inner consolidation. Even if twenty more emergency decrees are rained down upon our people, they will not be able to change the course leading to our ruin. If one day the path leading upwards is to be found again, then the German people must first be straightened out. That is a process which no one can avoid! It is not acceptable to say, "It's all the fault of the proles!" No, believe me: our entire German people, all strata of society, are to blame for our collapse—some because they wanted it and consciously brought it about, others because they stood by and were too weak to prevent it! In history, failure is weighed just as heavily as intentions or deeds themselves. Today, no one can escape the responsibility to carry out the regeneration of the German national body through his personal participation and integration.

When I speak to you today, it is not to persuade you to vote, or to get you to do this or that favor for the Party on my account. No, I am presenting to you a view whose victory I am convinced represents the only possible starting point for a German resurgence, and which is also the last asset the German people possesses. Often I hear from our opponents, "You will not be able to overcome today's hardships either." Suppose, gentlemen, that were true. But what would that mean? It would mean that we were facing a terrible time, with nothing at all to oppose it but a purely materialistic view on all sides. The crisis, however, would be felt a thousand times more acutely as a purely material one, if no ideals were restored to the people.

I am so often told, "You are only the drummer of nationalist Germany!" And what if I were only the drummer? It would be a greater statesmanlike deed today to drum a new faith into this German people than to slowly squander the existing one. Take a fortress and burden this fortress with the harshest privations — as long as the garrison sees a possible salvation, believes in it, has hope for it, then it can bear the reduced rations. Take away the last belief in a possible salvation from the hearts of the people, in a better future, and you will see how these people suddenly regard the reduced rations as the most important thing in their lives. The more they are made aware of being only the pawns of other actors, only prisoners of geopolitics, the more they, like every prisoner, will turn only to material interests. Conversely, the more you lead a people back into the sphere of idealistic faith, the less they will regard material need as an exclusively determining factor. The strongest proof of this has been our German people. Let us never forget that for 150 years it fought religious wars with enormous dedication, that hundreds of thousands of people once left their homeland and their possessions for the sake of an idea and a conviction! Let us never forget that for 150 years not a single ounce of material interest was involved! And you will then understand how enormous the power of an idea, of an ideal, is! Only in this way can it be understood that in our movement today hundreds of thousands of young people are prepared to risk their lives to oppose the enemy. I know very well, gentlemen, that when National Socialists march through the streets and there is suddenly a commotion and racket in the evening, then the bourgeois pulls back the curtain, looks out, and says, "Once again I'm disturbed in my night's rest and can't sleep. Why do the Nazis always have to agitate and march around at night?" Gentlemen, if everyone thought like that, the night's rest would not be disturbed, but then the bourgeoisie would not be able to go out on the streets by day either. If everyone thought like that, if these young people had no ideal to animate them and propel them forward, then they would gladly dispense with these nocturnal fights. But do not forget that it is a sacrifice when today many hundreds of thousands of SA and SS men of the National Socialist movement have to go out on their trucks every day, protect meetings, perform marches, sacrifice night after night, only to return at dawn—either back to the workshop and the factory, or else as unemployed to receive their few pennies in stamps; when they buy their uniforms, their shirts, their badges, even when they pay for their own transportation — believe me, therein lies the power of an ideal, a great ideal! And if the whole German nation today had the same faith in its vocation as these hundreds of thousands, if the whole nation possessed this idealism, then Germany would look different to the world today! For our situation in the world has such disastrous effects for us only because of our own underestimation of German strength. Only once we have changed this fateful assessment will Germany be able to take advantage of the political possibilities which, in the distant future, will put German life back on a natural and sustainable basis: either new living space with the expansion of a large domestic market, or the protection of the German economy from the outside by employing unified German strength. The manpower of our people and the skills are there — no one can deny our industriousness. But the political conditions must first be created again; without them, diligence and skills, industriousness and thrift will be in vain in the end, for an oppressed nation will not even be able to use the results of its thrift for its own good, but will have to sacrifice them on the altar of extortion and tribute.

Thus, in contrast to our official government, I see the means of German resurgence not in the primacy of German foreign policy, but in the primacy of the restoration of a healthy, national-minded, and powerful German body of people. I founded the National Socialist movement thirteen years ago to accomplish this task and have led it for twelve years, and I hope that one day it will indeed accomplish this task, that the most beautiful result of its struggle it will be to leave behind a completely internally regenerated German national body, intolerant of anyone who interferes with the nation and its interests, intolerant of anyone who sins against the nation and its interests, intolerant of anyone who does not recognize its vital interests or who opposes them, intolerant and intransigent against anyone who seeks to destroy and divide this body of the people—and, moreover, ready for friendship and peace with anyone who wants friendship and peace!

ADOLF HITLER'S FIRST RADIO
BROADCAST AS CHANCELLOR

February 1st, 1933

The Background

The circumstances in which Hitler came to power in 1933 were the result of a combination of popular support, shrewd political maneuvering, chance, the inability of his enemies to cooperate, and the mistaken belief that he could be manipulated and controlled. In 1930, Centre Party Chancellor Heinrich Brüning was at an impasse with his parliament, unable to get the squabbling parties of a coalition of the SPD and conservative *Deutsche Volkspartei* (German Peoples' Party, DVP for short) to agree to pass a budget, and instead forced it through via emergency decree, the beginning of a pattern of "rule by decree" by the democratic parties in the last years of the Weimar Republic. This was indicative of a transition to a more authoritarian form of "democracy," wherein parliamentary gridlock was bypassed in favor of rule through bureaucratic institutions. The weakening of parliamentary authority helped prepare the ground for Hitler and the NSDAP to muscle their way into absolute power.

In the Weimar system of democracy, a President was elected every seven years, while a Chancellor was appointed by the President after every federal election. Any party or coalition that attained a 51 percent majority of seats would automatically be awarded the chancellorship. If there was no absolute majority, the

President would appoint the Chancellor, usually, but not always, from the largest party or coalition.

Even with the growth and electoral success of the NSDAP in the late 1920s and early 1930s, Hitler himself was unable to stand for elections because he was still not a citizen of Germany. Before the presidential elections of 1932, he scrambled to scheme up a way to get his citizenship quickly so that he could run in the election. An NSDAP official and minister of the interior and education in the Free State of Braunschweig named Dietrich Klagges appointed Hitler as a staff member of the Braunschweig legation in Berlin, a low-level and purely ceremonial post that allowed Hitler to gain citizenship in the country he had always identified with. Now he could stand for elections.

The 1932 presidential election boiled down to a race between Hitler and the aged general and war hero Paul von Hindenburg, another symbolic figurehead of the nationalist right and military, who had ruled alongside Ludendorff in the quasi-dictatorship of the last years of the war. Although he was not a member of any party, he was an arch-reactionary and nationalist. The left thus had very little to hope for from this election. Against the rising Hitler and the legendary Hindenburg, the other candidates stood no chance. The final results of the presidential election were 53 percent for Hindenburg, 37 percent for Hitler, and 10 percent for KPD candidate Ernst Thälmann.

Hindenburg was moving the government towards an authoritarian, conservative, anti-democratic military dictatorship. In May 1932, President Hindenburg dissolved the Reichstag, set the next election for the end of July, and appointed the conservative catholic Centre Party member Franz von Papen as Chancellor, who left the Centre Party to accept the post, and went on to rule almost exclusively by emergency decree.

During the fevered Reichstag election campaign, during which Hitler delivered speeches in fifty-three different towns within two months, the communists ramped up their campaign of terror against his supporters. *Antifaschistische Aktion* (Anti-Fascist

Action), the successor to the banned *Roter Frontkämpferbund* (Red Front Fighters' League) was founded in 1932 as the paramilitary wing of the KPD to oppose both the government and the Nazis, gaining a membership of over 130,000. But the Nazis met terror with terror: in the month of July 1932 alone, there were eighty-six political murders, almost all of them committed by either Nazis or communists.[82] The SA's own membership by now numbered over four hundred thousand. During this period, the Communist International sent instructions to the KPD from Moscow not to cooperate with the Social Democrats, deeming the SPD "social fascists," instead directing them to try to steal the workers' support away from the rival SPD. Thus, as was typical of the period, the moderate left and far left were never able to effectively cooperate to oppose the far right or the National Socialists.

The July 1932 Reichstag election resulted in massive gains for the NSDAP. They won over 37 percent of the vote, resulting in 230 seats in the Reichstag, making them easily the largest party, but still not quite enough to win them the chancellorship automatically.

After the election, Hitler met with General Kurt von Schleicher, who was officially the *Reichswehr* minister, but had made himself into a political adventurer and important power-broker in the new authoritarian, military-dominated shell of a democracy that was the late Weimar system. Schleicher was a confidant and advisor of President Hindenburg, and it was on this basis that Hitler appealed to him with a list of conditions for his cooperation with a Hindenburg-Papen government as leader of the largest party. These ambitious demands included chancellorship for himself and ministerial posts in the cabinet for several of his men, including the Ministry of Education for Goebbels, and Labor Ministry for Gregor Strasser.

Hindenburg balked at these demands, especially at giving Hitler the chancellorship, still eyeing the NSDAP with suspicion from his haughty and aristocratic vantage point as plebeians and potentially dangerous socialists. Instead he proposed Papen

---

[82] Deuerlein, *Der Aufstieg der NSDAP*, 392-393.

remain Chancellor, and Hitler be appointed Vice-Chancellor. Gregor Strasser urged him to accept. But as the leader of the largest party, Hitler refused what he viewed as the consolation prize of a vice-chancellorship, and threatened stubborn opposition to the Papen government.

The conservatives in the Hindenburg-Papen government now had to contend with a hostile Reichstag split mainly between the NSDAP and the KPD. Consulting legal scholars such as Carl Schmitt, who would later serve as the chief jurist and legal scholar in National Socialist Germany, the regime came up with a technically unconstitutional but pseudo-legal scheme to dissolve the intransigent Reichstag, postpone elections as long as possible by way of emergency decree, and finagle a new two-chamber system into place, with an unelected higher chamber, and the powers of the Reichstag greatly reduced.[83]

The KPD put forward a vote of no confidence in the government. In a bid to demonstrate his displeasure with the President and Chancellor, as well as to embarrass and frustrate the government, Hitler and the NSDAP supported the motion.

Papen tried to move forward with the order to dissolve the Reichstag, but Hermann Göring simply talked over him, pushing the vote of no confidence through despite Chancellor Papen's efforts. The Reichstag voted 512 to 42 against the government, with only the conservative DVP and bourgeois-nationalist DNVP supporting it. Technically the dissolution and order for new elections was legally binding, but the vote of no confidence was demoralizing to the Hindenburg-Papen regime, and demonstrated that they had very little public support.

The new election would be the fifth of the year, and the public was growing tired of campaigns and politicking. The NSDAP put forth an enormous propaganda effort nonetheless. Between October 11th and November 5th, Hitler embarked on a grueling campaign schedule, flying all around the country by plane to fifty different rallies in a campaign called "The Führer Over Germany,"

---

[83] Winkler, *Weimar 1918–1933*, 518-519.

focusing his speeches on attacking governmental chaos and incoherence, and portraying the regime as a small circle of stubborn reactionaries acting against popular will.

These efforts were not quite able to overcome electoral fatigue, and the overall lower voter turnout resulted in slightly worse performance for the NSDAP. Still, with over 33 percent of the vote and 196 seats, they remained the largest party in the Reichstag.

Negotiations after the election in November between Hitler and Hindenburg again fell through. Hitler would not budge on his demand for the chancellorship, and Hindenburg would not budge on his refusal.

Meanwhile, the *Reichswehr* reported to Hindenburg that in the event of a general strike by the SPD or KPD-affiliated trade unions, they would be unable to restore order, and the situation could descend into a civil war. Hindenburg reluctantly replaced Papen, who was still unable to secure a solid base of support in the Reichstag, with General Kurt von Schleicher as the new Chancellor.

The perpetual plotter Schleicher began scheming behind the scenes to bring about an unlikely scenario that would depend on a coalition of the SPD, DVP, DNVP, and NSDAP with Gregor Strasser at its head as vice-chancellor instead of Hitler. Schleicher's repeated overtures to Strasser put the latter in a bad spot. He was forced to choose between betraying Hitler to accept the vice-chancellorship, and continuing to back Hitler in what he increasingly viewed as an unrealistic and stubborn demand for full chancellorship. In the end he chose neither. In December of 1932, he resigned from his offices and withdrew from politics to return to his work in a chemical and pharmaceutical business.

Chancellor Schleicher's ambitions were foiled by Strasser's resignation. He ran into yet more trouble when his chancellorship was opposed by major agricultural interest groups due to his refusal to impose the high tariffs they requested on imported produce. These interests had sway with the government due to their support for the DNVP and especially the NSDAP, and their opposition could prove politically costly.

A series of meetings took place in January 1933 between Papen, Hitler, and Paul von Hindenburg's son Oskar. Hitler still insisted on the chancellorship for himself, but made more modest demands for ministerial posts for his supporters. These meetings resulted in a tentative agreement to propose a coalition between the bourgeois-nationalist DNVP and the NSDAP, with Papen as Vice-Chancellor, and Hitler as Chancellor.

A desperate Schleicher prevailed upon President Hindenburg for yet another new election, hoping for a more favorable distribution of seats, but Hindenburg refused to dissolve the Reichstag yet again. Schleicher threatened to resign in protest and take his entire cabinet with him. Hindenburg consulted Papen, who put forth the plan he and Hitler had agreed to previously. For the first time, Hindenburg had to seriously consider appointing Hitler as Chancellor.

Hindenburg, Papen, and DNVP leader Alfred Hugenberg eventually reached an agreement: Hindenburg as President, Papen as Vice-Chancellor, all but two cabinet posts occupied by conservative ministers, only two National Socialists in the cabinet, a coalition government with the DNVP, and finally, after more than two years of holding out for the position, relentless campaigning, and refusing to be bought off with consolation prizes or half measures, Adolf Hitler as Chancellor of Germany.

This plan amounted to a futile attempt by a coalition of right-wingers, including conservatives, aristocratic reactionaries, and bourgeois-nationalists, to control Hitler and the National Socialists. Hugenberg, leader of the DNVP, was confident that this maneuver would "box Hitler in." Despite misgivings from "respectable" conservatives, Papen was confident. When cautioned about being manipulated by Hitler, Papen answered, "You are mistaken. We've hired him."[84] Historian Karl Dietrich Bracher notes:

[A]s far as Hitler was concerned, the alliance with rightist parties, industrial circles, agrarian interests, and the military was merely

---

[84] von Krosigk, *Es geschah in Deutschland*, 147.

one of expediency.... Hitler's allies had initially overestimated
their own power, and later they tried to steer the revolution into
orderly channels.[85]

During its meteoric rise in the late 1920s and early 1930s, the Party had formed something like a state within a state, designating its top members as ministers of government-like "ministries" such as foreign policy, press, industrial relations, agriculture, economy, interior, justice, science, and labor.[86] This quasi-state apparatus helped Party officials prepare themselves for future ministerial posts in a real government, and allowed the Party to slide into these positions of power surprisingly smoothly.

Chancellor Adolf Hitler assumed his new office on January 30th, 1933. The following speech is his first official radio broadcast to the German people in this capacity, in which he reiterates his commitment to do his duty to the country, his gratitude for the people's support, outlines his vision for the future, and asks the German people to give him a four-year trial period to show what he can do for them.

---

[85] Bracher, *The German Dictatorship*, 69-70.
[86] Ibid., 179-180.

The Speech

More than fourteen years have passed since that unfortunate day when, blinded by promises at home and abroad, the German people forgot the highest goods of our past—the Reich, its honor, and its freedom—and lost everything in the process. Since those days of betrayal, the Almighty has withdrawn His blessing from our people. Discord and hatred have taken hold. In the deepest distress, millions of the best German men and women from all walks of life see the unity of the nation fading away and dissolving into a jumble of political and egotistical opinions, economic interests, and ideological opposition.

As so often in our history, since that day of revolution, Germany has presented a heartbreaking picture of disunity. We did not receive the promised equality and brotherhood, but we did lose our freedom. The dissolution of the unified spirit and will of our people at home was followed by the decline of its political position on the world stage.

Imbued with the burning conviction that the German people went into the great battle in 1914 without any thought of their own guilt and filled only with the burden of having to defend the Reich from attack and preserve the freedom and the existence of the German people, we see in the shattering fate that has haunted us since November 1918 only the result of our inner decay. But the rest of the world has been no less shaken by major crises since then. The historical balance of powers, which once contributed greatly to the understanding of the necessity of internal national solidarity, with all its positive economic consequences, has been eliminated.

The delusion of victor and vanquished destroys the trust between nations and thus also the global economy. But the misery of our people is appalling! The millions of unemployed, starving industrial proletariat are followed by the impoverishment of the entire middle class and the craftsmen. If this deterioration finally takes hold among the German peasantry, we will be faced with a catastrophe of incalculable proportions, for it is not only the Reich that will then disintegrate, but a two-thousand-year heritage of the highest form of human culture and civilization.

The phenomena around us threaten to herald the completion of this downfall. In an unprecedented onslaught of willpower and violence, the communist method of madness is attempting to poison and divide the people, which is shaken and uprooted to its core, in order to drive it towards an age which would be even worse according to the promises of the communist spokesmen of today than the time behind us has been according to the promises of the same apostles of November 1918.

Starting with the family, extending to all concepts of honor and loyalty, nation and Fatherland, culture and economy, to the eternal foundation of our morals and faith, nothing is spared from this purely negating, all-destroying idea. Fourteen years of Marxism have ruined Germany. One year of Bolshevism would destroy Germany. The richest and most beautiful cultural areas in the world today would be turned into chaos and a field of ruins. Even the suffering of the last decade and a half could not compare with the lamentation of a Europe in whose heart the red flag of destruction was hoisted. May the thousands of wounded, the countless dead that this internal war is already costing Germany, be a flash of lightning warning of the coming storm.

In these hours of overwhelming worries about the existence and future of the German nation, the aged leader of the World War[87] called upon us men of the nationalist parties and associations to fight once again under him, as once we had on the front, this time at home, in unity and loyalty, for the salvation of the Reich. As the venerable President of the Reich had joined hands with us in this generous spirit, we as national leaders pledge to God, to our conscience, and to our people that we will resolutely and steadfastly fulfill the mission thus entrusted to us as a national government.

---

[87] Referring to Paul von Hindenburg.

The legacy we are inheriting is a terrible one.

The task we must accomplish is the most difficult that has been set for German statesmen since time immemorial. But our confidence is unlimited, because we believe in our people and its everlasting values. Peasants, workers, and bourgeoisie, together they must provide the building blocks for the new Reich.

Thus, the national government will consider its first and foremost task to be restoring our people's unity of will and spirit. It will preserve and defend the foundations on which the strength of our nation rests. It will take Christianity as the basis of our entire morality, and staunchly defend the family as the nucleus of our national and state body. It will reawaken in our people the consciousness of their national and political unity and the duties arising from it, across all ranks and classes. It will make reverence for our great past and pride in our old traditions the basis for the education of German youth. In doing so, it will wage a merciless war against spiritual, political, and cultural nihilism. Germany must not and will not sink into anarchic communism.

In place of turbulent instincts, it will again make national discipline the guiding force of our lives. In doing so, it will give the highest consideration to all those institutions that are the true guarantors of our nation's strength and vigor.

The national government will solve the great work of reorganizing the economy of our people with two great four-year plans: saving the German farmer to preserve the nation's food supply and thus its basis for life, and saving the German worker through a massive and comprehensive campaign against unemployment.

In fourteen years, the November parties have ruined the German peasantry. In fourteen years they have created an army of millions of unemployed.

The national government will implement the following plan with iron determination and the most tenacious perseverance: within four years the German peasant must be freed from destitution; within four years unemployment must be finally overcome.

At the same time, this will create the conditions for the rest of the economy to flourish.

The national government will combine this gigantic task of reorganizing our economy with the task of reorganizing the Reich, the federal states, and the municipalities in administrative and fiscal terms.

Only then will the idea of promoting the preservation of the Reich become a living reality.

One of the cornerstones of this program is the idea of compulsory labor service and settlement policy.

The provision of daily bread will also include the fulfillment of social duties towards the sick and the elderly.

Frugality of administration, the promotion of labor, the preservation of our peasantry, and utilizing the initiative of the individual are the best guarantee for avoiding any experiment endangering our currency.

In terms of foreign policy, the national government will view the preservation of the rights and the recovery of the freedom of our people as its highest priority. By being determined to put an end to the chaotic conditions in Germany, it will integrate Germany into the community of nations as a state of equal value, and thus also with equal rights. In doing so, the national government is conscious of the greatness of its duty to stand for the preservation and consolidation of peace, which the world needs today more than ever before.

May the understanding of other states also help to fulfill this most sincere wish of ours for the good of Europe, indeed of the world.

As great as our love for our army as the bearer of our arms and symbol of our great past is, we would be happy if the rest of the world, by limiting its armaments, would never again make it necessary to increase ours.

But if Germany is to experience this political and economic resurgence and conscientiously fulfill its obligations to the other nations, then this presupposes a decisive act: overcoming the communist subversion of Germany.

We men of this government feel responsible to German history for the restoration of an orderly body of the people, and thus for finally overcoming class madness and class struggle. We do not see class, but the German people, the millions of its peasants, bourgeoisie, and workers, who will either overcome the strife of this time together, or else succumb to it together.

Resolutely and true to our oath, in view of the inability of the present Reichstag to support this work, we thus wish to set before the German people themselves the task we represent.

Reich President Field Marshal von Hindenburg has called upon us and given the order to give the nation a chance at recovery through our unity.

We therefore now appeal to the German people to co-sign this act of reconciliation themselves.

The government of national revival wishes to work, and it will work.

We did not spend fourteen years wrecking the German nation, but we wish to lead it back to the top.

It is determined to pay off the debt of the last fourteen years in the next four years. But it cannot subject the work of reconstruction to the approval of those who were responsible for the collapse.

The parties of Marxism and its fellow travelers have had fourteen years to prove their mettle. The result is a field of ruins.

Now, German people, give us four years, and then pass judgment upon us!

True to the command of the Field Marshal General, let us begin our work. May Almighty God give our work His grace, lead our will on the right path, bless our insight, and grace us with the trust of our people, for we do not wish to fight for ourselves, but for Germany!

ADDRESS TO THE REICHSTAG REGARDING THE
PURGES OF THE NIGHT OF THE LONG KNIVES

July 13th, 1934

The Background

Much has been made of the supposed ideological differences that led to the purges of the Night of the Long Knives, but the reality is that they were motivated much more by the contingencies of *Realpolitik* and personal grievances. This mistaken view is based on a kernel of truth, but more so on politically-motivated reasoning, misunderstanding, overemphasis on the importance of ideology, and a corresponding under-emphasis on considerations of *Realpolitik*.

Even after being appointed Chancellor, Hitler's power was by no means absolute. It depended rather on a reluctant and mistrustful alliance with establishment conservatives in his early cabinet, in the Reichstag, in the aristocracy, and in the military. In 1933 and 1934, the NSDAP was still in the process of consolidating its power.

By this time, the SA membership had ballooned massively to over two million men, far eclipsing the military, which was only just beginning to rearm. Tensions began to mount between the military and the NSDAP regarding the role of the SA. The military aristocracy, bearers of a Prussian tradition dating back hundreds of years, felt that their position and prestige was threatened by what they largely viewed as little better than a semi-organized street gang, an oversized mob of thugs with no ties to the proud military tradition of Germany, and none of its military discipline.

Their fears were proven well-founded when SA leader Ernst Röhm began to publicly toy with the idea of abolishing the military entirely and replacing it with his SA, with himself as chief of staff. He dressed this proposal up in terms of "completing the revolution" to replace the "reactionary" military establishment with a "people's army," which only further alienated and added to the panic of the conservatives and military on which Hitler's rule still depended. But it is obvious that this idea was based on personal ambition, not on sincere ideological belief. From the outset, and often against Hitler's wishes, Röhm had endeavored to build up the SA as a paramilitary force, for Röhm, above all else, was a soldier. He was interested exclusively in military matters, and though an early member of the Party the days when it was still the DAP, had always scorned politics.

When Hitler disabused Röhm of these notions of replacing the Army with his SA and instructed him to tone down his rhetoric, Röhm refused, and Hitler became concerned that the SA chief was instead plotting against him.

Furthermore, after Hitler became Chancellor, there were numerous complaints of unacceptable behavior and outrageous abuses of power by SA men — and here I am not referring to the homosexuality of Röhm and some of the officers he appointed, though later propaganda made use of lurid innuendo about this detail as justification for Röhm's murder, to make it more difficult to defend Röhm lest one be accused of defending a sexual deviant. But in fact, Röhm's homosexuality had long been an open secret among those who knew him well, and Hitler certainly knew him well enough to be aware of it, especially considering Röhm made little secret of it, sparing his confidants the details but openly admitting that he was "same sex oriented." Röhm's affinity for thrusting himself upon younger men was the subject of disgust and scorn, something that nobody in the Party condoned or wanted to be associated with, but was begrudgingly tolerated and swept under the rug as long as Röhm was politically useful. And up until 1934, he was extremely politically useful: he had been instrumental in setting up, supplying, arming, training, and recruiting for the SA, and his high-ranking connections in the military and on the nationalist scene were instrumental in getting Hitler taken seriously by powerful people, to the extent that without him, the early movement probably would not have survived.

Much more important than the sexual deviancy were the many well-documented instances of SA thugs abusing their newfound privilege and authority to harass and bully civilians, settle personal vendettas, extortion, drunken public rowdiness, and a contemptuous attitude toward police attempting to discipline them—after all, now that their man was in charge, who were the police to tell them what to do? Many of them behaved as though they were untouchable. Thugs, gangsters, barroom brawlers, rowdies, and roughnecks who wouldn't hesitate to mix it up with the enemy in a good scrap had been useful, even indispensable, during the Party's early days and rise to power. The problem arose when the time came to transition from an upstart revolutionary movement to a mature government. The internal culture of the SA under the war-obsessed Röhm was not able to adapt to being in power and acting responsibly with that power. As Hitler notes in the following speech, there are certain personality types who are simply agents of chaos, who instinctively oppose all order, who could be useful as pure muscle during the *Kampfzeit*, but once the Party was in power represented a destructive element that proved difficult to reign in and threatened to strain the Party's relationship with traditional authorities like the police, and to make the public resent its apparently frivolous and petty abuse of power, making Hitler's new regime look bad by association. Thus, to use the parlance of our times, in many ways the SA under Röhm was "bad optics" for Hitler. *Reichspräsident* Paul von Hindenburg even threatened to declare martial law and put the Army in charge of enforcing it if the rowdiness of the SA were not curtailed. Röhm was informed of these abuses of power and ordered to reign them in, which he not only did not do, but in fact actively promoted personal friends of his who were engaged in them to positions of leadership within the SA.

It was primarily for these reasons, and not due to ideological disagreement or personal dislike, that Röhm and a cadre of officers around him had to go. All evidence indicates that the decision was a difficult one for Hitler. Röhm had been a member of his inner circle for over a decade. In his speeches at his trial for the Beer Hall Putsch, he refers to Röhm as his personal friend. He was one of the few men whom Hitler allowed to use the informal "du" when addressing him.[88] And when a list of names was drawn up of those to be executed, Röhm's did not appear on it. It was only after much deliberation, and at the insistence of his subordinates that it would not be fair to spare Röhm while executing his officers, that his name was finally added.[89]

In the final analysis, Röhm was always much more warlord than politician — yes, a domineering, homosexual, fascist warlord, who had disdain for politics and ideology, and was only interested in power, violence, and the military camaraderie of soldiers. This was useful for many years, but when it came time for the NSDAP to grow out of its rebellious revolutionary mindset and settle into its new role as government, Röhm resented this new role. Ever since his service in the First World War, his wartime mindset had never left him. He chafed under any sort of stability and order other than whatever version of it he himself imposed on his subordinates, to the extent that he engaged in insubordination against Hitler. Allegations were made, which Hitler repeats in the following speech, that Röhm was in contact with French spies and, even more foreboding, that eternal intriguer Kurt von Schleicher, whose specter continued to haunt German politics after Hitler's ascent to power and inspire paranoid suspicions of subterfuge and

---

[88] "Du" is the informal way to say "you" (singular) in German. The formal version is "Sie" (pronounced "zee")
[89] Irving, *Hitler's War*, 30-31.

double-dealing. Schleicher and his cronies had in fact inserted themselves into the intrigue, drawing up a list of names for a new cabinet to replace the current one in the event of a putsch by Röhm, although the role of Röhm himself in this scheme is not clear, and the connection to French spies is dubious at best. Regardless, when Röhm's ambition, rebellious spirit, and insubordination threatened Hitler's relationship with the traditional military and position as Chancellor, Hitler had to make the difficult decision to liquidate his old comrade. He was left alone in a cell with a pistol loaded with one bullet, but refused to kill himself, telling his guards that if "Adolf" wanted him dead, he ought to do it himself. On July 1st, 1934, he was shot to death in his cell.

The other most prominent member of the old inner circle liquidated on the Night of the Long Knives was Gregor Strasser, and this is another very complicated case, shrouded in misunderstanding and outright misrepresentation. Historians in the Marxist tradition have constructed a narrative that this purge constituted the suppression of the "left wing" of National Socialism, and from this premise concluded that National Socialism was never a revolutionary movement, but merely a tool of capital to be wielded against genuine socialism all along. On the other side, many who come to sympathize with National Socialism from a right-wing background accept this framing, but count it in favor of National Socialism instead of viewing it as discrediting, without ever really examining whether the premise itself is even true. The fact is that there is a kernel of truth to it, but the issue of ideological disagreement is so muddled and confused, and so blown out of proportion, that it is much more accurate to assert that Gregor Strasser's murder, just like Ernst Röhm's, was motivated more by *Realpolitik*, and in his case even personal vengeance, than ideology.

On the left today, one can see people who espouse socialist economic views but, in the eyes of their peers, are not sufficiently progressive on social issues, accused of "Strasserism" or "National Bolshevism." Similarly, on the nationalist right, those who augment their nationalism and social traditionalism with strong critiques of capitalism risk being labelled "Strasserists" or "National Bolsheviks." Both of these concepts originate in this period. But what do they actually mean?

National Bolshevism, in its original sense, is a murky and ill-defined concept, blending the ideas of socialism in one country, admiration for the Soviet Union and the planned economy, and nationalism. It was mainly propagated in Germany by Ernst Niekisch, a writer, politician, and malcontent who bounced around his whole life from party to party, and even country to country, always finding reasons to be disillusioned and dissatisfied with the politics of whichever milieu in which he found himself. He was a member of the SPD, governed in the central executive committee in the Bavarian Soviet Republic for about a month, left for the USPD over political differences, went back to the SPD to try to turn it in a more patriotic direction, got kicked out, helped found ARPLAN (Association for the Study of the Russian Planned Economy) with Ernst Jünger, the renowned author of *Storm of Steel*, went to Soviet Russia, came back to Germany where he criticized the National Socialist regime but never joined the resistance, got thrown in a concentration camp for his writings, became disillusioned with nationalism and reverted to orthodox Marxism, moved to communist East Germany after the war, and then became disillusioned with that state too and moved back to West Germany. Before Hitler's rise to power, a mutual friend introduced him to Joseph Goebbels, one of the more socialistic and intellectual high-ranking members of the NSDAP, in an attempt at rapprochement. Instead the two intellectuals immediately hated each other so much they almost came to blows.

In the end, National Bolshevism in its original German incarnation was nothing more than a loose literary circle centered around Niekisch, with half-baked syncretic beliefs, which was never able to attract much support, and was never taken seriously. Others with similar anti-capitalist, pro-Soviet, but still nationalistic beliefs would call themselves National Bolsheviks in later years —

perhaps some still do—but it seems more often to be used derisively by both the socialist left and the nationalist right to suggest that someone in or close to their circles holds unorthodox and incompatible views. This is certainly the sense in which Hitler used it in the following speech, relaying to the Reichstag that he had received reports of rumors of a "National Bolshevik" plot against him. Ernst Niekisch and the self-styled National Bolsheviks were not involved; he simply meant a disruptive tendency within the SA that was agitating for a "second revolution" to disband the Army and replace it with the SA.

"Strasserism" is a slightly more difficult subject, because it is a label that has been applied almost exclusively as a pejorative; nobody in the National Socialist era called themselves Strasserists, and it is only in later years that very fringe tendencies adopted that label for themselves, or more often, that people used it to insinuate subversive tendencies. The issue is further confused by the fact that the two Strasser brothers, Gregor and Otto, were actually quite divergent in their politics, and in their paths in life.

Gregor Strasser, certainly, never saw himself as anything other than an orthodox National Socialist. He joined the Party very early on, way back in 1920, and marched by Hitler's side in the failed Beer Hall Putsch of 1923. His organizational skills, energy, and commitment were crucial to building up the NSDAP into a nationwide movement, and especially in reaching industrial workers in bigger northern cities. His worker-oriented National Socialism was never inherently in conflict with the main Party line; it was rather a particular focus under the big tent of National Socialism, meant to appeal to a particular demographic, the same way Richard Walther Darré's "Blood and Soil" agrarianism was a particular focus meant to appeal to peasants and rural landowners. His disagreements with Hitler were rather of a tactical nature, for example during the election years in the early 1930s he thought Hitler's insistence on accepting nothing less than the full chancellorship was stubborn, unrealistic, and foolish, and he constantly urged the Party to take whatever pieces of power it could get in order to advance at least some of its agenda. In economic terms he was on the left end of the National Socialist spectrum, but then so were Gottfried Feder and Joseph Goebbels. Furthermore, he was at times perceived as one of the more moderate and sensible members of the Party, even by some industrialists.[90]

His brother Otto, on the other hand, only joined the Party in 1925 at his brother's urging, after having been a member of the SPD for years, even taking part in putting down the right-wing Kapp Putsch attempt. During his membership in the Party, he propounded his ideas in the newspaper *Nationaler Sozialist*. These included support for strikes and unions, closer ties with the Soviet Union, and expropriation and redistribution of land and property. Hitler at first took little notice of these ideas, but when it came to his attention that they were causing a bad look for the Party among the middle and upper classes and ruining his chances of finally gaining some credibility for the Party among that demographic, Hitler shut down the paper. Gregor must have supported at least some of these ideas, as he was a co-publisher and occasional contributor to *Nationaler Sozialist*, but when Otto left the Party, repudiating National Socialism and Hitler's leadership, Gregor remained close to Hitler, and as late as 1932 Hitler proposed him for Labor Minister in his cabinet. After leaving the Party, Otto formed the Black Front in an attempt to split the Party and carry forward his ideas, but it never had significant support. After Hitler came to power, Otto fled the country. Later on, the Black Front, with its insignia of the crossed sword and hammer, began to actively resist the NSDAP regime, even plotting a failed assassination attempt on Hitler by Jewish Black Front member Helmut Hirsch. After his brother's murder, Otto devoted himself to supplying "intelligence" to the allied powers fighting Germany in the form of misinformation and false rumors. Many malicious and salacious rumors about top NSDAP officials, including those surrounding Hitler's sexuality and his relationship with his niece,

---

[90] Turner, "Big Business and the Rise," 65.

were spread by Otto Strasser — perhaps these were his revenge for Gregor's murder. [91] After the war, he continued writing and expanding on his ideas, but by then these had little in common with orthodox National Socialism, repudiating race realism and antisemitism, and emphasizing a pro-Soviet, anti-Western stance.

Whatever the brothers had in common ideologically, then, was eclipsed by their differences: Otto Strasser disavowed both National Socialism and Hitler's leadership, while Gregor remained faithful to both. This raises the question of why exactly Gregor was murdered.

The obvious answer is that, although he had withdrawn from politics in 1932 and requested not to be involved in any political issues, and had nothing whatsoever to do with his brother's Black Front, NSDAP officials feared that he might return to politics and try to challenge Hitler's power. The repeated attempts on the part of Kurt von Schleicher in 1932 to convince Gregor to take up a position in the government as Vice-Chancellor and split the Party by bringing his faction with him made this seem like a credible threat. But the fact remains, Gregor had no involvement in politics after he resigned from his posts, and there is no evidence he had any designs on challenging Hitler's power. His name was nowhere on the hit list that Hitler drew up, which originally named only seven men including Röhm, but through a process that is not entirely clear, expanded to include many more. The memoirs of Alfred Rosenberg, as well as historian David Irving, seem to imply that Strasser was killed against Hitler's wishes, quite possibly on Hermann Göring's own initiative, and with the approval of Goebbels, who for some time had regarded Strasser as a personal rival. [92][93]

In both cases, the tendencies that both socialists and reactionaries might label "National Bolshevism" or "Strasserism" very often have little to do with the actual ideas of Ernst Niekisch

---

[91] Kershaw, *Hitler*, 219.
[92] Irving, *Hitler's War*, 31.
[93] Rosenberg, *Memoirs*, 65.

or Otto Strasser, but are either simply orthodox socialism without liberal social progressivism, or would in fact fall under the umbrella of orthodox National Socialism.

A factor that contributes to the narrative that these purges were rooted in irreconcilable ideological disputes is the fact that this narrative is usually put forth by people who are themselves very interested in ideology and politics, whatever their political persuasion happens to be. There is an apt saying that when you're a hammer, everything looks like a nail. Those who are very interested in and motivated by ideology and politics tend to project this motivation onto others, and thus attribute undue importance to ideological factors in world-historical events, while under-estimating the influence of the hard realities of non-ideological political maneuvering, summed up in that German term *Realpolitik*. For example, while religion certainly played a role in the crusades of the Middle Ages, so did wealth, personal power, prestige, and economics. To this day there are regions of Germany that are Protestant by default because their princes converted during the Reformation, not necessarily because they read and were strongly persuaded by Martin Luther's *Ninety-five Theses*, but perhaps because they wanted more independence from the Holy Roman Emperor, or even wanted to divorce their wife without waiting for the pope's permission. Countless wars, probably the vast majority, have been fought without any ideological disagreement between the two sides, but rather over factors like land, women, wealth, or the personal ambitions of rulers. To be sure, ideology is an important motivating factor, and can fuel the flames of a conflict with other causes, but other factors are very often more important. And such was the case in the purges of the Night of the Long Knives.

In the end, at least eighty-five people were killed during the purge, and possibly more, some by mistake, some resisting arrest, some due to personal vendettas. Kurt von Schleicher was gunned down in his home, and his wife was killed by accident when she got in the way. Other prominent victims included Otto Ballerstedt, the former Bavarian separatist politician and early rival to Hitler, SA Obergruppenführer Edmund Heines, who was caught in bed with a younger man when he was arrested, and immediately dragged out of bed and shot, Gustav Ritter von Kahr, the former Prime Minister of Bavaria who had helped foil the Beer Hall Putsch, and Willi Schmid, a music critic killed in a case of mistaken identity, as the SS mistook him for a member of Otto Strasser's Black Front.

In the aftermath of the purges, Hitler referred to the Night of the Long Knives as "twenty-four hours of the most bitter decisions [he had] ever had to make." His list of six names had turned to a bloodbath of dozens, including some of his oldest comrades. But these growing pains were necessary for Hitler to demonstrate to the military establishment and to the people of Germany that he was no longer merely the upstart firebrand and beer hall rabble-rouser, but a proper statesman, ready to drop his previously rebellious stance towards the government and social order, and mature into his new role as the representative of a new government and a new order. The following speech outlines Hitler's version of events leading up to and including the purges — or at least, the version that he wished to present to the Reichstag and the German public.

The Speech

Deputies! Men of the German Reichstag!

On behalf of the Reich Government, the President of the Reichstag, Hermann Göring, has called you together today to give me the opportunity to enlighten the people before this highest forum of the nation about events which should live on in our history for all time as a sad reminder and cautionary tale.

From a combination of objective causes and personal guilt, from human incompetence and human defects, a crisis arose for our young Reich that could all too easily have had truly devastating consequences for the foreseeable future.

The purpose of my remarks is to explain before you and thus before the nation how this emerged and how it was overcome. The content of my statement will be unreservedly open; I have only had to limit the scope. This is necessitated on the one hand by consideration for the interests of the Reich, and on the other hand by the boundaries drawn by a feeling of shame. [...]

Street riots, barricade fighting, mass terror, and an atomizing, divisive propaganda are today disturbing almost all countries of the world. In Germany, too, some fools and criminals are still trying to carry out their destructive activities again and again. Since the defeat of the Communist Party, we have nevertheless seen one attempt after another, albeit weakening, to establish communist organizations of a more or less anarchist character. Their method is always the same. While describing the present situation as intolerable, they sing the praises of the communist paradise of the future, and yet in practice they are only waging a war for hell, for the consequences of their victory in a country like Germany could be nothing other than devastating. The National Socialist state will, however, eradicate and destroy the last remnants of this poisoning and madness of the people in a war lasting a hundred years, if necessary.

The second group of malcontents is commanded by those political leaders who feel that their future has been settled by January 30th,[94] without being able to come to terms with the irreversibility of this fact.

A third destructive element is comprised of those revolutionaries who in 1918 were shaken and uprooted in their former relationship to the state, and thus have lost any inner relationship to a regulated human social order. They have become revolutionaries who worship revolution for its own sake, and want it to become the permanent state of affairs. We all once suffered the terrible tragedy of being obedient and dutiful soldiers suddenly faced with a revolt of mutineers who managed to take control of the state. Each of us had once been taught to respect the law, respect authority, obey the orders and commands emanating from it, and an inner devotion to the representation of the state. Now the revolution of the deserters and mutineers forced us to inwardly detach from these concepts.

We could not have any respect for these new usurpers. Honor and duty forced us to refuse to obey; love of the nation and the Fatherland obliged us to wage war on them; the immorality of the law extinguished in us the belief that it was necessary to comply with it — and thus we became revolutionaries.

However, even as revolutionaries, we had not disassociated ourselves from the obligation to recognize and respect the natural law of the sovereign rights of our people.

We did not wish to violate the sovereign will and rights of the German people, but only to drive away those who violated the nation.

For us, the revolution that shattered the Second Reich was the mighty act of birth that brought the Third Reich into being. Nevertheless, we wanted to create a state to which every German could cling with love, to establish a regime that everyone could look up to with respect, to pass laws that corresponded to the morals of our people, to secure an authority to which every man

---

[94] The date Hitler was appointed Chancellor.

would happily submit and obey.

Among the countless other files I have been obliged to read through in the past week, I have studied a diary containing the notes of a man who was thrown onto the path of resistance to the law in 1918, and now lives in a world in which the law itself seems to provoke resistance. A harrowing document. An incessant conspiring and constant plotting, a glimpse into the mentality of people who, without suspecting it, have found in nihilism their ultimate creed. Incapable of any real cooperation, willing to take a stand against any order, filled with hatred for all authority, their restlessness and agitation only find satisfaction in the constant mental and conspiratorial preoccupation with the destruction of what exists. Many of them ran in our circles against the past state in the early days of our struggle. But most of them, in the course of the struggle, were driven away from the disciplined National Socialist movement by their inner lack of discipline.

The last remnant seemed to have left after January 30th. Their bond with the National Socialist movement was severed the moment this movement became a state, and thus the object of their pathological aversion. They are enemies of every authority on principle and therefore cannot be converted at all. Achievements that seem to consolidate the new German state arouse their increased hatred, for all these contrarians have one principle in common: they do not see before them the German people, but the institution of order that they hate. They are not filled with the desire to help the people, but rather with the burning hope that the government will fail in its work to save the people. They are therefore never prepared to admit the benefit of an action, but rather deny on principle every success and nitpick every achievement for possible faults and weaknesses.

This third group of pathological enemies of the state is dangerous because they represent a reservoir of willing accomplices for every attempt at revolt until a new order begins to crystallize out of the state of conflict.

But I must now also address the fourth group, which truly

wreaks havoc, even if perhaps unintentionally. These people belong to a relatively small social class. In doing nothing, they find time and occasion to report orally on everything that, from their own point of view, is an interesting and important diversion in their otherwise completely trivial lives. For, while the overwhelming majority of the nation has to work hard to earn its daily bread, there are still people in various walks of life whose sole activity is doing nothing, and then taking breaks to recover from this idleness. The more pathetic the life of such a drone is, the more eagerly he will seize upon anything that can give his empty life some excitement. Personal and political gossip is then eagerly picked up and even more eagerly passed on.

Since these people, as a result of their idleness, do not have a living relationship with the masses of the nation, their lives are marked out by the circumference of their own circles in which they move. Any gossip that ends up in this circle is passed back and forth again and again, as if between two concave mirrors. Because their own selves are filled with a void that they always find confirmed in their peers, they see it in everything. They mistake the views of their circle for the views of everyone. Their concerns, they imagine, are the concerns of the whole nation. In reality, this little tribe of drones is only a state within a state, without any living contact with the life, feelings, hopes, and concerns of the other people. But they are dangerous, because they carry the germs of unrest, uncertainty, rumors, allegations, lies, suspicions, calumnies, and fears, and thus contribute to a state of anxiety in which it becomes difficult to recognize or find the natural demarcations in the people. As they do their mischief in every other nation, so also in the German nation. For them, the National Socialist revolution was just as interesting a topic of conversation as, conversely, the struggle of the enemies of the National Socialist state against it.

One thing, however, is clear: the work of rebuilding our people, and thereby the work of our people itself, is only possible if the German people follow its leadership in inner peace, order and discipline, and above all if they trust its leadership! Only confidence and faith in a new state made it possible for us to tackle and solve the great tasks that earlier times had bequeathed us.

Even if the National Socialist regime had to come to terms with these various groups from the beginning, and did indeed come to terms with them, nevertheless, for some months now a mood has been emerging which could no longer be taken lightly.

Chatter about a new revolution, a new upheaval, a new insurrection, which had been suppressed at first, gradually became so intense that only a careless state leadership could have overlooked it. It was no longer possible to simply dismiss all the hundreds and eventually thousands of oral and written reports about it as mere idle talk. Only three months ago the Party leadership was convinced that it was simply the frivolous gossip of political reactionaries, Marxist anarchists, or other sorts of idlers, and lacked any actual substance. In the middle of March I had preparations made for a new propaganda campaign. It was intended to inoculate the German people against the attempt at a new poisoning. At the same time, however, I gave orders to some of the Party offices to investigate the rumors of a new revolution which kept appearing and, if possible, to find the source of these rumors. It turned out that tendencies were appearing among some high-ranking SA leaders which gave rise to very serious concerns. In the end, these were general trends whose inner connections were not readily apparent.

First: contrary to my express orders and contrary to explanations given to me, a build-up of the SA occurred under former SA leader Ernst Röhm to an extent which must have threatened the inner homogeneity of this unique organization.

Second: instruction in the National Socialist worldview was neglected more and more in the aforementioned areas of certain high-ranking SA offices.

Third: the natural relationship between the Party and the SA slowly began to loosen. Deliberate and systematic efforts were made to remove the SA more and more from the mission I had given it, in order to make it serve other tasks or interests.

Fourth: the promotions of these SA leaders, when examined, were revealed to be based on a completely one-sided evaluation of purely external ability, or even of alleged intellectual aptitude. The majority of the oldest and most loyal SA men increasingly took a back seat when it came to leadership positions and appointments to posts, while those who joined in 1933, who were not particularly highly regarded in the movement, received incomprehensible preferential treatment. A membership in the Party, sometimes lasting only a few months, or even only in the SA, was enough for promotion to a higher SA position which an old SA leader had not been able to attain even after years.

Fifth: the conduct of these individual SA leaders, most of whom were not integrated into the movement at all, was a disgrace to National Socialism, and sometimes downright repulsive. It could not be overlooked, however, that it was precisely in these circles that one source of unrest in the movement was also found, caused by the fact that their lack of practical National Socialism was disguised by very inappropriate calls for a new revolution.

I pointed out these and a number of other grievances to Chief of Staff Röhm. No tangible improvement, or even a recognizable response to my statements, was forthcoming. In the months of April and May these complaints came to me incessantly. For the first time, however, I also received documentary evidence of meetings which had been held by certain higher SA leaders, and which could only be described as gross insubordination. [...]

In the month of May, several Party and state offices received numerous accusations of violations by higher and middle-ranking SA leaders, which were supported by documentary evidence and could not be denied. The offences ranged from disruptive speeches to intolerable excesses.

I have always emphasized that an authoritarian regime bears particularly great responsibility. If the people is asked to place its blind trust in its leadership, then that leadership must earn this trust by its achievements and by particularly good conduct.

Mistakes and errors can occur now and then, but they must be corrected. Improper conduct, drunken excesses, harassing peaceful, upstanding citizens—this is unworthy of a leader, contrary to National Socialism, and supremely detestable. Thus I have always insisted that higher demands be placed upon the behavior and conduct of National Socialist leaders than upon the other members of the people. He who would command more respect for himself must in turn achieve more.

The National Socialist state leadership was determined to put an end to the excesses of these unworthy elements, who brought only shame to the SA and the Party. This led to a very ugly reaction by the then Chief of Staff. The first of the National Socialist fighters, some of whom had struggled for almost fifteen years for the victory of the movement, now representing the movement as high officials in leading positions in our state, were called to account for their actions against such unworthy elements. That is to say, Chief of Staff Röhm attempted to have the Party's oldest fighters reprimanded by courts of honor, some of which were composed of the youngest Party members or even people who were not Party members at all. [...]

Without ever informing me of it, and without my even suspecting it at first, Chief of Staff Röhm established relations with General Schleicher through the mediation of a thoroughly corrupt swindler, a Herr von Alvensleben [95], whom all of you know. General Schleicher was the man who now gave external expression to Chief of Staff Röhm's inner desires. It was he who expressed in concrete terms the opinion that firstly, the present German regime was untenable; secondly, that above all the Wehrmacht and all national units should be united in one hand; thirdly, that the only man who could do this was Röhm, the Chief of Staff; and fourthly, that Herr von Papen would have to be removed and he would be prepared to take up the position of Vice-Chancellor. Furthermore, he claimed that fundamental changes would have to be made in

---

[95] Werner von Alvensleben, a conservative German businessman and friend of General Kurt von Schleicher.

the Reich Cabinet later on.

As always in such cases, the search for the men to form the new government now began, under the assumption that I myself would be allowed to remain in my position, at least for the time being. I could only meet these proposals of General von Schleicher with unshakable resistance, even on the basis of the second point alone. It would never have been objectively or humanly possible for me to give my consent to a change in the *Reichswehr* Ministry and to propose its replacement by Chief of Staff Röhm.

Firstly, for objective reasons. For fourteen years I have steadfastly maintained that the Party's fighting organizations are political institutions which have nothing to do with the Army. In my eyes, it would have been a disavowal of this view and fourteen years of policy to appoint the leader of the SA as head of the Army. Even in November 1923[96] I proposed an officer, General Ludendorff, to head the entire Army, and not my SA leader at the time, Captain Göring.

Secondly, it would have been humanly impossible for me ever to consent to General von Schleicher's line of reasoning. By the time I became indirectly aware of these intentions, my image of the intrinsic value of Chief of Staff Röhm was already such that I could never have proposed or approved him for this position, for the sake of my conscience and of the Army's honor. But above all, the head of the Army is the Field Marshal General and President of the Reich. As Chancellor, I have sworn my oath to him. His person is inviolable for all of us. The promise I made to him to preserve the Army as an apolitical instrument of the Reich is binding to me, from my innermost conviction and from my word. However, it would also have been humanly impossible for me to take such action against the Minister of Defense of the Reich. There are duties of loyalty which one should not and must not violate. And I believe that, above all, a man who has brought the nation together in his name must not act disloyally under any circumstances, lest all trust in good faith disappear both internally and externally. Since Chief

---

[96] The date of the Beer Hall Putsch attempt.

of Staff Röhm himself was uncertain whether these attempts would meet with resistance from me, he made plans to force the issue. [...]

At the beginning of June, as a last attempt, I summoned Chief of Staff Röhm once more for a discussion lasting almost five hours, which lasted until midnight. I told him that I had gained the impression from countless rumors and from numerous assurances and statements by old and loyal Party Comrades and SA leaders that unscrupulous elements were plotting a national-Bolshevik operation which could only bring unspeakable misfortune to Germany. I further explained to him that I had also heard rumors about the intention to include the Army in the scope of these schemes. I assured Chief of Staff Röhm that the assertion that the SA was to be dissolved was a malicious lie, that I would not even deign to comment on the lie that I myself wanted to take action against the SA, but that I would also personally quell any attempts to create chaos in Germany immediately, and that anyone who attacked the state must count me among his enemies from the outset. I implored him for the last time to oppose this madness on his own initiative and to use his authority to prevent a development that could only end in disaster one way or another. I again objected in the strongest terms to the increasing number of intolerable excesses committed by SA members, and now demanded directly that he eradicate these elements of the SA, so that the SA itself, millions of decent Party Comrades, and hundreds of thousands of old fighters would not be deprived of their honor by inferior individuals. Chief of Staff Röhm left me with the assurance that the rumors were partly untrue and partly exaggerated, and that he would do everything in his power to set things straight.

The result of the discussion, however, was that Chief of Staff Röhm, realizing that he could under no circumstances count on me in his plot, now prepared to eliminate me. [...]

The magnitude of the danger was proven by the statements which now came to Germany from abroad. English and French newspapers began to speak more and more frequently of an imminent upheaval in Germany, and more and more reports indicated that the conspirators were giving foreign powers the impression that the "revolution of the true National Socialists" was imminent in Germany, and that the existing regime was no longer capable of action. General von Bredow, who, as a kind of foreign affairs agent of General von Schleicher, was in charge of establishing these connections, worked only in accordance with the activity of those reactionary circles which, though perhaps not directly connected with this conspiracy, allowed themselves to be misused as a willing underground intelligence asset for foreign countries. At the end of June I was therefore determined to put an end to this impossible state of affairs, before the blood of tens of thousands of innocent people could seal the catastrophe.

Since the danger and tension weighing on everyone had gradually become unbearable, and certain Party offices and staff positions had to take defensive measures as a matter of duty, the strange sudden extension of the SA's service before a holiday seemed suspect to me, and I therefore decided on Saturday, June 30, to relieve the Chief of Staff of his office, to take him into custody for the time being, and to arrest a number of SA leaders whose crimes were clearly evident. Since it was doubtful whether, in view of the threatening escalation, Chief of Staff Röhm would have come to Berlin or anywhere else he was summoned, I decided to go in person to the SA leaders' meeting in Wiessee. Relying on my personal authority, and on the powers of determination which had always served me well, I intended to relieve the Chief of Staff of his position there at noon, arrest the main guilty SA leaders, and put out an urgent appeal for the rest to return to their duties. In the course of June 29th, however, I received such threatening news about final preparations for action that I had to break off the tour of the labor camps in Westphalia at noon in order to be ready for any eventuality.

At one o'clock in the morning I received two urgent alerts from Berlin and Munich. Firstly, that an alert had been ordered for

Berlin at four o'clock in the afternoon, that the requisitioning of trucks for the transport of the shock troops had been ordered and was already under way, and that the action was to begin at twelve o'clock sharp with the occupation of government buildings. This was the reason why Röhm had not travelled to Wiessee, but had stayed behind in Berlin — to personally lead the operation. Secondly, the SA was verbally ordered to be alerted at seven in the evening in Munich. The SA formations were no longer sent to the government buildings. The SA formations were no longer to be given leave to go home, but were to be placed in the high alert barracks. This is mutiny! The commander of the SA is me, and no one else!

Under these circumstances, there was only one decision I could make. If disaster was still to be averted, then action had to be taken at lightning speed. Only a ruthless and bloody intervention would perhaps still be able to stifle the spread of revolt. There could then be no question that it was better to destroy a hundred mutineers, plotters, and conspirators, than to let ten thousand innocent SA men bleed to death on one side, and ten thousand innocent people on the other. [...]

It was then finally clear to me that there was only one man who could confront the Chief of Staff. He had broken faith with me, and I alone had to hold him responsible.

Where just a few days before I had been willing to be lenient, now there could be no such leniency. Mutinies are broken according to the eternal iron law. If someone reproaches me that we did not use the ordinary courts for sentencing, then all I can say is this: at that hour I was responsible for the fate of the German nation, and thus the supreme judge for the German people.

Mutinous divisions have always been brought under control by decimation. Only one state did not make use of its articles of war, and this state collapsed as a result: Germany. I did not want to give over the young Reich to the fate of the old. I gave the order to shoot the main culprits of this treason, and I further gave the order to burn out the ulcers of our internal poisoning and poisoning by foreign powers down to the raw flesh. And further I gave the order that at any attempt by the mutineers to resist arrest, they should be put down at once with the gun.

The nation must know that its existence, which is guaranteed by its internal order and security, will not be threatened by anyone with impunity! And everyone must know for all time to come that if he raises his hand to strike against the state, certain death is his lot. And every National Socialist must know that no rank and no position can exempt him from personal responsibility or from due punishment. I have prosecuted thousands of our former opponents for their corruption. I would have to reproach myself if I tolerated the same phenomena among our own ranks. [...]

The punishment for these crimes was a harsh and severe one. Nineteen senior SA leaders and thirty-one ordinary SA leaders and SA members were shot, as were three SS leaders as co-conspirators in the plot. Thirteen SA leaders and civilians who tried to resist gave up their lives in the process. Three others ended by suicide. Five non-SA Party members were shot for participation. And last of all, three members of the SS who were guilty of disgraceful abuse of prisoners in protective custody were shot. In order to prevent political passion and indignation from heightening into lynch mobs against further incriminated persons, after the danger had been eliminated and the revolt could be considered defeated, the strictest order was given on Sunday, July 1st, to refrain from any further retaliation. [...]

The SA has maintained its inner loyalty in these last days that have been so difficult, for itself and for me. It has thus proven for the third time that it is mine, just as I will take the oath at any time that I belong to my SA men. In a few weeks, the brown shirt will once again dominate the German streets, so that everyone understands clearly that National Socialist Germany has only grown stronger by overcoming a severe hardship.

When our young revolution roared through Germany last March, it was my greatest endeavor to shed as little blood as possible. I offered millions of my former opponents a general amnesty in the new state and on behalf of the National Socialist Party. Millions of them have since joined us and are faithfully cooperating in the rebuilding of the Reich. I hoped that it would no longer be necessary to defend this state once again with a gun in my fist. But now that fate has imposed this test on us, let us all vow to hold on all the more fanatically to what was first fought for with so much of our best men's blood, and which today had to be defended again with the blood of our German comrades.

Just as I offered reconciliation to our former opponents a year and a half ago, I would also like to offer redemption to all those who were complicit in this insane act. May they all look inwards and, reflecting on this sad plight of our recent German history, devote themselves with all their strength to making amends. May they now recognize with more clarity than before the great task that fate has set before us, and which will not be solved by civil war and chaos. May they all feel responsible for the most precious good that can ever exist for the German people: order and peace, at home and abroad, just as I am ready to take responsibility before history for the twenty-four hours of the most bitter decisions I have ever had to make, in which fate has once more taught me to anxiously cling with every thought to the most precious thing given to us in this world: the German people and German Reich!

REICHSTAG SPEECH: FOUR YEARS OF NATIONAL SOCIALISM

January 30th, 1937

The Background

The following speech takes place on the anniversary of Hitler's ascent to power, and in many ways is a follow up on his first radio broadcast, in which he had asked the German public to give him four years to show what he could do for them. Now he would reflect on the last four years in Germany under National Socialism.

When Hitler assumed responsibility for the leadership of Germany, he was faced with three parallel challenges: secure the position of the NSDAP as the sole ruling party so that it could implement its vision for the nation, rebuild Germany's defense capabilities, and restructure the economy to pull the country up out of the depression. He set about these tasks immediately, moving his top men into place in important administrative positions to bring culture and education in line with the National Socialist worldview, earning the trust of the military—part of which involved the purges and curtailing of the SA in 1934—on which German sovereignty would depend, and launching a massive campaign against unemployment.

Beginning with the premise that it is better for the state to pay people to work than to hand out unemployment benefits, the National Socialist government embarked on a gigantic public works campaign to rebuild and expand the country's infrastructure, giving hiring preference to those who had been out of work the longest and the men with the largest families. In order to ensure that there were enough labor hours to employ as many full-time workers as possible, none were allowed to work more than forty hours per week. [97] This required massive public spending, but it also gave workers purchasing power, which stimulated spending, thus increasing consumer demand, and thus production, which provided an enormous and much-needed boost to the economy. It was also a long-term investment in critical infrastructure, some of which is still in use today, including railways and the *Autobahn* network.

Multiple agricultural, horticultural, and fishing organizations were combined to form the *Reichsnährstand* (Reich's Food Producers), which sought to make Germany self-sufficient in food production, to promote the interests of farmers, peasants, and all those involved in supplying sustenance to the country, and to reverse the trend of young people leaving the countryside for the cities to find work. This organization reduced property taxes on farmers and cancelled their mortgages and debts to give them a fresh start. The *Landhilfe* (Rural Aid), an organization with a similar focus, recruited approximately 120,000 unemployed workers to move to the countryside as farm workers, paying and housing them at the state's expense to assist the farmers, and arranged and promoted temporary farm work programs for university students on their summer break.[98] These measures had several benefits at once: they reduced unemployment, improved the circumstances of peasants and farmers, moved the country towards food security, which was also critical for national security as it would reduce the effects of a potential future blockade. They allowed young city folk to connect with nature and with their rural countrymen, which was ideologically important according to the "Blood and Soil" doctrine of the National Socialist worldview. Hitler saw the peasantry as the foundational material on which the German

---

[97] Reinhardt, *Die Beseitigung der Arbeitslosigkeit*, 49.
[98] Tedor, *Hitler's Revolution*, 47-48.

ethnos was built. In a speech addressing farm folk at Bückeberg, he stated:

> *In the same measure that liberalism and democratic Marxism disregard the farmer, the National Socialist revolution acknowledges him as the soundest pillar of the present, as the sole guarantee for the future.*[99]

Cancelling debts, public works projects, interest-free loans for the expansion of small businesses and farms, and large-scale infrastructure projects were the primary methods by which Hitler's government accomplished the goals of ending the unemployment crisis, bringing inflation under control, and "rescuing" the German farmers and peasants which he had outlined in his radio broadcast of 1933, and revisited in the following speech.

He speaks of overcoming the divisions in German society, especially political and class divisions. He asserts that four years of National Socialism have already overcome many of the old social prejudices, and replaced class warfare with class cooperation, class consciousness with national consciousness.

He also addresses Germany's foreign policy situation. Germany was not yet at war at this time, and had not even annexed Austria or the ethnic German-inhabited Sudetenland, but its foreign relations with Britain and France, which had already been strained since Hitler took power, were deteriorating. He still hoped for good relations with England, which had been a cornerstone of his foreign policy goals since he wrote *Mein Kampf*,[100] but this hope was probably naïvely optimistic from the outset. With the vengeful France, any ideas of friendly relations were certainly hopeless, especially when Germany began to rearm.

Indicative of his lifelong artistic and architectural aspirations, he ends the speech with his future vision of renovating several

---

[99] Zitelmann, *Hitler Selbstverständnis eines Revolutionär*, 204-205, quoted in Ibid., 48.
[100] Hitler, *Mein Kampf, Vol. II*, C. 13.8, 473.

cities, especially Berlin, with grand monuments and architectural projects, some of which did come to fruition, but most of which were never realized due to the demands of fighting the Second World War.

The Speech

Men of the German Reichstag!

Today The Reichstag convenes on an important day for the German people. Four years have passed since the moment that marked the greatest internal transformation and reorganization that Germany has ever experienced. I asked the German people to give me four years as trial period. What could be more logical than to use this occasion to enumerate in detail all the successes and progress that these four years have brought to the German people? Of course it will not be possible to mention in such a short rally all the remarkable results of what might be the most astounding epoch in the life of our people. This is rather the task of the press and propaganda. In addition, an exhibition will take place this year in the capital of the Reich, Berlin, in which a more comprehensive and in-depth picture will be presented of what has been created, achieved, and begun than I could possibly do in a two-hour speech. I will therefore use today's historic meeting of the German Reichstag to look back on the past four years and point out some of the general insights, experiences, and conclusions that are important to understand, not only for us, but also for posterity.

I would also like to take a position on the most important problems and tasks that face us, and finally I would also like to outline in the briefest possible terms the projects that I have in mind, some for the near future and some for the more distant future. […]

Who can doubt that in these four years that lie behind us, a revolution of the greatest magnitude has indeed swept over Germany? Who can compare this Germany of today with what existed on January 30th, four years ago, when I took the oath from the venerable President of the Reich? […]

This National Socialist revolution was first and foremost a revolution in the conduct of revolutions. By this I mean the following: for thousands of years, not only in German minds, but even more so in the minds of our neighbors, the view has prevailed that the characteristic feature of every true revolution must be a bloody destruction of the former bearers of power, and the ensuing destruction of public and private institutions and property. Mankind has become accustomed to regarding revolutions with these accompanying consequences as legal processes, which is to say, accustomed to facing the tumultuous destruction of life and property, if not with approval, at least with forgiveness, as the necessary accompaniments to revolution.

This is the greatest difference between the National Socialist revolution and other revolutions, perhaps aside from the Fascist uprising in Italy.

The National Socialist revolution was almost completely bloodless. It did not cause any material damage at all during the time when the Party took power, despite overcoming great resistance in Germany. I may say this with a certain pride: this was perhaps the first revolution in which not even one window pane was smashed.

But I don't want to be misunderstood: if this revolution was bloodless, it was not because we were not men enough to see blood! For over four years I was a soldier in the bloodiest war of all time. I never once lost my nerve in any situation or under any pressure. The same is true of my comrades.

We saw the task of the National Socialist revolution not as destroying human lives or property, but rather in building a new and better life. It is our greatest pride to have carried out what is certainly the greatest transformation in our people with a minimum of sacrifice and loss. Only where the Bolshevik bloodlust tried, even after January 30th, 1933, to prevent the victory or the realization of the National Socialist idea by force, did we also respond with force, and with lightning speed. Other elements, whose lack of restraint we recognized as being due to their political ignorance, we only took into safe custody, in order to give them back their freedom after a short time. There were only a few whose political activity was merely a cover for their criminal inclinations, as evidenced by numerous prison sentences, whom we later prevented from continuing their pernicious work of destruction by putting them, probably for the first time in their lives, into productive employment. Has there ever been a revolution of such sweeping proportions as the National Socialist one, which nevertheless allowed innumerable former political functionaries to go about their work unmolested and in peace, and even awarded to numerous former bitter enemies the highest state offices and the full enjoyment of the pensions and annuities to which they were entitled? [...]

When we managed to form a government, the National Socialist revolution as such was over. From the moment of the Party's secure seizure of power in the Reich, I always intended that the revolution would be transformed into an evolution. [...]

The National Socialist worldview has already undoubtedly had a revolutionary effect in countless areas of our lives.

Fundamentally, our National Socialist program replaces the liberal concept of the individual and the Marxist concept of general humanity with the concept of a blood-bound and soil-bound people. This is a very simple and succinct statement, yet it carries enormous implications. Perhaps for the first time in the history of mankind, we have come to the realization in this country that of all the tasks set before us, the noblest and most sacred for man is the preservation of the blood ties given to us by God. [...]

It is only through this inner recognition that, for the first time in our history, the German people have found their way to a greater unity than ever before. Countless prejudices have been broken down, numerous reservations have been cast aside as immaterial, bad traditions are fading, old symbols are being discarded. From the weakness of the old familial, dynastic, ideological, religious, and partisan divisions, the German people are rising and carrying before them the banner of unification which symbolizes the victory not of a state principle, but of a racial principle. For four and a half years, German legislation has been in the service of the victory of this idea. [...]

How this blood community of the German people was realized by the state at that time will probably be the most beautiful memory of our lives. Like a spring storm, our movement roared across the German land four years ago. The fighting troops of our movement, who had defended the swastika banner for many years against an overwhelming force of opponents, and had carried it ever forward through fourteen long years, now thrust it deep into the soil of the new Reich.

In a few weeks, the political residues as well as the social prejudices of the last thousand years in Germany were cleared away and eliminated.

Or can one not speak of a revolution when, in barely three months, parliamentary confusion is replaced by a regime of order, discipline, and vitality, such as Germany has never before possessed? The revolution was so great that even now its intellectual foundations have not yet been recognized by the outside world that judges it superficially.

People talk of democracy and dictatorship, and have not yet grasped that a transformation has taken place in this country, the result of which, if democracy has any meaning at all, can only be described as democratic in the highest sense of the word. With infallible certainty we are working towards an order which will ensure a natural and rational selection process in the realm of the political leadership of the nation, by which the most truly capable minds of our people will be chosen for the political leadership of the nation only according to the higher calling given to them, without regard to birth, origin, name, or wealth. The great Corsican's[101] most beautiful insight, that every soldier must carry the marshal's baton in his pack, will find its political expression in this country. Is there a more glorious and beautiful socialism and a truer democracy than National Socialism, which, thanks to its organization, makes it possible for any one of the millions of German boys to find his way to the top of the nation, if Providence

---

[101] Referring to Napoleon Bonaparte, who was Corsican by birth.

wishes to make use of him?

And this is no mere theory! In today's National Socialist Germany this is an observable reality. I myself, as the leader appointed by the trust of the people, come from among the people. All the millions of German workers know that at the head of the Reich there is no strange man of letters or international revolutionary apostle, but a German from their own ranks. And numerous former workers' and peasants' children are now in leading positions in this National Socialist state, indeed some of them are among the highest leaders and representatives of the people as ministers, Reich governors, and *Gauleiters*.[102]

Of course, here too National Socialism sees only the whole people and never one class. The purpose of the National Socialist revolution was not to turn a privileged class into a class without rights, but to turn a class without rights into a class with equal rights. We did not destroy millions of bourgeoisie in order to degrade them into forced laborers; our aim was to raise forced laborers into German citizens. All Germans will understand one thing: revolutions, as acts of violence, can only be short-lived. If they are not able to build something new, they will consume what already exists in a short time. From the violent act of taking power, a beneficial work of peace must develop in short order. But he who eliminates classes in order to create new classes lays the seed for new revolutions! That which is bourgeois and rules today, will be proletarian again tomorrow as a forced laborer in Siberia, and will then hope one day for liberation in exactly the same way as the proletarian who was first oppressed and now believes he can rule. The National Socialist revolution, therefore, never intended to put one particular class of the German people in power in order to eliminate another, but on the contrary: its only aim was to secure for the whole German people, by marshalling the masses, the possibility not only of economic but also of political engagement. It confines itself, however, to the elements belonging to our people, and refuses to give a foreign nation influence over our political,

---

[102] NSDAP governor of a *Gau*, an administrative district.

spiritual, or cultural life, or to grant it economic predominance. [...]

Nothing confirms the extent to which the German people have understood this change and this transformation and have grasped its significance more than the approval that the nation has given us so many times since then. And to all those who so often and so readily endeavor to portray democratic governments as institutions supported by the people as opposed to dictatorships, I say this: no-one has more right to speak in the name of his people than I do! [...]

However great the confusion we found in other spheres of life in 1933, it was still surpassed by the collapse of the German economy. This was also the aspect of the German collapse which the broad masses felt most keenly and directly. That state of affairs still stands out in your memory and probably in the memory of the entire German people. There were two phenomena as testament to this catastrophe: more than six million unemployed, and an apparently doomed peasantry. [...]

When I appear before the German people today after four years, and also give an account before you, men of the German Reichstag, then you will not deny me and the National Socialist government the confirmation that I have kept my promise from that time to resolve this situation.

This was not an easy undertaking. I am not speculating when I say that even the so-called "experts" at that time no longer believed such salvation was possible. [...]

If you trace the development even of only the known history of our people from prehistoric times to the present day, you will appreciate the ridiculousness of the posturing of those lily-livered chatterers who, as soon as a piece of paper is devalued somewhere in the world, immediately start going on about economic collapse, and thus also the collapse of human life. Germany and the German people have already overcome very serious catastrophes. Admittedly, it always took men to take the measures necessary and to get things done without regard to naysayers and know-it-alls. However, a bunch of parliamentary cowards are ill-suited to lead a people out of crisis and despair!

I had the firm belief and the most sacred conviction that the German economic catastrophe could be overcome as long as one believed in the immortality of the people, and assigned the economy its proper role as the servant of the people.

I was not an economist, which means above all that I have never been a theorist in my life. [...]

In the relationship between the economy and the people, there is only one thing that cannot be changed, and that is the people. Economic activity, however, is not and will never be a dogma.

There is no economic conception or economic theory that could somehow claim to be sacred. What is decisive is the will to always assign the economy the subservient role towards the people, and capital the subservient role towards the economy.

National Socialism, as we know, is the fiercest opponent of the liberal view that the economy is at the disposal of capital, and the people at the disposal of the economy. We were therefore determined from the very first day to break with the fallacy that the economy could lead an independent, uncontrollable, and unsupervised life of its own within the state. [...]

The national community does not live by virtue of the imaginary value of money, but by virtue of real production, which is what gives money its value in the first place.

This production is the primary backing of a currency, and not a bank or a vault full of gold! And if I increase this production, I actually increase the income of my fellow citizens, and if I decrease it, I decrease the income, no matter what kind of wages are paid.

In these last four years we have created an extraordinary increase in German production in all fields. And the increase in this production benefits the German people as a whole. For if, for example, countless millions of tons of coal are extracted today, it is not in order to heat the rooms of a few millionaires to a few thousand degrees, but in order to be able to increase the standard of living for millions of German citizens. [...]

The way we understand the tasks of the economy in such a

folkish sense, the former distinction of employer and employee becomes invalid. The new state will not and does not want to be an entrepreneur. It will only regulate the use of the nation's labor power to the extent necessary for the benefit of all. And it will only supervise the labor process to the extent that it must in the interest of all concerned. In doing so, it will under no circumstances attempt to tyrannize economic life. Every instance of real and practical initiative benefits all the people in its economic effect. The value of an inventor or a successful business leader is often impossible to estimate at the moment for the entire national community. In the future it will be all the more the task of National Socialist education to make the respective value of each of our national comrades clear to them. [...]

Our entire German educational system, including the press, theatre, film, and literature, is today run and shaped exclusively by Germans. How often we used to hear that the removal of Jewry from these institutions would lead to their collapse or desolation! And what has happened now? In all these areas we are experiencing a tremendous blossoming of cultural and artistic life. Our films are better than ever before, our theatrical productions now stand at the peak of achievement in our top theatres, our press has become a formidable instrument in the service of our people's self-assertion, and helps to strengthen the nation. German science is achieving successes, and enormous monuments to the creative will of our people will one day bear witness to this new epoch!

An unparalleled immunization of the German people has been achieved against all the corrosive tendencies from which the rest of the world has to suffer. Some of our institutions, which only a few years ago were not understood, are now taken for granted. The *Jungvolk*,[103] the Hitler Youth, the League of German Girls, the National Socialist Women's League, the Labor Service, the SA, the SS, the National Socialist Motor Corps, and above all the German Labor Front in its enormous structure are keystones in the proud

---

[103] An organization similar to the Hitler Youth, but for younger boys aged ten to fourteen.

construction of our Third Reich.

Four years ago, when I was entrusted with the chancellorship and thus with the leadership of the nation, I took on the bitter duty of restoring honor to a people that for fifteen years had been forced to lead the life of a leper among the other nations. To secure the internal order of the German people required the reconstruction of the German Army, and from both at the same time grew the possibility of throwing off those fetters which we felt to be the deepest stigma that had ever been branded on a people. Today, as I conclude this process, I have only a few explanations to give:

The restoration of equal rights to Germany was a process that exclusively affected and concerned Germany itself. We have not taken anything from any nation, and have not caused any suffering to any nation!

I announce to you that, in the spirit of restoring German equality, I will strip German National Rail and the German Reichsbank of their previous private character and place them once again entirely under the sovereignty of the Government of the German Reich.

I hereby declare that the effect of the section of the Versailles Treaty which deprived our people of their equal rights and degraded them to an inferior people is at an end.

Above all, however, I solemnly withdraw the German signature from the declaration that was forced upon a weak government against its better judgment, that Germany was to blame for the war!

Men of the German Reichstag, this restoration of the honor of our people, which found its most visible outward expression in the introduction of compulsory military service, the creation of a new air force, the rebuilding of a German navy, the reoccupation of the Rhineland by our troops, was the most difficult and daring task of my life. On this day, I must humbly thank Providence, whose grace allowed me, once an unknown soldier of the World War, to succeed in thus winning back our nation's honor and righteousness.

[...]

Now I will comment on the general questions of the present, and this is perhaps most appropriately done along the lines of those statements which were recently made in the English House of Commons by the British Foreign Secretary, Mr. Eden. [...]

What is the justification for the view that Germany is pursuing a policy of isolation? [...]

I do not believe at all that any state could intend to consciously declare itself politically disinterested in what is going on in the rest of the world. Especially not when that world is as small as Europe is today. I believe that if a state really has to resort to such an attitude, it is only under the compulsion of a foreign will imposed on it. I would like to begin by assuring Minister Eden that we Germans do not in the least wish to be isolated, nor indeed do we feel that we are isolated. In recent years, Germany has established, re-established, and improved a whole range of political relations and has established close and friendly relations with a number of states. From our point of view, our relations in Europe are normal with most states, and very friendly with a large number of states. I place at the top of the list the excellent relations that unite us above all with those states that have come to similar conclusions from similar sufferings as we have. Through a series of agreements, we have eliminated earlier tensions and have thus contributed significantly to improving European conditions. I need only remind you of our agreement with Poland, which is to the advantage of both states, of our agreement with Austria, of our excellent and close relationship with Italy, of our friendly relations with Hungary, Yugoslavia, Bulgaria, Greece, Portugal, Spain, et cetera, and finally also of the no less cordial relations with a whole series of states outside Europe.

The agreement which Germany has reached with Japan to combat the Comintern movement is living proof of how little the German government wishes to isolate itself, and how little it therefore actually feels isolated. Incidentally, I have more than once expressed the wish and the hope of achieving a similarly good and cordial relationship with all our neighbors. Germany, and I solemnly reiterate this here, has repeatedly declared that there can be no humanly conceivable point of contention between it and France, for example. The German Government has also assured Belgium and Holland that it is prepared to recognize and guarantee these states as inviolable neutral territories at any time.[104] In view of all the declarations we made earlier and the actual state of affairs, I do not quite see why Germany should feel isolated, or even pursue a policy of isolation. [...]

I am afraid, however, that I must infer from Mr. Eden's words that he regards the implementation of the German Four-Year-Plan as evidence of Germany's rejection of international relations. I would therefore like to leave no doubt that the decision to carry out this plan is not going to change. The reasons which led us to this decision were compelling. And I have not been able to discover anything in recent times that would have been able to dissuade us in any way from making this decision.

Let me take just one practical example: the implementation of the Four-Year Plan will ensure an additional annual production of twenty to thirty million metric tons of coal in our country for the synthetic production of petrol and rubber alone! And that means the guaranteed employment of many tens of thousands of coal miners for the rest of their lives. I really have to ask: which statesman would be in a position to guarantee me the purchase of twenty or thirty million metric tons of coal by any other economic factor outside the Reich if I were to forego implementing this Four-Year Plan? And that is what it is all about. I want work and bread for my people. And not temporarily through the granting of loans for my sake, but through a solid, permanent production process, which I can either exchange for the goods of the rest of the world, or for my own goods in the cycle of our own economy. [...]

Mr. Eden believes that in future all states should only possess the armaments necessary for their defense. I do not know whether

---

[104] Of course, with the changing geopolitical situation in Europe and a typically Germany *Realpolitik* response to it, Germany would find itself unable or unwilling to respect these declarations within a few short years from the date of this speech.

and to what extent Moscow has already been contacted about the realization of this pleasant idea, or to what extent promises have already been given from there. But I must say one thing: it is quite clear that the necessary extent of armament for defense is determined by the extent of the dangers threatening a country. It is for each nation to judge, and each nation alone to judge. So when Great Britain today determines the extent of its requirement for armaments, everyone in Germany understands this, for we take for granted that London itself is exclusively competent to assess the protection requirements of the British Empire. But I would also like to emphasize that we are exclusively competent to assess the protection requirements, and thus the requirements for defensive armaments, for our people, and therefore this is decided exclusively in Berlin.

I believe that a general recognition of these principles will not contribute to aggression, but only to easing tension. Germany, at any rate, is fortunate to have found friends in Italy and Japan who share our view, and it would be even happier if this conviction were to spread throughout Europe. That is why no one has welcomed more warmly than us the visible easing of tensions in the Mediterranean as a result of the Italian-English agreement. We believe that this is also the most likely way to reach an understanding on remedying or at least limiting the disaster that has befallen poor Spain.[105] [...]

Our sympathies for General Franco and his government lie firstly in general compassion, and secondly in the hope that a consolidation of a truly national Spain will strengthen European economic possibilities, but conversely, that an even greater catastrophe could originate from there should the other side succeed. We are therefore prepared to do everything we can to contribute to a restoration of orderly conditions in Spain. [...]

As I conclude this part of my speech, I would like to take a very

---

[105] The Spanish Civil War, a conflict between the Nationalists on one side, a loose coalition of conservatives, monarchists, and fascists, and the Republicans on the other side, a loose coalition of liberals, anarchists, and communists.

brief look at the tasks of the future.

The implementation of the next four-year plan is at the top of the agenda. It will require enormous efforts, but will also be a great blessing to our people. It includes strengthening our national economy in all areas. The great projects which have begun outside of it will continue. Their aim will be to make the German people healthier, and their lives more comfortable.

As an outward testament to this great epoch of the resurrection of our people, the planned development of some of the great cities of the Reich will now take place. And at the top of the list is the development of Berlin into a real and true capital of the German Reich. For this reason, I have appointed today, as I did for the construction of our roads, a General Building Inspector [106] for Berlin, who is responsible for the structural development of the Reich capital and who will see to it that the chaos of Berlin's previous building development is brought into line with the spirit of the National Socialist movement and the nature of the German Reich capital. A period of twenty years is planned for the implementation of this plan. May Almighty God grant us the peace we need to be able to complete this tremendous task.

In parallel with this, there will be a generous enhancement of the Capital of the Movement, [107] the City of the Reich Party Rallies,[108] as well as the city of Hamburg.

This, however, is only to serve as the model for a general cultural development to which we aspire for the German people as the manifestation of its internal and external freedom. [...]

On this historic day I must again remember those millions of unknown Germans from all walks of life, from every profession and every factory and every homestead, who gave their hearts and their love and their sacrifices to the new Reich. And all of us, men and members of the Reichstag, want to give thanks together, above

---

[106] This man was Albert Speer, the leading architect of National Socialist Germany, and a member of Hitler's inner circle due to their shared passion for architecture.
[107] Munich, where the party was founded.
[108] Nuremberg, site of many massive party events.

all to the German woman, to the millions of our mothers who gave their children to the Third Reich. For what sense would all our work have, what sense would the uprising of the German nation have without our German youth? Every mother who has given a child to our people in these four years contributes through her pain and happiness to the happiness of the whole nation. When I consider these healthy youth of our people, my faith in our future becomes a joyful certainty, and I feel with deep fervor the meaning of that single word that Ulrich von Hutten[109] wrote before he put down his pen for the last time:

Germany!

---

[109] A German knight and poet of the late fifteenth to early sixteenth century.

ADDRESS TO THE NATIONAL SOCIALIST WOMEN'S LEAGUE

Reich Party Congress "Rally of Labor"
Nuremberg, September 10th, 1937

The Background

The following speech took place at one of the infamous "Nuremberg Rallies," celebratory gatherings of National Socialists with marching, performances, and speeches. The first of these took place in 1923, the next in 1926, then 1927, 1929, and annually every September after 1933 until 1938. After the inaugural rally in 1923, they were loosely centered on some theme such as "Re-founding," "Victory," or "Peace." The 1937 rally was dubbed the *Reichsparteitag der Arbeit* (Reich Party Congress of Labor).

In his speech, Hitler briefly addresses the National Socialist Women's League after its leader finishes her remarks. He addresses gender relations, answers charges that women are oppressed in National Socialist Germany, and outlines his vision for the role of women in National Socialism, which of course for most women he sees as primarily in building families and raising children, although he did warn male Party members that he would not tolerate them treating women as "baby-making machines or playthings."[110]

There were, however, many women whose talents in other spheres were officially recognized, such as photographer and

---

[110] Klüver, *Volksgemeinschaft*, 186, quoted in Tedor, *Hitler's Revolution*, 292.

filmmaker Leni Riefenstahl, who made the infamous propaganda film *Triumph des Willens* about the 1934 Nuremberg rally, which is universally recognized as having pioneered many film techniques, as well as the ace aviators Melitta von Stauffenberg[111] and Hanna Reitsch, both incredible and groundbreaking pilots who set numerous world records, and were decorated with numerous awards for their services in test-piloting German aircraft. In a 1970s interview with Ron Laytner, Reitsch lamented the defeat of National Socialism, said she still wore the diamond-encrusted Iron Cross Hitler had awarded her, reported that Hermann Göring told her that Germany's genocide of Jews was British and American propaganda, and asserted that Germany's only guilt for the war was that it had lost.[112]

Furthermore, from 1934 to 1937, the number of women in the workforce actually increased despite the government policy of incentivizing women to leave the workforce and have children. Women were encouraged, but not forced, to assume traditional social roles. They were eligible for all of the same tax incentives as men for starting their own businesses.[113] During the course of the war, with so many men away in the military, the role of women in the workforce expanded drastically. Despite Hitler's misgivings, chief of the German Labor Front Robert Ley insisted on equal opportunities, conditions, and pay for women,[114] and by the later years of the war approximately half of all university students were women.

Much has been made of Hitler's own personal relationships with women, or lack thereof. With all of the propaganda and pathologizing, and given his modest and private nature in regard to such matters, the truth is difficult to determine, and such a task

---

[111] Sister-in-law of Claus von Stauffenberg, who attempted to assassinate Hitler in the failed bomb plot of July 1944; she was briefly detained in relation to the assassination attempt, but released and reinstated as a *Luftwaffe* pilot when it was understood she had no involvement in it; she continued flying in the *Luftwaffe* until she was shot down by an American fighter and died in April 1945.

[112] Laytner, "The first astronaut: tiny, daring Hanna."

[113] Reinhardt, *Die Beseitigung der Arbeitslosigkeit*, 89.

[114] Klüver, *Volksgemeinschaft*, 192-195, quoted in Tedor, *Hitler's Revolution*, 292.

is beyond the scope of this work. What is certain is that he was a bachelor and single man throughout the 1920s; any youthful relationships before that time, or any romantic affairs during that time, are unknown and have to be regarded as mostly rumor and conjecture. He did eventually settle down with the young photographer Eva Braun in 1932, though this relationship was kept very private and largely out of the public eye. Whatever the exact nature of Hitler's relationships with women before he met Eva Braun, it cannot be denied that he was popular with the women of Germany at the time. He was inundated with love letters and marriage proposals, and many of his early benefactors and supporters were women. There is another fact that is not disputed, though it is little known: three different wealthy women over the years gave Hitler whips as presents, which he carried with him to public appearances in the old tradition of military officers. [115] Whatever significance one attaches to these facts, they do shed light on Hitler's standing with the women of Germany, as does the content of the following speech.

---

[115] Kershaw, *Hitler*, 115-116.

The Speech

Women of the Party!

I have read through the report of your women's leader, and of course it is not easy to expand on these questions after such a comprehensive report. I can only express my gratitude for the great work that has been done, and I must express this gratitude above all to your leader herself, who has succeeded in building up the largest women's organization in the world. This is not only a proof of the ability of the German woman and the German girl, but especially proof of the ability of your leader.

I would nevertheless like to address you very briefly, limiting myself to the subjects that are inherently in the purview of our National Socialist movement. For many foreigners, and especially, as I have seen, for many foreign women, it seems impossible to understand why we have a women's movement in Germany, and how it is even possible that we have it. They are all convinced — I hear this very often when they come and talk to me — that in Germany women are being enslaved and oppressed, and that they really only have one task, namely to do the bidding of the barbaric men. Yes, that is more or less how people out there, instructed by an "open" press, imagine the position and life of the German woman and the German girl. They cannot understand why or how we have a German women's movement, because they themselves see these problems from a completely different angle than we do.

We approached this question under the guidance of the most natural and safest rule in this life — namely, the guidance of reason. Certainly, the difficulties of men and women coexisting have always been raised, recognized, and dealt with. These difficulties give nourishment primarily to the organizations that dealt with women's problems before the National Socialist revolution; indeed, these organizations were often based solely on these difficulties. They saw this as the object of all women's organizing. We started from a different point of view: that this should not be a problem at all, for nature has already solved this problem for us. Whether the two sexes want to or not—and indeed they do want to—but even if they did not want to, they still have to come together. They have to come to terms with each other and get along with each other. This is perhaps the best recipe for every marriage—namely, the realization that there is no point wishing things could be otherwise, for either party. They depend on each other, they have to stay together, they have to live together, and they have to figure out how they can arrange their lives. They can arrange them easily if they are reasonable, or they can arrange them with difficulty if they are unreasonable. But—praise and thanks be to God for this—in most cases they don't separate anyway.

The same points of view that we apply on a large scale to the organization of our national body naturally apply even more to the life of the two sexes together. We started out from the conviction that class divisions within a people are senseless, in that they are all absolutely dependent on each other, and none is able to exist without the others. It was then only a question of whether one wanted to be reasonable or unreasonable about this. We can make life bearable by showing consideration for each other and taking into account the necessities of nature, or be unreasonable by making life sour and difficult for each other. That would not help at all. In the end, the intellectuals and the manual laborers will have to live together, whether they want to or not. And this is exactly how the problem is, of course, even more so in the relationship between the two sexes. Men and women have to get along with each other. And so far, thankfully, they have always managed to get along with each other. This state of affairs has lasted for millions of years. Nothing has changed. Men have remained men and women have remained women. So it can be assumed that we will probably not change in the coming millennia, or at least not at all in our present time. So we are working with quite well-known variables here, the male variable and the female variable. And now that the two are there, and we also know that they would no longer be there if they could not form relationships with each other, they must find a reasonable way to relate to each other. That was the basis on which we started our women's movement from the beginning. Here too we started from the realization that the question is not up for discussion as to which of the two sexes rules or governs — every woman knows that appearances are often deceiving here — but only the questions of how they should live together, whether they want to organize their lives reasonably, intelligently, and thus in accordance with nature, or unreasonably, i.e. contrary to nature. And we chose the former, not only because it is the most reasonable, but also because it is the most pleasant; for there is no doubt that in the long run any other way of living would begin to get on one's nerves, on a large scale as well as on a small one.

It is said, however, that in almost every marriage the two spouses have to wrestle with each other in order to be completely happy. Now let us assume that this wrestling has already taken place in the times before ours, and that in our time the two sexes are now living in a happy marriage with each other, a marriage of reason, of understanding, of prudence, of insight, of consideration for each other, but above all of knowledge of what nature has prescribed for the two sexes in the world. For we cannot doubt that if humanity, like many other beings, has divided itself into two sexes, then this has a definite purpose by nature, and if these beings are not the same outwardly, then this also has a purpose by nature. Providence could have done otherwise. We are very happy that that is not the case. Men are happy that things are the way they are, and so are women. I believe that many of the charms of life in this world would be lost if nature were suddenly to make it possible, through some invention, for men to live without women without going extinct. But it would also become somewhat monotonous for women if the deeper bass of life were suddenly to disappear and everything were only soprano. Then, too, one would very quickly discover that the beauty of woman is only apparent because one can always contrast her with man, and conversely, no one would notice the strength of man if the allegedly weaker sex did not stand opposite him. Believe in this: nature has not only given the two sexes certain predispositions, but has also assigned them and predisposed them to certain tasks. And it is only in the spirit of a reasonable interpretation of this nature that we now endeavor to consciously lead the two sexes further in the direction of the purpose already given to them by nature. That is to say, we do not want to see men suddenly become women, but we also do not want to see women suddenly become men. We want women to remain women in their nature, in their whole being, in the purpose and fulfillment of this being, just as we want men to remain men, also in their nature and also in the purpose and fulfillment of their nature and aims.

As soon as this solution is accepted, the problem itself is no longer so difficult. Then it is no longer a question of so-called equal rights, but more a question of respective duties. There is no longer a dispute about which of the two sexes is privileged; rather, the profound realization arises that these sexes together make up the people, and that the continuation of the people is only possible through their cooperation.

There are then two tasks, but in one world, just as there are two sexes, but in one people, in one community. This is the basis of the organization of the life work of men and of women.

And the more these two sexes are absorbed in their tasks, the more they are occupied by the fulfillment of these tasks, the less the problem of the earlier time of the dispute between man and woman can arise between them. The more masculine the man is, the more uncontested he will be in his sphere of activity, and the more feminine the woman is, the more uncontested and undisputed she will be in her own work and thus also her own position. And mutual respect between the sexes is ultimately not achieved by the statements of two different associations, the men's association and the women's association, but is acquired on a daily basis through practical life. The more a man is faced with a woman who is truly a woman, the more he is disarmed from the outset in his arrogance, so much so that he is sometimes almost overcome; and on the other hand, the more that a man is completely a man, and fulfills his activity and his task in life in the highest sense of the word, the more a woman will gravitate to the position towards him which is natural and self-evident to her. The two can never cross each other on their paths in life, but can only unite in a great shared mission, and this mission ultimately means the continuation of the human community as it is now, and its safeguarding for the future as we wish it to one day be.

Thus, of course, the individual covenant of man and woman always emerges from this overall covenant of the two sexes. Here too we know that this union, if it is to be a lasting one, must be supported by the knowledge of this great companionship in life. But in light of this, we must also understand that the search for and finding of this life companionship cannot be commanded or ordered, that this too is ultimately a problem not only of reason, but of the heart. And it is therefore understandable that for many people, and especially for women, the solution to this problem of finding a life companion might fail, because the heart cannot always follow reason. We must have the greatest compassion for this, for there is still the second great work, namely work for our broader community.

But the ultimate goal must and will always be the formation of that germ of life which itself gives life again, for what would be the point of our whole struggle if the next young generation were not to come about? Everything we do, at the bottom of it all, we do for the child. We might believe we are taking care of ourselves, of our generation, of our time, and are simply unable to express correctly what nature makes us think, what it makes us do. We may speak of a present, speak of a Germany that now stands before us, and yet all of us unconsciously act for a Germany that will come after us. That is the way it is in all of nature, that is the concern of every individual being, that is the impulse for founding a small family, but it is also the impulse for the formation of the people and the state. All this has only one purpose: that this flesh and blood does not die out, but that it continues to flourish, that it gains immortality through its children, as far as immortality can be spoken of in this earthly world.

And that is ultimately also the highest and most rewarding expression of gratitude, the gratitude to a leader just as much as the gratitude to each individual participant in this great work of education, upbringing, and preservation of a nation. The individual sees his survival in his child, and in the whole and on a large scale we can only live on through the child. In the end, it is the highest and most beautiful reward there is.

There are hundreds of thousands of men marching here, tens of thousands of women. All this is wonderful. But what a gap it would be if this young generation didn't come after them, these tens of thousands of *Pimpfen*,[116] Hitler Youth boys, and BDM girls.[117] Only here does one's heart really sing, only here does one know what one is actually fighting for, and why one is creating all this: not for us, who represent a living generation in our people, one link in the chain of life, but for that which we see sprouting up, that which is already here, that is now actually the beneficiary of this life, and also the goal of this whole life. And this happiness is not exclusive to a leader. Every single man can have it, and above all every single woman can have it. This happiness can also be given to every mother, to know, "I am not living in vain, but have a purpose, because here are my children. All that I create now will not perish with me, but will remain, will benefit those who are of my own blood." It is a wonderful thought to know this on a large scale, but also to be able to experience it on a small scale.

Once we have come to this realization, then the work of the two sexes on a large scale is mapped out just as it is mapped out for the individual members of the two sexes on a small scale. And each and every member of the two sexes can now fulfill his or her duty here within his or her own framework. Every man and every

---

[116] An affectionate term for young boys, becoming an official term for members of the Deutsches Jungvolk; the sense is something like tyke, squirt, or scamp.
[117] *Bund Deutscher Mädel*, the girls' equivalent of the Hitler Youth.

woman, from this great point of view, can also help for their part not to live in vain, but to give their own lives a higher meaning. No matter where they stand, no matter how they accomplish their particular life's work, no matter how they fulfill their task. In the end, after an honestly fulfilled duty, there will always be the awareness of having worked not in vain, not for today's fleeting time, but for a later posterity, for generations that will come after us, and who will experience suffering just as we do, but who will also experience joy just as we do, great and glorious and beautiful joy. That is the meaning of our struggle, the meaning of the organization, of our movement, and thus also the meaning of our National Socialist Women's League. And this League is one of the main pillars of this struggle. Its value cannot be expressed by association statements, but every woman and every girl carries its value within herself; no one can give it to her, and no one can take it away from her. The sum total of all these values gives value to the organization as a whole. And I am absolutely convinced that we have achieved this in Germany in a higher sense and to a greater extent than in other countries.

This is valid not only for men, but also for women. The men we train to be a tough sex. German women can rest assured that the coming generations will be real protectors and active supporters of women, and conversely, men have the happy awareness that in the future, more than in any other state, women will be the most faithful companions of men, that they will really embody in themselves that eternal femininity which has always attracted and will always attract men. The ultimate arrangement of the relation-ship between the sexes will then take place in these millions of processes of seeking each other, finding each other, and finally staying together, in these innumerable life processes, which may seem insignificant taken individually, but which nevertheless constitute the most decisive destiny of each individual human being. It is in all these millions of individual processes that the final community formation between the two sexes takes place. It is our most sublime task to facilitate and promote this for the education of both sexes. And I can tell you this, Comrade Scholtz-Klink[118] the way you have begun to go about this is correct, and it will now help to facilitate the achievement of this goal, for you have understood wonderfully how to avoid creating an opposing force to men through the organization of women, but on the contrary, how to make the German women's organization a complement to the male fighting organization.

When I thank you for this, it is the thanks of a single person, but in the future, many millions of people will thank you, especially all the young men who have found the girl of their dreams, and all the millions of girls who have discovered the man of their heart. All of them will thank you for making it easier through your education to bring the two sexes together, instead of making it more difficult, as happens elsewhere. And this is the most beautiful and by far the most effective thanks, for it will be experienced in the form of the greatest happiness by countless

---

[118] Gertrud Scholz-Klink, the second leader of the National Socialist Women's League after the first, Guida Diehl, left to raise her family. She led an interesting and well-rounded life of her own, having six children, one of whom, Ernst Klink, went on to become an SS officer himself, and later on a member of HIAG, a Waffen-SS veterans' association that aimed to advocate for maligned veterans and rehabilitate the reputation of the SS. He was also a prominent military historian who contributed to research showing that the invasion of Russia was a preemptive strike to head off a planned Soviet invasion of Western Europe, and questioning the often unexamined narrative that Hitler was an incompetent military commander (*Germany and the Second World War*. Oxford/New York: Clarendon Press/Oxford University Press, 2000). Gertrud was born with the maiden name Treush; Schotz was the name she took from her first husband, Klink from her second after she was widowed; when she was widowed a second time, she married high-ranking SS officer Obergruppenführer August Heißmeyer, but did not take his name – perhaps by then she figured it might be bad luck. After the war, she was briefly detained in a Soviet POW camp but managed to make a daring escape and reunite with her third husband, living in hiding for three years under the aliases Heinrich and Maria Stuckebrock, until they were eventually caught and spent several years in prison. Schotz-Klink remained an unrepentant lifelong National Socialist; in 1978 she published a book titled *The Woman in the Third Reich*, in which she defended Adolf Hitler and the NSDAP regime, elaborated on her own National Socialist beliefs, and gave detailed insight on the role and lifestyle of women in that period. In a 1980s interview with feminist historian Claudia Koonz, she rebuked the view that women were oppressed and marginalised in the Third Reich, and once again defended National Socialism. She passed away of old age in 1999 at the age of ninety-seven.

millions of human beings who are already living among us today and who will surely come after us.

On Church and State — Excerpt

Berlin Reichstag, January 30th, 1939

The Background

The following speech was yet another one delivered on the anniversary of Hitler's ascent to power. Every year on this date he addressed the Reichstag, discussing the issues of the past year and the future. As such, the following speech was quite long, lasting more than two hours, and covered many topics, including the Sudetenland crisis, foreign policy, rearmament, and the Jewish question.

Notoriously, this was the speech in which Hitler warned that if international finance Jewry managed to stir up another world war against Germany, the result would not be the destruction of Germany, but the annihilation of Jewry in Europe. This is probably the most famous line from any of his speeches, and frequently cited as evidence that as early as 1939 he was already planning a systematic genocide of Jews, although all mainstream scholarship indicates that the "final solution" to the Jewish question had not been decided on yet, and here he was very likely referring to deportation.[119] In future speeches in later years, he often quoted himself, repeating his "prophecy" that at some point in the future the other nations would join Germany in removing the Jews from their midst. Elsewhere in the speech, he makes clear that Germany intends to deport as much of its Jewish population as possible,

---

[119] Mommsen, "Hitler's Reichstag Speech," 147–61.

removing them especially from elite positions to open up these positions to the children of the peasants and working classes.[120] He did not miss the opportunity to castigate the countries condemning Germany for this policy as hypocrites, as they decried Germany's attempts to deport Jews, while themselves refusing to take in Germany's Jews as refugees. He points out that these countries should be happy to take in Germany's Jewish population, as these countries are the ones going on about how indispensable Jews are as "apostles of culture."[121]

But these remarks are only a brief segment of the rather long and rambling address to the Reichstag, and are not the main focus. Nor, admittedly, is the part where he addresses the religious question, but I believe this section is of historical interest as well.

Already by the time Hitler delivered the following speech, religious issues had plagued Germany for over four hundred years. A hundred years after Martin Luther posited his *Ninety-five Theses*, Germany was plunged into the most destructive religious war in world history, the Thirty Years' War of 1618–1648, which killed at least several million people and, in some of the most war-torn parts of what was then the Holy Roman Empire, reduced the population by more than half. Other factors played a role in that conflict, especially expansionism and power politics on the part of foreign powers, but the advent of Protestantism left deep divisions in Germany, some of which endure to the present day, though in a less extreme form. In broadest possible terms, the country was, and still is to an extent, divided into a predominantly Protestant North, and a predominantly Catholic South.

The issue of the respective authority and roles of church and state plagued Chancellor Otto von Bismarck in what has come to be known as the *Kulturkampf* (cultural struggle, or "culture war"), conflicts between Catholicism, Protestantism, and secular state authority at a time of increasing secularization, but during which

---

[120] de Sales, *My New Order*, 584.
[121] Ibid.

the Catholic Church especially still wielded tremendous cultural power.

To further complicate the issue, on the fringes of the Romanticist and nationalist movements, a revival of interest in, and even attempted reconstruction of, pre-Christian Germanic Paganism began to grow, associated with mystical nationalism and Pan-Germanism. These ideas were very influential, even dominant, among the esoteric-Nordicist *Germanenorden* (Germanic Order), the precursor to the Thule Society, which in turn helped fund the early National Socialist movement in the days of the DAP. Several early NSDAP members were also members of the Thule Society, including Rudolf Heß, and similar esoteric-Aryanist, pagan, and even anti-Christian ideas were widespread in the broader *völkisch* movement; the influence of such ideas is evident, for example, in the writings of Alfred Rosenberg. Hitler himself was mostly dismissive of these ideas, and especially expressed distaste for esotericism,[122] but they were still a factor with which he had to contend as head of state.

"Positive Christianity," as referred to in the rather vague plank of the original 25-Point Program of the NSDAP, came to be embodied in an abortive attempt to create a new state religion by uniting the various Protestant sects into a single Church, whose doctrine proclaimed that Christ was not ethnically Jewish but in fact Aryan, downplayed the Old Testament, and clumsily attempted to shoehorn themes of a struggle between Aryans and Jews into the New Testament. Its half-baked ideas were never clearly elucidated, and it never caught on in any significant way, even among the pro-NSDAP Protestant group the German Christians. Though it is quite ill-defined, the "positive Christianity" mentioned in the 25-Point Program was not originally conceived of as a new religious sect of its own, but merely indicated a secular and non-denominational but vaguely pro-Christian attitude on the part of the NSDAP.

---

[122] Hitler, *Mein Kampf, Vol. I,* C. 12.15, 659-667.

There was tension between the regime and the Catholic Church over issues of divided loyalties and hostility towards National Socialism among Catholic clergy. Among Protestants, the Confessing Church sprang up as a dissident movement that opposed the German Christians, the attempt to unify all the Protestant churches into a single German Evangelical Church, and the NSDAP regime itself.

Hitler's own religious beliefs are the subject of debate and controversy, and the issue is too complicated to properly address here. He frequently appealed to Christians on the basis of protecting Christian Europe from atheistic communism. He certainly believed in God, or at least in something he found convenient to call God, and he certainly was not a pagan in the sense of the esoteric-Aryanists, but whether he believed in the divinity of Christ and the literal truth of the scriptures, and thus could properly be called a Christian, is questionable. Every indication from his writings, his speeches, and his actions suggests that, while he did believe in God, or at least in a higher power he frequently called "the Creator" or "Providence," he viewed sectarian religious issues primarily from a pragmatic perspective, as troublesome distractions that could cause divisions among Germans and detract from the national unity that he viewed as of primary importance.

These various religious issues, as well as accusations from rival foreign powers of persecution of priests and pastors, were what prompted Hitler to address the question of church and state in the following excerpts from his address to the Reichstag.

The Speech

Among the accusations that the so-called democracies against have levelled Germany is that National Socialist Germany is hostile to religion. I would like to make the following solemn declaration before the entire German people:

First of all, to date, no one in Germany has been persecuted for their religious beliefs, nor will anyone be persecuted for them.

Secondly, since January 30th, 1933, the National Socialist state has made the following sums available to the two Churches in public tax revenues through its state organs: in the fiscal year of 1933, 130 million Reichsmarks; in the fiscal year of 1934, 170 million; in the fiscal year of 1935, 250 million; in the fiscal year of 1936, 320 million; in the fiscal year of 1937, 400 million; and in the fiscal year of 1938, 500 million Reichsmarks.

In addition, the churches receive about 85 million Reichsmarks annually from grants from the *Länder*, and about 7 million Reichsmarks from grants from the municipalities and municipal associations.

Apart from that, the churches are the largest landowner after the state. The value of their agricultural and forestry property exceeds 10 billion Reichsmarks. The income from this property is estimated at over 300 million annually.

Added to this are the countless donations, bequests in wills and, above all, the proceeds from their church collections. Furthermore, the churches in the National Socialist state are tax-privileged in various areas, and their donations, inheritances, and so on are all tax exempt.

It is therefore, to put it mildly, an insolent impertinence when foreign politicians in particular dare to speak of hostility to religion in the Third Reich.

But if the German churches really should consider this situation unbearable for them, then the National Socialist state is prepared at any time to enact a clear separation of church and state, as is the case in France, America, and other countries.

I would now like to take the liberty of asking: how much did France, England, or the USA deliver to their churches through the state from public funds during the same period?

The National Socialist state has neither closed a church, nor prevented a service, nor has it ever had any influence on the form of a service. It has neither influenced the doctrine nor the confession of any denomination. In the National Socialist state, everyone can seek salvation in his own fashion.

However, the National Socialist state will deal with priests who, instead of being servants of God, make it their mission to denigrate our present Reich, its institutions, or its leading minds, by making them realize that the destruction of this state by anyone will not be tolerated. As soon as a priest steps outside the bounds of the law, he will be held accountable to the law just like any other German citizen.

But it must be stated here that there are tens of thousands of priests of all Christian denominations who fulfill their ecclesiastical duties just as well as, or probably better than, the political agitators, without ever coming into conflict with the laws of the state. The state sees it as its duty to protect them, and to destroy its enemies.

When leading figures of the National Socialist Party were guilty of these crimes five years ago, they were shot. If other persons in public or private life, even priests, commit the same offences, they are punished by law with imprisonment. Transgressions of priests against their other vows, of chastity for example, do not interest us at all, nor has a word ever appeared about the subject in our press.

Incidentally, this state has intervened only once in the internal affairs of the churches, namely when I myself tried in 1933 to unite the impotent and fragmented regional Protestant churches in Germany into a large and powerful Reich Protestant Church. This failed due to the resistance of individual regional bishops. This attempt has thus also been abandoned; after all, it is ultimately not our task to defend or even strengthen the Protestant Church by force against its own leaders.

When foreign countries, and especially certain democratic statesmen, make a show of standing up so strongly for individual German priests, then there can only be a political reason for this, for the same statesmen remained silent when thousands of priests were being massacred or burned in Russia. They remained silent when thousands of priests and nuns were slaughtered in Spain in the most brutal way, some even burned alive.

They could not deny these facts, but they kept quiet and remained silent. I must reproach the democratic statesmen for this. Meanwhile, in response to these slaughters, numerous National Socialist and Fascist volunteers placed themselves at the disposal of General Franco in order to help prevent a further extension of this Bolshevik bloodlust over Europe, and thus over the majority of civilized humanity. [...]

It was concern for European culture and for real civilization that led Germany to take sides in this struggle of nationalist Spain against the Bolsheviks trying to destroy it. It is a sad sign of the mentality in various countries that they cannot even imagine acting out of such selfless motives. National Socialist Germany alone took part in General Franco's uprising only out of the fervent hope that he might succeed in saving his country from a danger to which Germany itself once almost succumbed.

So it cannot be sympathy or pity for persecuted men of God that motivates the interest of democratic citizens in individual priests who have come into conflict with the law in Germany; they are only interested in them as enemies of the German state.

On this subject they should be aware of one thing: we will protect the German priest who is a servant of God; we will destroy the priest who makes himself a political enemy of the German Reich.

We believe that this is the best way to prevent a development which, as the experience in Spain shows, would otherwise all too easily lead to a confrontation of unimaginable proportions.

I would like to explain the following axiomatically:

There seems to be an opinion among certain circles abroad that the particularly loud expression of sympathy for elements who have come into conflict with the law in Germany could ease their situation. Perhaps it is hoped that through certain journalistic methods a coercive influence can be exerted on the German leadership. This opinion is based on a grave error.

The support from certain hostile foreign elements for these men is proof to us that they are traitors. Mere opposition to a regime has never elicited sympathy from a foreign democracy, nor has the prosecution or punishment of such a political offender. When was there ever a stronger opposition movement in Germany than the National Socialist movement? Never was an opposition suppressed, persecuted, and hounded by baser means than was the National Socialist Party. Thus it is all the more an honor to us that we have never enjoyed the sympathy, let alone the support of these foreign powers.

DECLARATION OF WAR ON THE
UNITED STATES OF AMERICA

Berlin Reichstag, December 11th, 1941

The Background

If Hitler's own account is to be believed, then it was only reluctantly that he entered into a fight against America. Though in this speech he does express certain biting criticisms of the American government and American culture, he also emphasizes that National Socialist Germany has no enmity towards the American people, nor even any interests that conflict with theirs. In *Mein Kampf*, Hitler even expresses admiration for American immigration policy, which at the time he was writing was very restrictive toward those of poor health and of non-European descent.[123]

Hitler's declaration of war on the United States of America came only after great deliberation and a long campaign of escalating tensions carried out by the American government. By this point, America was already at war with Germany in every sense except on paper. Its material support for Britain and the Soviet Union, and later its direct entry into the war in Europe, would certainly contribute to the downfall of Hitler's Germany, but even more significantly, would determine the fate of Europe and the very shape of world history up to the present day.

---

[123] Hitler, *Mein Kampf, Vol. II*, C. 3.1, 137.

The following is Hitler's address to the Reichstag regarding the declaration of war, outlining the reasons behind it, the perceived aggression and offences towards Germany on the part of the USA, and his vision of the war as a great European crusade against the forces of Bolshevism and what he dubs a "new Mongol horde" threatening to sweep over Europe from the steppes of Central Asia.

The Speech

Men of the German Reichstag!

A year of world-historical events is drawing to a close; a year of great decisions lies before us. At this grave hour, I am speaking to you, Members of the Reichstag, as the representatives of the German nation. Moreover, the entire German people should take note of this retrospective, and of the decisions which the present and the future impose upon us.

After the repeated rejection of my peace proposal in 1940 by the present British Prime Minister and the clique which supports, or rather controls him, it was clear by the autumn that this war must be fought through to the end, contrary to all logic and necessity. You know me, my old Party Comrades. I have always been an enemy of half-hearted and weak decisions. If Providence has deemed that the German people cannot be spared this struggle, then I am grateful that it has entrusted me with the leadership of a historic struggle that will decisively shape not only our German history, but the history of Europe, indeed of the whole world, for the next five hundred or one thousand years.

The German people and their soldiers work and fight today not only for themselves and their own time, but for generations to come. A historical revision of unparalleled magnitude has been entrusted to us by the Creator, and we are now obliged to carry it out. [...]

As early as 1940 it was becoming clearer month by month that the plans of the men in the Kremlin were consciously aimed at the domination — and thus destruction — of the whole of Europe. I have already given the nation a picture of the build-up of Russian military power in the East at a time when Germany had only a few divisions in the provinces bordering Russia. Only a blind man could fail to see that a mobilization of unparalleled historical dimensions was taking place. And this was not in order to defend something that was threatened, but to attack something that did not appear capable of defense. Even if the sudden end of their campaign in the West deprived the ruling powers in Moscow of the possibility of counting on an immediate exhaustion of the German Reich, this in no way eliminated their intentions, but only postponed the timing of the attack. The summer of 1941 seemed to be their ideal time to strike. A new Mongol horde would pour over Europe.

At the same time, Mr. Churchill also promised a change in the British struggle against Germany. Today he tries to deny in the most cowardly way that in 1940, in a secret session of the British House of Commons, he cited Soviet entry into the conflict as an essential factor for the successful continuation and completion of this war. This was to come in 1941 at the latest, and would then put England in a position to go on the offensive.

In the spring of this year, and ever conscious of our duty, we observed the build-up of a world power that seemed to have inexhaustible reserves of men and materiel. Dark clouds began to gather over Europe.

After all, my deputies, what is Europe? There is no geographical definition of our continent, only an ethnic and cultural one. It is not the Urals that mark the border of this continent, but the line that separates the outlook on life in the West from that of the East.

There was a time when Europe was confined to Greece, which had been reached by Nordic tribes, where the flame was first lit which since then has slowly but steadily begun to enlighten the world of man. And when these Greeks repelled the invasion of the Persian conquerors, they were not only defending their immediate homeland, which was Greece, but that concept which today is called Europe.

And then Europe spread from Hellas to Rome.

Roman thought and Roman statesmanship were combined with Greek spirit and culture. A world empire was created that even today has not been equaled, let alone surpassed, in its significance and creative power. But when the Roman legions defended Italy against the African onslaught of Carthage in three terrible wars, and finally achieved victory, it was once again not only Rome for which they fought, but the Europe of that time, which encompassed the Greco-Roman world.

The next invasion of the home soil of this new human culture came from the far reaches of the East. A horrific storm of uncivilized hordes poured from the interior of Asia deep into the heart of what is now the European continent, burning, ravaging, and murdering, like a true scourge of God.

In the Battle of the Catalaunian Plains,[124] in a fateful conflict of incalculable significance, Romans and Germanic men stood together for the first time for a culture which, starting with the Greeks, had now spread beyond the Romans to the Germanic tribes.

Europe had matured. The Occident emerged from Hellas and Rome, and its defense was now for many centuries not only the task of the Romans, but also the task of the Germanic peoples. What we call Europe is the Occident, enlightened by Greek culture, inspired by the mighty heritage of the Roman Empire, and territoriality expanded through Germanic colonization. No matter whether it was German emperors fighting off invasions from the East on the Unstrut and the Lechfeld,[125] or Africa being pushed back from Spain in long battles, it was always a struggle of the nascent Europe against a profoundly foreign outside world. Just as Rome once earned its immortal credit with the creation and defense of this continent, the Germanic peoples have now taken up the defense and protection of a family of nations, which, although they may differ and diverge in their political structures and goals, in the big picture represent a sum of blood and culture whose components are partly unified, and partly complimentary to each other. [...]

---

[124] A historic battle in 451 AD fought by a coalition of the forces of the late Roman Empire under General Flavius Aetius, often called the last of the true Romans, and a confederation of German tribes under Theodoric, King of the Visigoths, against the invading hordes of Attila the Hun.

[125] Battles in the mid-tenth century AD between the Germans and Magyar invaders.

I have to make these remarks because the struggle which gradually began to appear inevitable in the first months of this year, and which this time the German Reich is called upon to lead first and foremost, also goes far beyond the interests of our own people and country. Just as once the Greeks defended not only Greece against the Persians, the Romans defended not only Rome against the Carthaginians, Romans and Germanic tribes defended not only the Empire against the Huns, German emperors defended not only Germany against the Mongols, Spanish heroes defended not only Spain against Africa, but all of Europe — so today Germany is fighting not only for itself, but for our entire continent.

And it is an auspicious sign that this realization is so deeply rooted in the subconscious of most European peoples today that they are taking part in this struggle, whether with open support or with streams of volunteers. [...]

Fate has destined a number of peoples to prevent or parry this blow through the sacrifice of their blood. If Finland had not immediately decided to take up arms for the second time, the leisurely bourgeois life of the other Nordic states would have come to an abrupt end.

If the German Reich had not stood against this opponent with all its soldiers and weapons, a storm would have burned over Europe which would have swept away the ridiculous British idea of maintaining a "balance of powers" in Europe once and for all, in all its mindlessness and traditional stupidity.

If Slovaks, Hungarians, and Romanians had not helped to protect this European world, the Bolshevik North would have roared over the Danubian lands like Attila's Hunnic horde, and on the shores of the Ionian Sea today Tatars and Mongols would be forcing the revision of the Montreux Convention.[126] If Italy, Spain and Croatia had not sent their divisions, a European defense front would not have arisen that proclaimed a new conception of Europe

---

[126] The international agreement governing maritime transit through the Turkish straits connecting the Black Sea and the Mediterranean, notably prohibiting the transit of warships in times of war.

and radiated its recruiting power to all other peoples. It was out of this foreboding recognition that the volunteers came from Northern and Western Europe: Norwegians, Danes, Dutch, Flemish, Belgians, and so on, even French, who together give the struggle of the allied Axis powers the character of a European crusade in the truest sense of the word. [...]

On what grounds could President Roosevelt fall into such fanatical hostility towards a country that has never done America or himself any harm in its entire history? As far as Germany's position on America is concerned, the following can be said:

First, Germany is perhaps the only great power that has never possessed a colony or otherwise been politically active on either the North or South American continent, except through the emigration of many millions of Germans and their cooperation, from which the American continent, and the United States in particular, have only benefited.

Second, throughout the history of the creation and existence of the United States, the German Reich has never taken a hostile or even politically unfriendly stance, but it has helped to defend the United States with the blood of many of its sons.

Third, the German Reich has never taken part in any war against the United States, but in 1917 the United States did go to war against Germany for reasons which have been fully clarified by a committee appointed by the current President Roosevelt himself to examine this question.

It was precisely this investigative committee looking into the reasons for America's entry into the war in 1917 that clearly established that the reasons were due exclusively to the capitalist interests of a few small groups, and that Germany itself had no intention whatsoever of coming into conflict with America. Nor is there any other antagonism between the American and German peoples, whether territorial or political, which could somehow affect the interests or even the existence of the United States. [...]

And on the personal side: I understand all too well that there is a world of difference between President Roosevelt's outlook and attitude towards life and my own.

Roosevelt comes from an obscenely rich family, and has always belonged to that class of people for whom birth and background pave the way of life in democracies, and thus ensure advancement.

I myself was the child of a small and humble family, and had to struggle my way through life by means of work and diligence.

When the World War came, Roosevelt, in his position under the shadow of Woodrow Wilson, had witnessed the war from the position of the privileged. He therefore knows only the pleasant consequences that arise from conflicts between peoples and states for those who do business where others bleed to death.

During this same period, my own life was again the complete opposite. I was not one of those who made history or even profits, but only one of those who followed orders.

As an ordinary soldier, I endeavored to do my duty in the face of the enemy during these four years and, of course, returned from the war just as poor as I went into it in the autumn of 1914. So I shared my fate with millions, while Mr. Franklin Roosevelt shared his with the so-called upper ten thousand. While Mr. Roosevelt was already trying out his skills in financial speculation after the war in order to personally profit from inflation, which is to say from the misery of others, I was still in a field hospital, just like hundreds of thousands of others.

And when Mr. Roosevelt at last took up the career of the normal politician — business-savvy, with economic backing, and protected by his birth — I was fighting as a nameless and unknown man for the rebirth of my people, who had suffered the gravest injustice in all their history.

Two different paths in life! When Franklin Roosevelt became head of the United States, he was the candidate of a thoroughly capitalist party that looks after its own; when I became Chancellor of the German Reich, I was the leader of a people's movement that I myself had created.

The powers that supported Mr. Roosevelt were the powers that I fought against out of concern for the destiny of my people and my most sacred inner conviction. The "brain trust" at the new American President's disposal was made up of members of the same people that we in Germany fought against as a parasitic phenomenon of humanity, and began to remove from public life.

And yet we both had something in common:

Franklin Roosevelt took over a state with a decaying economy as a result of democratic influence, and I took the helm of a Reich that was also on the brink of total ruin thanks to democracy.

The United States had thirteen million unemployed, Germany seven million, and another seven million part-time workers.

In both states, public finances were in ruins and the decline of general economic life seemed almost unstoppable.

From that moment, a development began in the United States and in the German Reich which will make it easy for posterity to pass a final judgment on the correctness of the two opposing theories. While in the German Reich, under National Socialist leadership, a tremendous flourishing of economic, cultural, and artistic life took place in a few years, President Roosevelt had not succeeded in bringing about even the slightest improvements in his own country.

And how much easier this work should have been in the United States, where barely fifteen people live per square kilometer, compared to 140 in Germany!

If it is not possible to bring about economic prosperity in that country, it is either due to a lack of will on the part of the ruling leadership, or to the complete incompetence of the people in charge.

In barely five years, the economic problems in Germany were solved and the unemployment problem was eliminated.

In the same period, President Roosevelt increased his country's national debt to monstrous proportions, devalued the dollar, further disrupted the economy, and maintained the unemployment rate.

This is not surprising, however, when one considers that the minds whom this man called to his support, or rather who had called him to theirs, belong to that element who, as Jews, are only interested in disruption and never in order. While we combated financial speculation in National Socialist Germany, it has flourished astonishingly during the Roosevelt era. [...]

He was encouraged in this by the circle of Jews who surrounded him and who, out of an Old Testament desire for revenge, saw the United States as the instrument with which to prepare a second Purim[127] for the European nations, which were becoming increasingly antisemitic. It was the Jew in all his satanic baseness who rallied around this man, and whom this man also sought out. [...]

From November 1938 onwards, he [Roosevelt] began to deliberately sabotage any possibility of a European peace policy. He pretended to be interested in peace, but threatened every state that was prepared to pursue a policy of peaceful understanding with the blocking of credit, economic reprisals, cancellation of loans, et cetera. The reports of the Polish ambassadors in Washington, London, Paris, and Brussels provide a shocking insight into this.

In January 1939, this man intensified his smear campaign, threatening the authoritarian states before Congress with every measure short of war.

While constantly claiming that other states are trying to interfere in American affairs and insisting on upholding the Monroe Doctrine,[128] since March 1939 he has begun to interfere in internal European affairs, which are none of the business of the President of the United States. In the first place, he does not understand these problems, and in the second place, even if he did understand them and their historical context, he would have just as much right to concern himself with the Central European sphere as, for example, the German head of state has the right to judge or

---

[127] The holiday celebrating the Jewish uprising against the Persian Empire characterized by ruthless slaughter of non-Jews in Palestine, as related in the Book of Esther.

[128] The US foreign policy doctrine of opposing European colonialism or influence in the Americas, guarding the entire New World as an American sphere of influence.

even comment on the conditions in a state of the USA. [...]

From July 1940 onwards, Roosevelt's measures were increasingly aimed at war, whether through allowing American citizens to join the British Air Force, or through training British airmen in the United States. And as early as August 1940, the United States and Canada formed a joint defense policy. But in order to make the necessity of establishing a joint American-Canadian defense committee seem plausible, at least to the biggest fools, he invented crises from time to time, in which he pretended that America was threatened by an invasion, which he suggested to his pitiable followers by suddenly cutting trips short and driving back to Washington in the greatest haste, in order to underline the danger of the situation.

In September 1940, he came even closer to war. He delivered fifty destroyers from the American fleet to the British fleet, but in return he took over military bases in the British possessions of North and Central America. There is one thing which only posterity will be able to clarify, which is to what extent all this hatred of Socialist Germany was also motivated by the ambition to take over the British Empire as safely and securely as possible in its hour of decline.

Now that England was no longer in a position to pay for American supplies in cash, he imposed the Lend-Lease Act on the American people. As President, he was given the power to lease and lend support to countries whose defense Roosevelt considered vital for America. [...]

On June 14th, German assets in the United States were frozen, again in violation of international law. On June 17th, President Roosevelt demanded the withdrawal of the German consuls and the closure of the German consulates under false pretexts. He also demanded the closure of the German *Transocean* press agency, the German Library of Information, and the *Deutsche Reichsbahn* headquarters.[129] On July 6th–7th, American forces occupied Iceland,

---

[129] *Transocean* was a print news agency established in 1915 by a conglomerate owned by Alfred Hugenberg to facilitate journalistic connections between foreign

which is within the German military zone of operations, on Roosevelt's orders. He certainly hoped firstly, to finally force Germany to war, or secondly, to at least render the German submarine force just as ineffective as it was in 1915–1916.

At the same time, he sent a promise of American aid to the Soviet Union. On July 10th, Navy Secretary Frank Knox suddenly announced that the US Navy had orders to fire on Axis warships. On September 4th, the US destroyer *Greer,* operating on his orders, took part in an operation with British aircraft against German submarines in the Atlantic.

Five days later, a German submarine spotted US destroyers acting as escort vessels in a British convoy. On September 11th, Roosevelt finally delivered the speech in which he himself confirmed and reissued the order to fire on all Axis ships. On September 29th, US patrols attacked a German submarine east of Greenland with depth charges. On October 17th, the US destroyer *Kearny*, acting as an escort for England, again attacked a German submarine with depth charges. Finally, on November 6th, US forces captured the German steamer *Odenwald* in violation of international law, towed it into an American port, and took the crew prisoner.

I will disregard the insulting attacks and accusations of this so-called President against me personally as inconsequential. The fact that he calls me a gangster is all the more meaningless, because this concept does not originate from Europe but from the USA, perhaps because there is a lack of such subjects here.

But apart from that, I cannot be offended at all by Mr. Roosevelt, because I consider him, as Woodrow Wilson once was, to be insane as well.

---

countries and Germany. In 1933 the propaganda department of the National Socialist government took control of its operations. The German Library of Information was another press operating in New York City in 1939 that periodically distributed a free pamphlet titled *Facts In Review*, which had the tagline "*That's not news... that's propaganda!*" It attempted direct outreach to the American public, claiming to counter Allied propaganda and present people with the facts from the German point of view. At the time of this publishing, an archive of its issues is available at: https://germanlibraryofinformation.wordpress.com

We know that this man and his Jewish supporters have been fighting Japan for years with the same means. I do not need to bring that up here. In that case, too, the same methods have been employed. First this man incites war, then he falsifies its causes, and makes baseless assertions. He wraps himself disgustingly in a cloak of Christian hypocrisy, and slowly but surely leads humanity towards war, and not without then, as an old Freemason, calling God as witness that his actions are honorable. [...]

We know the power behind Roosevelt. It is that eternal Jew who believes that his time has come to carry out on us what we all saw and experienced with horror in Soviet Russia. We have now become acquainted with the Jewish paradise on earth. Millions of German soldiers have been able to gain a personal insight into a country in which this international Jew destroyed and annihilated people and property. The President of the United States may not understand this himself. If so, this only speaks for his intellectual limitations. [...]

When Mr. Roosevelt or Mr. Churchill declare that they want to establish a new social order one day, it is about the same as a bald hairdresser recommending a sure-fire hair restorer. These gentlemen, who live in the most socially backward states, should have taken care of their unemployed instead of agitating for wars. They have enough need and misery in their countries to keep them busy there with the distribution of food. As far as the German people is concerned, it does not need charity from Mr. Churchill nor from Mr. Roosevelt, nor even from Foreign Secretary Mr. Eden, but it does demand its rights. And it will secure its right to live, even if a thousand Churchills or Roosevelts conspire against it. This people here now has almost two thousand years of history behind it. In all those years it has never been so united and determined as it is today, and as it will be from now on, thanks to the National Socialist movement. [...]

The sincere and incredibly patient efforts of Germany and Italy to prevent an expansion of the war and to maintain relations with the United States, despite years of intolerable provocations by

President Roosevelt, have been ruined.

Germany and Italy accordingly now regard themselves as finally compelled, in accordance with the provisions of the Tripartite Pact of September 27th, 1940, to fight side by side with Japan against the United States of America and England for the defense, and thus the preservation, of the freedom and independence of their peoples and empires. [...]

Ever since the rejection of my last peace proposal in July 1940, we have been aware that this struggle must be fought through to the end. It is no surprise to us National Socialists that the Anglo-Saxon Judeo-capitalist world has formed a united front with Bolshevism. We have always found that they are inwardly in the same community.

But we succeeded in our struggle at home and finally destroyed our opponents after sixteen years of struggling for power.

Twenty-three years ago, when I decided to enter political life to lead the nation back from its decline, I was a nameless unknown soldier. Many of you know how difficult the first years of this struggle were. The path from a small movement of seven men to taking power as the responsible government on January 30th, 1933 was so miraculous that only the blessing of Providence itself could have made it possible.

Today I stand at the head of the strongest army in the world, the mightiest air force, and a proud navy. Behind me and around me as a sworn community, I recognize the Party which made me great, and which became great through me. [...]

The American President and his plutocratic clique have dubbed us the "have-not" nations. That is correct! But the have-nots want to live, and they will by all means ensure that what little they have to live on is not robbed from them by the haves. You know, my Party Comrades, my unrelenting determination to carry through a struggle, once begun, to its successful conclusion. You know my will to stop at nothing in such a struggle, to break all resistance that must be broken.

In my first speech on September 1st, 1939, I assured you that in this war neither force of arms nor time could bring Germany down. I also want to assure my opponents that not only will the force of arms or time not defeat us, but also that no inner doubts can make us waver in the fulfillment of our duty. When we think of the sacrifices of our soldiers, of their commitment, then every sacrifice in the homeland seems completely trivial and insignificant. But when we consider the numbers of all those who have fallen in the generations before us for the existence and greatness of the German people, then we become all the more aware of the greatness of the duty that weighs upon us. [...]

Let our opponents not deceive themselves. In the two thousand years of known German history, our people have never been more united and more determined than they are today. The Lord of the world has done such great things for us in recent years that we bow in gratitude to a Providence that has allowed us to be members of such a great people. We thank Him that, in view of the past and future generations of the German people, we too can write our names in honor in the immortal book of German history.

THE FÜHRER'S FINAL RADIO BROADCAST TO THE GERMAN PEOPLE

January 30th, 1945

The Background

The following speech is yet another delivered on the anniversary of Hitler's ascent to power. This was to be the last.

With the clarity of hindsight, Hitler's continued desperate hope for final victory even at this late hour appears, depending on one's perspective, either hollow if it was not genuine, or delusional if it was, and perhaps even pathetic. By the end of January 1945, the war was essentially lost. Although it dragged on for over three more bitter months, at the time Hitler delivered this speech, Germany was in no position to achieve any sort of victory, and most of its officers were aware of this. The best that might have been hoped for would have been to fight the Allied powers to a stalemate and force a peace deal, but by then even that possibility was fast becoming unfeasible as the Soviet empire threw wave after wave of its seemingly inexhaustible manpower against the war-weary German forces, and the Western Allies bombed German cities into rubble. The main theme of this speech is resistance to the very end, an attempt to inspire courage and hope, but with the clarity of historical hindsight, it is clear that it had little to no impact militarily other than to prolong the fighting for a few more brutal months.

The scale of human suffering experienced by soldiers and civilians alike during the last months of the war was unfathomable and tragic. For the second time in as many generations, Europe tore itself apart in a war of unprecedented destruction, especially on the Eastern Front, where National Socialist Germany and the Communist Soviet Union were locked in a death struggle between states, worldviews, and peoples, the likes of which had never before occurred in world history, and, God willing, will never occur again.

Although it was the Soviet Union whose gigantic military formations were by then rapidly pushing German forces back, Hitler's most fatal mistake had been underestimating the depths of the hostility towards him, his country, and his worldview in the Anglosphere. Even as late as 1941 he was still hoping for peace with Britain.

He had gone to war against the four most powerful empires in world history: the French, the Soviet, the British, and the American; one he had taken by surprise and quickly overwhelmed; against one he had been bogged down in a brutal war of attrition, in which his relatively small country in the middle of Europe was hopelessly outmatched in terms of manpower and raw natural resources; with one he had underestimated the extent to which it was willing to sacrifice all of its wealth and resources, and lose its entire empire, just to defeat him; and of the final empire, America, already by then the most powerful, he had failed to understand its significance, both in terms of its unparalleled power and in terms of the extent to which it would devote itself to his destruction.

The following speech contains many of Hitler's predictions about the future of Europe should Germany fall to the Soviets, most of which proved incorrect. He had long railed against the timid weakness of liberal democracy and its inability to stand strong in the face of organized communism. He assumed that with Germany out of the way, no state would be strong enough to resist, and Bolshevik communism would sweep across Europe, toppling the liberal democracies, and plunging Europe into a new dark age.

But these apocalyptic predictions are indicative of a fatal error in Hitler's judgment: the severe underestimation of the power, danger, and adaptability of liberalism, and especially of the USA.

His fixation on communism as the ultimate enemy is understandable given his time. It represented the most immediate and direct threat to the continuity of European civilization. The biggest empire in the world by land mass underwent a brutal Bolshevik revolution and turned communist, right on the eastern borders of his own nation. The same revolution threatened to upend Germany during the formative years of his political awakening and rise to power. The destructiveness of communism was more visceral and more immediate—from the reports he heard and saw of the situation in Russia he could see how communism, in its chaotic early days, literally destroyed much of Russia's cultural heritage and plundered its wealth. To him, communism seemed to threaten a burst of chaos and rapid, violent destruction. Liberalism, on the other hand, results in a slow corrosion, which is harder to see because it is more gradual. Communism, unquestionably, was the more immediate threat from Hitler's perspective. He assumed that the same trend he witnessed in the East would continue if that worldview managed to conquer the West.

Speaking in the broadest possible terms, there were two world-changing historical developments which he could not foresee. One of these was that the liberal-democratic capitalist powers, which after the war were deeply indebted to and firmly in the sphere of influence of the United States of America, would succeed in halting the eastward advance of communism at Berlin. Roughly speaking, these borders became more or less fixed for the next fifty years, demarcating the divide between the American and Russian spheres of influence.

The other development, which was contingent on the first, was that communism would be forced to moderate and modernize itself in response to the geopolitical contingencies of competition with the Western powers. In fact, this process had already begun before and during its war against Germany. The Soviet Union became not only more patriotic to inspire the war effort, but also more competent to carry it out. No travesty on the scale of the famines of the 1920s and 30s would occur again, and, albeit slowly and with many hiccups along the way, it became less brutally repressive, although the bar for what might be considered "less repressive" had been set quite low in comparison to the paranoid brutality and scale of Stalinist terror.

As a result of the Cold War stalemate and cultural competition with the West, the destruction of European cultural heritage in the East slowed or even stopped. The Eastern Bloc arguably became a better steward of traditional European culture than the West, perhaps not in the field of architecture, but certainly in classical music, or even the preservation of traditional social norms, despite the best efforts of the early communists to the contrary. True enough, Christianity was never restored to its former role in public life, but a question then arises: where, on average, is the public more religious — in Eastern or Western Europe?

Simply put, Hitler's worldview led him to predict the destruction, or at least domination, of Europe by Soviet Russia should his country fall. This final broadcast is Hitler's attempt to inspire the German people to resist their destruction with their last reserves of strength. Eventually, of course, Hitler's Germany was defeated, brought down in the most titanic struggle in world history by the largest and most powerful empires the world has ever seen, and National Socialism has become the ultimate political taboo, the antithesis and arch-nemesis of the post-war liberal world order. But even in its defeat, and regardless of its doctrines, its significance in history is unquestionable and unparalleled. The political and cultural world we inhabit today is a result of the Allies' victory in the Second World War, and the form that victory took.

The Speech

My fellow Germans! National Socialists!

Twelve years ago, when the immortalized Reich President Paul von Hindenburg entrusted me with the chancellorship as leader of the strongest party, Germany was faced with the same situation internally as it is today externally in terms of geopolitics. The process of economic destruction and annihilation of the democratic republic, initiated and continued according to plan by the Treaty of Versailles, led to a phenomenon that was gradually becoming permanent of almost seven million unemployed, seven million part-time workers, a ruined peasantry, destroyed trade, and a corresponding breakdown of the economy. The German ports were nothing but ship graveyards. The financial situation of the Reich threatened at any moment to lead to the collapse not only of the state, but also of the provinces and municipalities. The decisive point, however, was this: beyond this methodical economic destruction of Germany loomed the specter of Asiatic Bolshevism, then as now. And just as it is now on a large scale, on a small scale the bourgeois world was completely incapable of offering effective resistance to this development in the years before we seized power. Even after the collapse of 1918, it was still not recognized that an old world was passing away and a new one was in the making, that it could not be a question of supporting and artificially preserving what had proven decayed and rotten, but that it was necessary to put what was obviously healthy in its place. An outdated social order had broken down, and any attempt to maintain it could only be in vain. It was therefore no different from what is happening today on a large scale, since the bourgeois states are also doomed to destruction, and only clearly aligned, ideologically consolidated national communities will be capable of surviving the most serious crisis in Europe in many centuries.

We were only given six years of peace since January 30th, 1933.

During those six years, we achieved tremendous things, and even greater things have been planned, so many and so great that they aroused the envy of our incapable democratic neighbors.

The decisive thing, however, was that in those six years, with superhuman efforts, it was possible to rehabilitate the German national body in terms of defense, to equip it not primarily with material military power, but with the spiritual will to resist and to assert itself. […]

It is hardly necessary to deal with those eternal airheads who hold that a defenseless Germany would certainly never have become a victim of this international Jewish conspiracy because of its impotence.

This means nothing other than turning all the laws of nature upside down. Since when does the defenseless goose not get eaten by the fox just because the goose is not aggressive by nature? And when will the wolf finally become a pacifist, since the sheep have no armaments? The existence of such bourgeois sheep, who believe this in all seriousness, only proves how necessary it was to do away with an age whose education system could produce and sustain such types. Indeed, it even granted them political influence.

Long before National Socialism came to power, the relentless struggle against this Jewish-Asiatic Bolshevism was already raging. If it did not overrun Europe in 1919–20, it was only because it was still too weak and under-equipped at that time. Its attempt to eliminate Poland was not abandoned out of compassion for the Polish, but only as a result of the lost battle of Warsaw. Its intention to annihilate Hungary was not abandoned because they thought better of it, but because the Bolshevik force could not be maintained militarily. The attempt to crush Germany was likewise abandoned not because they no longer desired success, but because it was not possible to eliminate our people's remaining natural resistance. Immediately, however, Jewry began with the planned internal disintegration of our people. And for this purpose it found the best allies in those obstinate bourgeoisie who did not want to recognize that the age of the bourgeois world was coming to an end, never to return, that the era of unbridled economic liberalism had outlived its usefulness and could only lead to its own collapse, and above all, that the great tasks of the time could only be managed by the authoritarian, united strength of the nation, based on the law of equal rights for all, and accordingly equal duties. [...]

The Almighty created our nation. By defending its existence, we defend His work. The fact that this defense is linked with unspeakable misfortune, suffering, and pain beyond compare only makes us more attached to this nation. But it also gives us the hardness we need to fulfill our duty even in the worst crises; that means not only the duty towards the decent eternal Germany, but also the duty towards those few dishonorable ones who try to separate themselves from their nationality. Therefore, there is only one commandment for us in this fateful struggle: whoever fights honorably might thereby save his own life and those of his loved ones; those spineless cowards who stab the nation in the back will die a shameful death no matter what.

The fact that National Socialism was able to awaken and strengthen this spirit in our German people is its greatest deed. Once the bells of peace ring out after this tremendous world drama has subsided, we will realize that the German people owe to this spiritual rebirth no less than their very existence in this world. [...]

I repeat my prophecy: England will not only not be able to tame Bolshevism, but its own development will inevitably follow the course of this degenerative disease. The democracies will not be able to get rid of the spirits that they themselves have summoned from the steppes of Asia. All the small European nations that capitulated in reliance on Allied promises are heading for total extinction. Whether this fate befalls them a little sooner or a little later is completely irrelevant. It is exclusively tactical considerations that cause the Kremlin Jews to proceed immediately with brutality in one case, and a little more cautiously in another. The end will always be the same. [...]

On this day I want to leave no doubt about another matter: in spite of an entirely hostile environment, I once chose my path and walked it as an unknown, nameless man until final victory. I was often pronounced dead, and always wished dead, but finally I was the victor! My life today, however, is determined just as exclusively by the duties incumbent upon me.

Taken together, they amount to one thing only: to work and to fight for my people. I can only be released from this duty by the one who called me to it. It was in the hands of Providence when the bomb that detonated one and a half meters away from me on July 20th failed to wipe me out and thus end my life's work.[130] I see the fact that the Almighty protected me on that day as a confirmation of the mission given to me. In the years to come, I will therefore continue to walk this path of uncompromising representation of the interests of my people, unperturbed by every crisis and every danger, and imbued with the holy conviction that in the end the Almighty will not abandon a man who in his entire life wanted nothing more than to save his people from a fate that they never deserved.

In this hour, therefore, I appeal to the whole German people, but above all to my old comrades in arms, and to all soldiers, to arm themselves with an even greater, hardened spirit of resistance, until we may, as we did once before, lay a wreath on the grave of the dead of this mighty struggle with a ribbon inscribed, "And yet you triumphed nevertheless!"[131]

I expect every German to fulfill his duty to the utmost, to make every sacrifice that is and must be demanded of him; I expect every healthy person to risk his life and limb in the struggle; I expect

---

[130] Referring to the July Bomb Plot of 1944, one of dozens of failed assassination attempts on Adolf Hitler, this time by a circle of high-ranking Army officers led by Claus von Stauffenberg, many of them of the old military aristocracy and resentful of Hitler for various political, pragmatic, ideological, or simply personal reasons, ranging from disagreement with his handling of the war, to aristocratic disdain for the upstart, petty-bourgeois corporal and his populism. Stauffenberg smuggled the bomb inside of a briefcase into a meeting, placing it as close as he could to Hitler, but Colonel Heinz Brandt moved it, unwittingly saving Hitler's life at the cost of his own. Four men were killed in the explosion, including Brandt, but Hitler escaped with only minor injuries.

[131] The same inscription as that on the monument to those who fell in the Beer Hall Putsch.

every sick and infirm or otherwise indisposed person to work to the utmost of his strength; I expect the inhabitants of the cities to forge the weapons for this struggle, and I expect the peasant to give bread for the soldiers and workers of this struggle with the greatest possible sacrifice. I expect all women and girls to support this struggle, as they have done up to now, with the utmost fanaticism. I turn with special confidence to the German youth.

By forming such a sworn community, we can rightly go before the Almighty and ask for his mercy and blessing, for a people cannot do more than ensure that everyone who can fight, fights, and everyone who can work, works, and all sacrifice together, filled only with the one thought of securing freedom, national honor, and a future for life.

No matter how difficult the crisis may be at the moment, it will be overcome in the end through our unshakable will, through our willingness to make sacrifices, and through our capabilities. We will survive this hardship. In this struggle, too, it will not be Central Asia that wins, but Europe, and at its head that nation which for one and a half thousand years has represented Europe as the supreme power against the East and will continue to do so in the future:

Our Greater German Reich, the German Nation!

BIBLIOGRAPHY

Bracher, Karl Dietrich. *The German Dictatorship: The Origins, Structure, and Consequences of National Socialism*. 1969. Reprint, UK: Penguin University Books, 1973.

Deuerlein, Ernst. *Der Aufstieg der NSDAP in Augenzeugenberichten*. Munich: Deutscher Taschenbuch-Verlag, 1974.

Dreier, Ralf and Wolfgang Sellert. *Recht und Justiz im ,,Dritten Reich."* Frankfurt am Main: Suhrkamp Verlag, 1989.

Evans, Richard J. *The Coming of the Third Reich*. Italy: Penguin Press, 2004.

Gerth, Hans. "The Nazi Party, Its Leadership and Composition." *American Journal of Sociology*, XIV (1940).

Hall, David Ian. *Hitler's Munich: The Capital of the Nazi Movement*. United Kingdom: Pen & Sword Books Limited, 2021.

Heinz, Heinz A. *Germany's Hitler*. 1934. Revised Edition, London: Hurst & Blackett Ltd., 1938.

Hitler, Adolf. *Mein Kampf, Volume I*. Translated by Thomas Dalton, PhD. 1925. Dual German-English Translation, New York/London: Clemens & Blair, LLC, 2017.

Hitler, Adolf. *Mein Kampf, Volume II*. Translated by Thomas Dalton, PhD. 1926. Dual German-English Translation, New York/London: Clemens & Blair, LLC, 2019.

Irving, David. *Hitler's War and the War Path*. London: Focal Point Publications, 2002.

Kershaw, Ian. *Hitler: A Biography*. New York: W.W. Norton & Company, Inc., 2008.

von Krosigk, Lutz Graf Schwerin. *Es geschah in Deutschland*. Tübingen/Stuttgart: Rainer Wunderlich Verlag/Hermann Leins Tübingen, 1951.

Kühnl, Reinhard. "Zur Programmatik der Nationalsozialistischen Linken: Das Strasser-Program von 1925/26," *Vierteljahrshefte für Zeitgeschichte* 14, no. 3 (1966).

Lane, Barbara Miller and Rupp, Leila J.. *Nazi Ideology before 1933: A Documentation.* New York, USA: University of Texas Press, 2021. https://doi.org/10.7560/755123

Laytner, Ron. "The first astronaut: tiny, daring Hanna." *The Deseret News*, February 19, 1981.

Lewis, Wyndham. *Hitler.* USA: Antelope Hill Publishing, 2020.

Maser, Werner. *Frühgeschichte der NSDAP: Hitlers Weg bis 1924.* Frankfurt am Main/Bonn: Athenäum Verlag, 1965.

Mommsen, Hans. "Hitler's Reichstag Speech of 30 January 1939." *History and Memory* 9, no. 1/2 (1997): 147–61. http://www.jstor.org/stable/25681003

von Müller, Karl Alexander. *Im Wandel einer Welt: Erinnergungen 1919–1931.* Munich, 1966.

Noakes, Jeremy. "Conflict and Development in the NSDAP 1924–1927." *Journal of Contemporary History* 1, no. 4 (1966): 3–36. http://www.jstor.org/stable/259890

Phelps, Reginald H. "Hitlers „Grundlegende" Rede über den Antisemitismus." *Vierteljahrshefte für Zeitgeschichte* 16, no. 4 (1968): 390-420.

Reinhardt, Fritz. *Die Beseitigung der Arbeitslosigkeit im Dritten Reich: Das Sofortprogramm 1933/34.* Kiel: Nordkieler Verlag, 2007.

Rosenberg, Alfred. *Memoirs.* 2000. Revised Edition, Ghent, Belgium: Skull Press Ebook Publications, 2013.

de Sales, Raoul de Roussy. *My New Order.* 1941. Reprint, New York/Tokyo: Ishi Press International, 2016.

Tedor, Richard. *Hitler's Revolution*, Expanded Edition. Chicago: Lightning Source UK/Milton Keynes UK, 2013.

Turner, Henry Ashby. "Big Business and the Rise of Hitler." *The American Historical Review* 75, no. 1 (1969): 56-70. https://doi.org/10.2307/1841917

Winkler, Heinrich August. *Weimar 1918–1933: Die Geschichte der ersten deutschen Demokratie.* 1st ed. Verlag C.H.Beck, 1993. http://www.jstor.org/stable/j.ctv116933g

SUGGESTIONS FOR FURTHER READING

Ian Kershaw, *Hitler: A Biography*
> In the genre of mainstream Hitler biographies, this is the standout. It is high quality, so well-written it is hard to put down, and extremely well-researched, though also, of course, extremely hostile towards its subject. Although every page is practically dripping with snark, it is probably the most comprehensive and detailed biography of Adolf Hitler ever written.

Heinz A. Heinz, *Germany's Hitler*
> This authorized biography was written while Hitler was still alive, and ends in 1939. It is unabashedly pro-Hitler, but it offers a refreshing inside perspective and interesting details.

David Irving, *Hitler's War*
> This is the best "wartime biography" of Adolf Hitler. It documents the story of the Second World War from Hitler's perspective.

Adolf Hitler, *Mein Kampf*, Dual English-German Version, Translated by Thomas Dalton, PhD
> Although there are some things I might have personally translated slightly differently, as a fellow translator, the Dalton translation is the only edition I can take seriously and recommend.

Richard Tedor, *Hitler's Revolution*, Expanded Edition
A particularly well-researched overview of National Socialism as it unfolded in Germany in terms of government policy.

Stephen Fritz, *The First Soldier: Hitler as Military Leader*
A military history book that aims to counter the persistent narrative that Hitler was an incompetent commander who had no business making strategic military decisions. Fritz argues that Hitler's strategy was mostly logical and competent.

Henry Ashby Turner, "Big Business and the Rise of Hitler"
A detailed breakdown of the issue of NSDAP funding and its alleged ties to big business.

Wyndham Lewis, *Hitler*
The perspective of an English writer and painter living in Germany on the rise of the NSDAP in the late 1920s and early 1930s.

Richard Walther Darré, *A New Nobility of Blood and Soil*
An elucidation of the National Socialist "Blood and Soil" doctrine, and its connections to agrarianism, environmentalism, and ruralism.

Frederic Spotts, *Hitler and the Power of Aesthetics*
An exploration of National Socialism as an aesthetic and artistic movement, and Hitler as a lifelong artist and lover of architecture.

https://www.nommeraadio.ee/rahvaraadio.php
This page has an extensive collection of Hitler's speeches in English available as a PDF file called "Adolf Hitler — Collection of Speeches — 1922-1945." The quality of the translations is serviceable. They are mostly accurate, if a bit clunky.

https://der-fuehrer.org/

Along with extensive collections of Hitler's speeches in both English and German, this page has many photographs, audio files, and videos.

ENJOYED THIS BOOK?

TO READ MORE, VISIT US AT

ANTELOPEHILLPUBLISHING.COM